The Great American Frontier

A Story of Western Pioneering

THE AMERICAN HERITAGE SERIES

The American Heritage Series

under the general editorship of
ALFRED F. YOUNG *and* LEONARD W. LEVY

The Great American Frontier

A Story of Western Pioneering

edited by

THOMAS D. CLARK
Eastern Kentucky University

THE BOBBS-MERRILL COMPANY, INC.
INDIANAPOLIS

for Elizabeth Turner Clark

The Bobbs-Merrill Company, Inc.
4300 West 62nd Street
Indianapolis, Indiana 46268

First Edition
First Printing 1975

Library of Congress Cataloging in Publication Data

Clark, Thomas D.
    The great American frontier.

    (American heritage series, AHS–87)
    Bibliography: p. xi
    Includes index.
    1. Frontier and pioneer life—The West.   2. The
West—History—Sources.   1. Title.
F591.C62   978   74–28026
ISBN 0–672–60146–X (pbk.)
ISBN 0–672–51511–3

Contents

Foreword

Enthusiasm and interest in the story of the American frontier is approaching new heights, and for several good reasons. At a time when the United States is celebrating two hundred years as a nation, Americans are recalling the early encounters of those who set out to conquer the western wilderness.

Now that the dust has settled in the long debate among scholars over Frederick Jackson Turner's exaggerated claims for the influence of the frontier, "even the unkindest of Turner's critics have conceded," as two of the most perceptive historians have put it, "that *some* relation most likely does exist between our history and our frontier."* Pioneering in a virgin land *was* central to this country's experience, and no collection calling itself *The American Heritage Series* would be complete without mention of it.

Current American discontents have justifiably led to a revival of interest in the frontier era as part of a general inquiry into the roots of our most persistent problems. The traditional nostalgia for a bygone period of fur trappers and cowboys and woodsmen, which era somehow seems simpler, more romantic, and more adventuresome, is now matched by the mood of those who ask, "How did we get this way?" or, more angrily, "How did we get into the mess we are in?" Sooner or later, Americans concerned about preserving the natural environment, coming to grips with the sources of violence, redressing the grievances of native Americans, or curbing the expansionist aspects of foreign policy, are led back to exploring the frontier. Frontier buffs are thus joined by frontier critics.

There is an especially good reason for a new volume of original sources on the frontier when collected by a man who

---

* Stanley Elkins and Eric McKitrick, "A Meaning for Turner's Frontier, Part I: Democracy in the Old Northwest," *Political Science Quarterly*, LXIX (September, 1954), 323.

has spent forty years with the subject. Thomas Clark has been recognized as a leading scholar of the West and the South by his fellow historians who have, among other things, elected him president of the Organization of American Historians and the Southern Historical Association. He knows the original literature of this field the way a fur trapper knew the nooks and crannies of the Rockies. It is fascinating to watch this sure-footed guide cull from the mountains of contemporary writings—the travelers' accounts, the pioneers' memoirs, the country newspapers—the single item that epitomizes an experience or vividly describes a scene. The selections in many ways are like the editor—earthy, full of vitality, and always able to tell a good story.

This book is one of a series created to provide the essential primary sources of the American experience, especially of American thought. The American Heritage Series constitutes a documentary library of United States history, filling a need long felt among scholars, students, libraries, and general readers for authoritative collections of original materials. Some volumes illuminate the thought of significant individuals, such as James Madison or John Marshall; some deal with movements, such as the Antifederalist or the Populist; others are organized around special themes, such as Puritan political thought or American Catholic thought on social questions. Many volumes take up the large number of subjects traditionally studied in American history for which surprisingly there are no documentary anthologies; others pioneer in introducing new subjects of increasing importance to scholars and to the contemporary world. The series aspires to maintain the high standards demanded of contemporary editing, providing authentic texts, intelligently and unobtrusively edited. It also has the distinction of presenting pieces of substantial length which give the full character and flavor of the original. The American Heritage Series is, we believe, the most comprehensive and authoritative of its kind.

Alfred F. Young
Leonard W. Levy

Selected Bibliography

This bibliography supplements the numerous entries made within the text itself. No cognizance is taken here or in the text of the enormously important body of periodical literature on the westward movement.

GUIDE TO SOURCES

Clark, Thomas D., ed., *Travels in the Old South*, 3 vols. (Norman, Okla.: University of Oklahoma Press, 1956, 1959).

Winther, Oscar O., *Classified Bibliography of the Periodical Literature of the Trans-Mississippi West* (Bloomington, Ind.: Indiana University Press, 1961).

TRAVEL ACCOUNTS

Audubon, John James, *Delineations of American Scenery and Character, by John James Audubon; with an Introduction by Francis Hobart Herrick* (New York: G. A. Baker, 1926).

Catlin, George, *Letters and Notes on the Manners, Customs, and Conditions of the North American Indians*, 2 vols. (London: Fosswill and Myers, 1841).

Clark, Thomas D., ed., *Gold Rush Diary: Being the Journal of Elisha Douglas Perkins on the Overland Trail in the Spring and Summer of 1849* (Lexington: University Press of Kentucky, 1967).

Clemens, Samuel L., *Life on the Mississippi* (Boston: James R. Osgood, 1883).

Cuming, Fortescue, *Sketches of a Tour to the Western Country, through Missouri and a Visit to Cuba and the Azores Islands*, 2 vols. (London: Richard Bently, 1839).

Read, Georgia and Ruth Gaines, eds., *Gold Rush: The Journals, Drawings, and Other Papers of J. Goldsborough Bruff, Cap-*

tain *Washington City and California Mining Association April 2, 1849–July 20, 1851,* 2 vols. (New York: Columbia University Press, 1944).

Trollope, Mrs. Frances Milton, *Domestic Manners of the Americans,* 2 vols. (London: Whitaker, Treacher, 1832).

Wied-Neuwied, Maximilian Alexander Philip, Prinz von, *Travels in the Interior of North America, by Maximilian Prince of Wied,* translated from the German, by H. Evans Lloyd. To accompany the original series of eighty-one elaborately colored plates (London: Ackerman, 1843).

CONTEMPORARY WORKS

Adams, Andy, *Log of a Cowboy* (New York: Houghton Mifflin, 1931).

DeVoto, Bernard, ed., *The Journals of Lewis and Clark* (Boston: Houghton Mifflin, 1953).

Hafen, Leroy, ed., *The Mountain Men and the Fur Trade of the Far West,* 2 vols. (Glendale, Calif.: Arthur H. Clark, 1965).

Ise, John, ed., *Sod House Days: Letters from a Kansas Homesteader, 1877–78,* by Howard Ruede, in Columbia University Studies in the *History of Agriculture,* vol. IV, edited by Henry J. Carmen and Rexford G. Tugwell (New York: Columbia University Press, 1937).

Jackson, Donald, ed., *Letters of the Lewis and Clark Expedition with Related Documents, 1783–1854* (Urbana, Ill.: University of Illinois Press, 1962).

Stuart, Granville, ed., *Forty Years on the Frontier,* by P. C. Phillips (Cleveland: Arthur H. Clark, 1925).

GENERAL STUDIES

Billington, Ray A. and James Blaine Hedges, *Westward Expansion* (New York: MacMillan, 1949).

Branch, E. Douglas, *Westward* (New York: D. Appleton, 1930).

Clark, Thomas D., *Frontier America, the Story of the Westward Movement* (New York: Charles Scribner's, 1959).

Reigel, Robert and Robert Athearn, *America Moves West* (New York: Holt, Rinehart, and Winston, 1966).

SPECIALIZED STUDIES

Abernathy, Thomas Perkins, *Three Virginia Frontiers* (Baton Rouge, La.: Louisiana State University Press, 1940).

Bodley, Temple, *Our First Great West* (Louisville: The Filson Club, 1938).

Bond, Beverly, *Civilization of the Old Northwest* (New York: MacMillan, 1934).

Brown, Dee and Martin Schmitt, *Trail Driving Days* (New York: Charles Scribner's, 1952).

Brown, John P., *Old Frontiers* (Kingsport, Tenn.: Kingsport Press, 1938).

Buley, Rosco C., *The Old Northwest Pioneer Period 1815–1840*, 2 vols. (Bloomington, Ind.: Indiana University Press, 1951).

Caughey, John W., *History of the Pacific Coast* (Los Angeles: the author, 1933).

Chittenden, Hiram M., *The American Fur Trade*, 2 vols. (Washington: Pioneer, 1932).

Clark, Thomas D., *The Rampaging Frontier* (Indianapolis: Bobbs-Merrill, 1939).

Crouse, D. E., *The Ohio Gateway* (New York: Charles Scribner's, 1938).

DeVoto, Bernard, *Across the Wide Missouri* (Boston: Houghton Mifflin, 1947).

Dick, Everett, *The Dixie Frontier* (New York: Knopf, 1948).

———, *The Sod House Frontier* (New York: D. Appleton-Century, 1937).

Foreman, Grant, *Indian Removal* (Norman, Okla.: University of Oklahoma Press, 1932).

Gard, Wayne, *The Great Buffalo Hunt* (New York: Knopf, 1960).

Hafen, Leroy, ed., *The Mountain Men and the Fur Trade of the Far West*, 2 vols. (Glendale, Calif.: Arthur H. Clark, 1965).

Hagan, William T., *American Indians,* The Chicago History of American Civilization, edited by Daniel J. Boorstein (Chicago: University of Chicago Press, 1961).

Hollon, Eugene, *The Great American Desert, Then and Now* (New York: Oxford University Press, 1960).

———, *The Southwest: Old and New* (New York: Knopf, 1961).

Ise, John, *Sod and Stubble* (New York: Wilson-Erickson, Inc., 1936).

Kercheval, Samuel, *A History of the Valley of Virginia* (Woodstock, Virginia: W. N. Grabill, 1902).

Kincaid, Robert L., *The Wilderness Road* (Indianapolis: Bobbs-Merrill, 1947).

MacCleod, William C., *The American Indian Frontier* (New York: Alfred A. Knopf, 1928).

MacBride, Thomas H., *In Cabins and Sod Houses* (Iowa City: The State Historical Society of Iowa, 1928).

McDermott, John F., *The Frontier Re-examined.* (Urbana, Ill.: University of Illinois Press, 1967).

Oglesby, Richard E., *Manuel Lisa and the Opening of the Missouri Fur Trade* (Norman, Okla.: University of Oklahoma Press, 1963).

Osgood, Ernest S., *The Day of the Cattleman* (Minneapolis: University of Minnesota Press, 1929).

Paul, Rodman, *Mining Frontiers of the Far West, 1848–1880* (New York: Holt, Rinehart, and Winston, 1963).

Pratt, Julius, *Expansionists of 1812* (New York: MacMillan, 1926).

Reigel, Robert, *The Story of the Western Railroads* (New York: MacMillan, 1926).

Reister, Carl Coke, *The Southwestern Frontier* (Cleveland: Arthur H. Clark, 1928).

Robbins, Roy, *Our Landed Heritage* (Princeton, N.J.: Princeton University Press, 1942).

Rusk, Ralph Leslie, *The Literature of the Middle Western Frontier*, 2 vols. (New York: Columbia University Press, 1925).

Saum, Lewis O., *The Fur Trader and the Indian* (Seattle, Wash.: University of Washington Press, 1965).

Smith, Henry Nash, *Virgin Land* (Cambridge, Mass.: Harvard University Press, 1956).

Stuart, Granville, ed., *Forty Years on the Frontier*, by P. C. Phillips (Cleveland: Arthur H. Clark, 1925).

Turner, Katherine, *Red Men Calling on the Great White Father* (Norman, Okla.: University of Oklahoma Press, 1951).

Webb, Walter Prescott, *The Great Plains* (Boston: Ginn, 1931).

Wright, Louis, *Culture on the Moving Frontier* (Bloomington, Ind.: Indiana University Press, 1955).

Wyman, Walker D. and Clifton B. Froeber, *The Frontier in Perspective* (Madison, Wis.: University of Wisconsin Press, 1937).

Editor's Note

Selecting materials that describe essentially the meaning of the westward movement is a difficult undertaking at best, and a frustrating experience at worst. The materials, both published and unpublished, which validate this phase of American history are voluminous, and the actors are legion. I have sought especially to present the writings of contemporary persons, who by presence and experience, were able to give a clear concept of the West in motion. I have used some travel materials sparingly, not because of a total lack of faith in their validity, but because there are so many more competent sources available.

The frontiersman's journals and diaries bore eye-witness testimony to his sense of the place he felt was his in both time and the destiny of the Republic. Besides the mounting volume of the native personal record of the pioneering drama, two other groups added both body and perspective to the contemporary account. These were numerous official observers such as Meriwether Lewis and William Clark, Zebulon Montgomery Pike, Stephen H. Long, and John Charles Fremont. Both federal and state governments created a significant official history in the forms of constitutional and legislative materials and in the endless number of public reports. Statutory acts, court decisions, debate journals, all gave indispensable meaning and understanding to the westward movement.

American pioneering was a drama played in the full glare of public observation. Amazingly, hundreds of travelers of various nationalities found their way onto the frontier and went away to write extended accounts of their experiences. However de-

fective much of their observation may have been, it is reflec-
tive and, with proper caution, it is informative.

The westward movement in American history has greater
pertinence to the understanding of national history than ever
before. At a time when conservationists are producing extensive lists of plants and animals that hover on the brink of
extinction, and when scarcely a newspaper appears in which
someone does not predict dire trouble for Americans in the
ecological and resource areas, the frontiersman's approaches
to virgin lands in two centuries of national history has fundamental meaning. Even that rugged economic fortress, the
American family farm, is disappearing, and a secretary of
agriculture talks in the strange terms of "agri-business," cit-
ing startling statistics, describing the ratio of individuals engaged in farm production to the rest of the productive population, to demonstrate the revolution in a cherished way of
American life.

Historians of the West have examined the frontier or pioneering experience from almost every conceivable angle: its
political significance, its human importance, as a factor in
foreign relations, as an expression of American chauvinism,
as a broad ethical venture, as the creator of a native culture,
and as a major extension of American economic institutions.
The thesis put forward by Frederick Jackson Turner in his
seminal article, "The Significance of the Frontier in American
History,"* has stimulated a constant flow of articles and books.
Some historians have chosen to treat the subject as one with
deep philosophical and ethical implications, while others have
viewed the pioneering experience as that of simple, earthy,
everyday common men.

The American frontiersman became a hero in his own eyes
as well as those of historians. He did not wait for the passage
of time to have his story revealed; he wrote much of himself.
He was the only American who enjoyed a fair amount of free-

Annual Report, American Historical Association (Washington: Government Printing Office, 1893), pp. 199–227.

dom of choice as to his environmental and physical location. He could move away from frustrations, often with complete abandon, if not with irresponsibility, and in the process of doing so gave his act a heroic coloration; his voice had weight in the making of national political decisions, and at the same time he assured himself almost a reverential chapter in national historical literature.

Every effort has been made to keep selections within the context and intent of the original authors, even to the retention of ancient spelling and punctuation. In some instances internal cuts have been made (indicated by ellipsis points ". . ."), but these in no way destroy the context or continuity of the subject. No doubt another editor would have selected other materials. The volume of writings is so great that no single group of selections alone reveals all of the central theme of this experience in American history. A half dozen volumes of this type could be compiled without serious duplication.

THOMAS D. CLARK
Lexington, Kentucky

Introduction

Prior to the rise of the late nineteenth-century industrial and technological age, pioneering was the great American adventure. This is of especial interest to us now, as we look back on two hundred years of America's development as a nation. Possibly in no other recorded history, except that of Canada, Australia, and two or three of the South American countries, did the term *frontier* have so specific a meaning. In countries like ancient Greece and the others around the Mediterranean the term itself is almost impossible of translation, especially into the Greek language, and even more difficult to describe in terms of historical experience. For Americans the word *frontier* was indelibly fixed in the national mind in both a regional and conditional sense. Irresistible seemed the challenges of natural forces in the back country, of Indians, enormous scopes of virgin lands, of rivers whose sources and mouths were undetermined, and of the inexhaustible supply of wild game and fur-bearing animals.

The westward movement was first of all a major challenge to physical man. Its conquest was in large measure a durability contest between man and nature. It was the place where older Americans and newly arrived people of the old world came into direct association with heady environmental conditions. Soil, climate, flora and fauna, topography, and natural resources promised an abundance of the necessities for a comfortable mode of human life. Even beyond this, in many places they promised the luxurious fruits of a "virginal garden." Few newly arrived European immigrants knew firsthand what it was like to have so readily available large boundaries of fresh lands. This basic frontier bounty was as plentiful as an extravagant wish and as extensive as a sweeping wave of the hand.

Most of the climate of the older valley-transmontane frontier was reasonably temperate where man, animal, and plant thrived, and only a minimum amount of human adjustment was necessary to achieve a fairly comfortable existence. In fact, the climate in most areas was moderate enough to be conducive to the intensive human activity so necessary to the claiming of the western lands from the wilderness. Fauna was indeed generous to frontiersmen; once they learned to take advantage of it, they could in many places sustain themselves for some time on the wild bounties of nature.

Except for a few uninhibited visionaries in the latter eighteenth century, no one in America had acquired the knowledge or perspective necessary to make the wild predictions of future population and economic expansion which later characterized the westward movement. Frontier lands seemed more extensive than the capacity of all contemporary civilized men to exploit them. So plentiful seemed its supply that few if any settlers in North America, except in the New England towns, had to go through the grueling labors of grubbing harvests from the limited confines of given plots of soil. In few instances of Anglo-European expansion onto the frontier did men reveal more clearly basic human greed than in the rush to possess lands. The psychologist perhaps would have a more acceptable answer than the historian in explaining why the raw possessive nature of men was so shamelessly revealed on the American frontier in the claiming of lands. Even beyond this, land claiming became a mania which in some way infected people at all social and economic levels. It was to prove a central fact in the history of the westward movement, so much so that no legislative body was ever able to devise entirely satisfactory legislative controls to insure proper administration of its distribution and control. It was in this area of frontier life that the westerner made some of his clearest political-social distinctions. In clear Jeffersonian terms he was landowner—a property holder, not a laborer in the more restrictive sense of the wage earner. His sense of freedom was expressed most forcibly in both his commitment to a republican way of life and in his ever-increasing volume of local legislation. The passion to own was a ruling one on the frontier, and this passion often brought the central government into conflict. Squatters claimed blocks of the most desirable lands and then enlisted enough supportive opinion to bring about enactment of settler-slanted legislation. No better examples of this can be found than the Land Law of 1820 and the subsequent Preemption Law of 1841. The passage of these laws reflected how far a central Jeffersonian agrarian ideal had spread, and how intense had become what George Dangerfield has called the centrifugal influence of the frontiersmen, speaking from the rostrum of multiplying western states.

Beyond the issues of individual exploitation of the soil, there arose the greater issue of creating national and international territories. Earlier rivalries among the nations of western Europe and England for territorial claims in North America gave earlier ventures of pioneering both an international flavor and sting. This was clearly demonstrated in mid-eighteenth century when in the contest between England and France for domination of the western country so many basic national decisions helped shape the future contours of the Anglo-American westward movement. Among the more important of these were shifting of colonial controls, institutional development, basic language and cultural foundations, the cultivation of folk culture forms, the making of Indian policy, and the development of a vast body of statutory laws.

The westward movement in American history began at the foot of gangplanks of English and European immigrant ships along the Atlantic Coast. The pioneering process, however, in terms of reducing the measures of human society and life to the minimum of human sophistication and culture began at that point where men first severed dependence upon Old World economic and cultural resources to sustain them in a New World environment. The exercise of trying to mark even the approximate spot where this occurred is little short of being an exercise in futility. Englishmen and Europeans became backwoodsmen at varying stages in the advances onto the frontier, but certainly those going directly to the frontier adjusted more quickly than did those who remained along the eastern coast and river estuaries.

It was little short of romantic coincidence that hordes of yeoman settlers arrived on the American scene just at the time explorers, Indian traders, and land scouts were opening the way into the second geographical tier of the frontier. Immigrants from Scotland, Ireland, and Germany especially moved into the valleys of Virginia, Pennsylvania, New York, and the Carolinas along with the newcomers from England and France to be transformed into American backwoodsmen. They experienced crushing Indian assaults in western border skirmishes and wars and survived physical hardships and deprivations born of frontier necessity. From the ranks of these early inhabitants of the western valleys came the long hunters, the Indian traders, trailbreakers, and venturesome settlers. Experience gained in the valley layers of the western movement conditioned settlers for all the rest of the American pioneering adventure. After 1810 little actual change was made in the fundamental act of pioneering; only the necessity for adaptations of old principles to new and peculiar environmental conditions occurred.

In remarkably short time, frontiersmen penetrated the first layers of the Appalachian wall to plant settlements in western Pennsylvania and Virginia, and along the headwaters of the eastern Tennessee rivers. As quickly, they filed through Cumberland Gap to establish Harrodstown, Boonesboro, Nashville, and lesser Ohio Valley outposts. Every move these nomadic pioneers made placed excessive pressures on the Indian frontier itself. The Indians' woods, rivers, and lakes in time were swarmed over by frontiersmen who turned the wilderness into farms and pastures, towns, counties, and territories. With every confrontation the Indian was driven back to make way for the new settlements. He was forced to withdraw, leaving behind loved regions, cherished monuments of his race and history, and the sources of his livelihood. The saga of the American Indians from the Appalachian frontier to the Dakota borderlands was one of conflict and retreat.

The advance of the first western settlement line was of central importance in the history of the whole western movement. Here both people and institutions made the initial social adaptations before moving on. These early settlers by no means invented the log cabin, but they brought it to a high degree of practicality, adaptability, and maturity. What they did introduce as original were the heavy log or defensive blockhouses and the crude puncheon forts which resembled those of medieval Europe only in the vaguest generality of form and purpose. Along the upper Ohio, on the outer western rim of the Blue Ridges southward to Tennessee, and inside the Great Smokies in the upper Tennessee Valley pioneers made preliminary preparations for almost all the rest of the frontier advance across the continent. Later, on the treeless plains, pioneers adapted the frontier log cabin to the use of native materials in the construction of the sod house and the dugout.

Settlement of the Ohio and Mississippi Valleys matured the whole pioneering activity. Men and women learned the art of existing in a harsh land where the utmost exertion was demanded of them to protect themselves against human and elemental enemies while extracting a livelihood from the soil. They learned to grow meager crops with a severely limited collection of tools and implements, and to take from the woods such materials as existed there. They learned the art of building by the use of virginal timber stock, and they even dug from the ground various minerals. In these early stages frontiersmen came to grips with forces that taxed their ingenuity, physical endurance, and persistence. These farmer-woodsmen and their immediate descendents were the forebears of still other men who enlarged upon the great American saga by sending forth mountain men, miners, wagon train settlers, cowboys and cattlemen, and farmers. Fortunately the historical record concerning these pioneers is fairly clear. There were recorders on every hand to preserve descriptions of the spread of American frontier civilization. Whether or not what the barely literate frontiersmen, or their more literate visitors and subsequently their historians, wrote was literature matters little at this stage.

The chronicle had color and verve, and its meaning was almost always clear. Collectively this material became the central American folk record.

As said above, the westward movement never really took the American pioneer beyond the challenges and conditions that he could not in some way control or surmount. Libraries and archival collections attest to this fact. The heroics of the frontier were made of hardships and deprivations. Human endurance in the face of austere conditions was a test of spiritual and physical qualities. If men wished to claim the land, they had to pitch much of their struggle to do so on the terms of the land itself.

Vast stretches of unbroken virgin lands, of course, beckoned men on as did the seas. Land in its abundance aroused in frontiersmen a desire of possession and possibly a state of disturbing indecision. Anyone who has come in contact with land in sizable tracts is well familiar with the seductiveness of adjoining areas, and so it was with men floundering in the wilderness. The conversion of western woodlands into cleared fields where cultivated crops could be grown was a herculean undertaking which required long and persistent effort. The building of a cabin was an equally arduous task requiring the labors of several men. At no time or place where any significant beginnings of settlement were made could it be claimed as the result of individual effort. The entire neighborhood made investments of labor in the enterprise. No community on the frontier could either survive long or grow without personal cooperation and contributions from every able-bodied person. Pioneering was decidedly a cooperative enterprise. Men tackled the jobs before them with severely limited technical knowledge or scientific and mechanical aids. The axe, froe, broadaxe, hand augur, drawing knife, and pegging awl were basic tools of the frontier. With a pair of capable hands and the shape of a problem defined for him the average frontiersman was able to fulfill his desires and needs from materials at hand. He was able to hack out and shape the forms which so eloquently symbolized the pioneering experience. He in time came even to supply a market for such surplus goods as he could produce.

Farming was a way of life from the outset. The clearing of fields and the planting of corn, small grains, tobacco, hemp and flax, and the grazing of woods and pastures, resulted in the productions of mountains of produce which sought markets far beyond the rim of the frontier itself. In time it was all but impossible to separate the period of basic pioneering from that which produced the yeoman farmers with settled farmsteads, grazing herds, smokehouses, hemp breaks, and flaxen looms. Agrarianism, with its relationship to the land and to the act of pioneering, became an impressive economic, social, and political force. To a large extent America's "common man," as the "peasant" in Europe, was a yeoman farmer.

Where men were called upon to pass through stages of adaptations and adjustments to physical and economic challenges, they had to adapt to fresh social demands. A vast majority of western communities were culturally cooperative ventures, whether crowded into the midst of heavily forested borderlands or strung along mosquito-ridden river bottoms, later in the move westward in covered wagon caravans or dispersed in mining regions and on arid plains. The plight of human loneliness was broken in all sorts of ways. Log-rollings, house-raisings, quiltings, hog-killings, community hunts, play parties, community sporting events, and religious revival meetings were important folk manifestations of pioneering and the conditions of life. Beyond these recreative activities were practical cultural needs which demanded more formal approaches. The organization of even the most rudimentary schools confronted backwoodsmen with the ultimate demand for public support. Long before the adoption of the Ordinance of 1787 with its basic educational provision there were schools of a sort on the frontier. In Kentucky in 1780 there was the legal beginning of Transylvania Seminary, and before this institution opened its doors there were dame and "old field" schools. The opening decades of the nineteenth century saw the organization of frontier schools, seminaries, and colleges in Tennessee, Ohio, Indiana, Illinois, and Alabama. Founding educational institutions became as much a part of the state organizational formula as the erecting of state and court houses. Western pioneers sought to serve two basic social needs with their schools. They desired religious instruction and sought to produce lawyers, statesmen, and other technically trained individuals—even though they were suspicious of the professional man who got his training at semipublic expense.

Religion had an influential bearing on the shaping and conditioning of the lives of people on the frontier. No amount of rowdiness, harshness, or apparent indifference to refinement obscured this fact. It would indeed be within factual reason to assume that a majority of people on all the American frontiers were fundamentalists holding to a fairly literal interpretation of the Bible and regional code of human conduct. The preacher, circuit rider, or church station servitor, was as much a pioneer cultural and everyday fixture as were sheriffs and magistrates. How much preachers helped to mold the political mind is difficult of precise determination, but they were personal forces. There is certainty, as expressed in various statutory laws of the states, that legislatures were influenced in the adoption of codes of human behavior in keeping with the protestant ethic of the age. Sabbatarian laws, the sanctity of marriage code, laws against swearing, carousing, gambling, drinking, and sexual irregularities all reflected this influence. The periodic or seasonal revivals were more important for social intercourse than were all the other gatherings on the frontier. It may well be true that looked at from its social significance the religiosity of the revival was highly secondary in its importance.

In many other ways the frontiersman enlivened his society. He enjoyed contests of every sort, so definitely was his daily life oriented in this way. He savored both physical and intellectual tests. Just as the conquest of the land called for prodigious expenditures of energy, so did sports of the West. Among these were foot-racing, wrestling, fist-fighting, hunting, horse-racing, ring-tournaments, and weight-lifting contests. In the less physical areas there was nothing the frontiersman loved more than attending court and listening to the arguments of rival lawyers. O. H. Smith of Indiana has left a good description of the role of the court gatherings in frontier life. Governor Thomas Ford described those of Illinois in his *History of Illinois,* and the biographers of Abraham Lincoln have given extensive coverage to the subject. Court day on the frontier was one part a judicial gathering and nine parts a social and economic institution.

Militia musters and political campaigns equaled court trials in public fascination; the former with mock heroics and drunken buffoonery, the latter with exchanges of wit and partisan venom. The larger political issues most often discussed by historians of the frontier touched only lightly the consciousness or direct personal interest of individual frontiersmen. For the most part their attention was focused on the local issues and candidates, and especially on the ponderous directions of the courthouse ring. Political hustings were as much amusement events as meaningful discussions of issues. Good examples were the War Hawk congressional campaigns, the Jeffersonian presidential campaigns, and later those which sent Andrew Jackson to the White House for two terms. The symbols of politics were simple and earthy: roosters, skinned coons, log cabins, hard cider, plowboys, millboys, and railsplitters. When the lawyers, strutting militia colonels and majors, and politicians were not on center stage, frontiersmen generated their own entertainment in spelling matches, debates, and "homemade" oratory. So long as the pretense to intellectuality was kept on an elementary rural level, most American pioneers kept abreast of their needs for emotional release.

The era of the American frontier was the last one in which Americans fitted into their environmental conditions with any sense of comfort and certainty. Even so, environmental pressures were harsh. Endemic diseases were an ever-present spectre to pioneering. The common ague was a natural threat to human vitality, if not human existence, in the sprawling inland valleys. Inrushing settlers appreciated, but for the wrong reasons, the fact that this disease had a natural origin associated with the condition of the land itself. Even the development of settlement patterns may have reflected the prevalence of this disease in many places.

Smallpox was for a time an even more threatening menace than malaria. Even though the practice of inocculation was introduced into the Ohio Valley before 1800, smallpox was not subdued until decades later. It was with a high degree of ignorant fatalism that men accepted its ravages and looked upon the incidence of its recurrences as one of the tribulations which had to be endured. Just as smallpox and the fevers took heavy tolls of life, so did other diseases and accidents. Obviously the accident toll was high where men worked constantly in association with such powerful natural forces with their primitive tools and mechanical devices. Clearing the forests, hunting and trapping, traveling crude trails and roads, performing the daily labors of the field, and navigating wild rivers all offered constant threat to life and limb.

The act of pioneering included man's search for remedies and preventatives for his ills and misfortunes. Folk medicine was as much a part of the backwoods social matrix as religion and politics. By drawing heavily from Indian lore and combining it with Old World folk practices and native ignorance, there came into existence a cure or preventative for every disease and physical disability. The remedies overwhelmingly involved the use of native materials, and as the botanical frontier was widened so was the stock of the folk apothecary. Beyond this, however, were the superstitions and customs which sustained the pioneer in his venture into the uncertainties of new land and new adventures.

Increase in the western population brought sophistication and social changes. There came into existence the western towns and cities, transferring in large measure the social customs and mores of the land to the more crowded communities. In the towns thousands of frontiersmen came into new associative bodies. Human congregation introduced contamination and pollution which menaced in its own particular way health and life. It was in the new towns, on steamboats, and in wagon trains that epidemics rendered their fiercest blows. These could be controlled only by instituting dramatic measures. Infectious yellow fever, for instance, was borne up stream by early flatboatmen and later by passengers aboard western steamboats. This technological advance was a boon to commerce, but often a threat to whole communities by the rapidity with which it transported infected people from one place to another. In 1833 the fierce outbreak of Asiatic cholera left not only a trail of death and human desolation in its path, but in many places threatened to halt the westward movement itself. Again in 1849 this black death struck the wagon trains responding to the first urge to reach the California gold field. It was prevalent again in the early 1850s.

There was, notwithstanding the epidemics and other threats to life, a desire to increase the national population. Locally, states, cities, and towns boasted of population increases. Each decennial census was in a sense a triumphant report of national growth. Articulate frontiersmen, such as Caleb Atwater of Ohio, saw in this national human expansion the force of progress which would bring the realization of a dream of progress. If there was a warning that the growth of the population would within itself constitute a national problem, it was confined to those pamphlets and special publications which opposed westward expansion itself. This opposition was a fact which is often overlooked by the historians of the frontier, and it created a considerable body of material of its own.

So long as frontiersmen remained within the ranges of constant and heavy rainfall, and along the wooded frontier, they scarcely gave the conservation of most natural resources a serious second thought. Trees were as much barriers to farming and grazing as they were sources for building materials, fuel, and timber resources for the future. Besides, from a highly enclosed perspective within the wooded frontier, a man in 1810 could not conceive of a future condition in which not only the choicest trees would disappear but likewise the forest itself. To boatmen who struggled with willful currents in flood tide and drouth it was inconceivable that the towns and cities, industries, and even the boats themselves would threaten within a century and a quarter to "kill" the rivers.

Farmers by the thousands sinned against the land. One of the reasons for the constant movement and the feverish hunt for new lands was the abuse of older farms. The lands were abused and neglected. Careless cultivation dredged nutritive chemicals from the soil, and erosion scarred the surfaces beyond efficient use. It was not an unusual boast at all for a man to say he had worn out two or three farms in a lifetime and as many wives. What tillers of the soil failed to accomplish in many places, herdsmen did by driving hundreds of thousands of miles across an arid frontier from one grazing ground to another to reach railheads and greener ranges. In doing so they gave little thought to overgrazing or upsetting the balance of nature. Plains farmers defiantly violated nature even in the face of warnings by astute men like John Wesley Powell and subsequent agricultural experts. The land and elements struck back in the more arid regions even though frontier farmers developed an ingenius system of dry farming and drawing sustenance from the land.

Men on the frontier did not live alone by the economy or folk customs of the land. The ever widening line of settlement with its constantly developing pockets of civilization offered frontiersmen genuine political challenges. In fact, some of the most intense studies of the westward movement as a phenomenon in American history have been centered on its political impacts and implications. It would be simple indeed to write that westerners transported in their cultural baggage a simple Jeffersonian philosophy of equalitarianism which flourished on the foundations of an agrarian society, but this was not the case. If political manifestations beyond the Appalachians had been only this, there would have been a vapidity, if not an aimlessness, about them which would not now merit the considerations of a serious historian. Often it almost appears that some historians have seemed to confuse the mere processes of cooperative neighborliness with an expression of genuine democracy. One of the troubles has been that too often insufficient analysis has been made of the nature of the times and of their political contexts, aside from mere expressions of local reactions. Local political issues and leaders were exceedingly important everywhere on the frontier. Repeatedly both issues and political protagonists were to prove microcosms of the greater mass of the national political experience.

In greater measure it was on the frontier that the actual theory of applied federalism underwent recurring tests. The federal formula was stated in the Land Ordinance of 1785 in dealing with a specialized issue, and much more fully in the Ordinance of 1787. It was then given more authoritative sanction in the United States Constitution in the Philadelphia Convention. The real testing came, however, each time a new state was carved out of the frontier and admitted to the Union. Despite the controversies that have flared from time to time among the constitutional historians, no really convincing reconsideration of the two federal ordinances has invalidated their meanings. The land ordinance underwent tremendously interesting political evolution between 1796 and 1862. The adoption of each new revision reflected an evolutionary stage and change and the rise of regional and sectional political influence. The land laws of 1820 and 1841 marked the focusing of attention directly upon the small land claimant and the squatter. The yeoman land purchaser was favored with terms which he could manage with his modest access to capital, and the Preemption Law insured the squatter security in his land jumping and booming activities.

State-making was both an art and a political pastime. Delegates to the first series of separation conventions in Kentucky, 1784–1792, did not engage in constitution-making activities, but rather an extended discussion of political theories which would help them shape the most effective popular constitution possible. Present in all of these discussions was a conscious fear of the common everyday man for whom the state was being devised as a servant in the first place. Men who had never before heard the name John Locke found themselves in time debating his theories. In the later period they were influenced by the experiences of the older states and by what happened in Philadelphia in 1787.

The product of the Kentucky Constitutional Convention of April and May 1792 was not a scintillating original document which embodied imaginative provisions that fitted a frontier society living near nature and in search of the quintessence of equality and democracy. It was a restrictive document, hastily carved out of the constitutions of New Jersey, Virginia, and Pennsylvania. In the classical sense the Bill of Rights embodied in this document represented about all of the victories of men for all time in the field of human freedom. The structural articles, however, were not eloquent expressions of the functions of state government. Nevertheless this was a seminal document. In time, it and the 1799 revision became models for the framing of other constitutions for new frontier states.

It was in the drafting of state constitutions, the organization of state governments, and the formulation of collected statute laws that the American frontiersman had his purest exposure to applied politics. In the emergence of courthouse rings he had his first taste of partisan politics which led him to become a militant supporter of one side or the other. It mattered not that he was ignorant of the operation of state governments or of pure political ideals; he had within the contexts of his simple understanding a cause or a party which he could emotionally possess in the same way he owned his farm or his horse. He also had an open channel by which he could ultimately have a voice in what happened in Congress and the White House.

Politics and law meant more than a classical legal expression to the frontiersman. In a day when lawbreaking and violence were common, almost accepted occurrences, there was a constant effort to establish law and order. In actuality the constable, sheriff, border marshall, and magistrate were more important functionaries to the individual citizen than governors and presidents. In far more colorful fashion, but not entirely by accident, these officials in time were to become stock folk characters, and even, in some cases, folk heroes. The westerner, whether in Kentucky or Oregon, had great love for the law and its processes as revealed in court trials. He appeared often as litigant, either as the aggrieved or offender, but more often as curious spectator. The bystanders came to hear lawyers, many of whom were cast as intellectual giants in courtroom arguments and oratory. Among these were John Breckinridge, who became Thomas Jefferson's attorney general; Henry Clay; Thomas Hart Benton; Andrew Jackson; Alexander Doniphan; and Abraham Lincoln. These were some of the top-liners; there were literally hundreds who shone as local lights, and sometimes in only a single trial. There is no more amazing fact relating to American history down to 1890 than the influence the local courtroom had in the training and conditioning of much of the national political leadership. This was especially true of those elected officials who came from states that had gone through extended periods of frontier existence. Likewise, this was the incubator of leaders who were of the soil as well as of the legislative chamber.

In a vague and largely undefined way the frontier experience etched an outline of what was perhaps the most important internal challenge, that of public management of natural resources. There was first the Indian trade in products of the forest such as skins, furs, and herbs, then land. Land, politically, was to be viewed in two dimensions. First, its international ramifications spread its pattern on large scales. The treaties of Paris, 1763 and 1783, gave near continental scope to this central frontier question. Subsequent treaties enlarged national and international sensitivities on the subject. Even when ultimately defined in terms of established national boundaries, territorial considerations were uppermost in negotiations.

Sharing parity of attention with territory and land were stream and river resources. Rivers everywhere in the world have been integral parts of human and political history, but nowhere more so than in North America. The presence of dense forests, of Indians, both fierce and commercially minded, treeless plains, peculiar topographical features, and great distances, all magnified the significance of the rivers. Even the fertility of the great valley, extended north and south across the continent, early figured in the creation of a rich national and international commerce. Equally as important, it created and shaped vital domestic political issues.

It may be that historians can never isolate and define clearly the full impact of expansionism in either objective fact or the forensics of political and nationalistic chauvinism. In the aggressive search of the record for the last decade of the eighteenth and the first half of the nineteenth centuries, revisionist historians have offered reappraisals of expansionist influences without denying their central importance. As the settlement thrust of the westward movement was broadened, the United States faced both internal and international complications, some of which resulted in wars. For instance, there was the Northwest Campaign during the Revolutionary War, the revolt in West Florida, the War of 1812, and the Mexican War. Besides there were the less chauvinistic Adams de Onis Treaty, The Webster-Asburton, and the Guadeloupe-Hildalgo treaties. All of these were political decisions made far apart from individual relationships with government and community.

Collectively, individuals on the frontier played key roles in either creating or sensing sectional interests and forces. Much of the sectional impact of political responses was cast in terms of individual reactions not only in reference to specific area and time, but also to the larger issues of recognition of sections and institutions. There was anxiety on the part of most political communities on the isolated frontier that they not be cut off culturally, economically, or politically from the central body of the nation. There was always the strong determination that laws formulated in the more sophisticated national or state capitals would injure neither frontier institutions nor economics. For instance, the Whisky Rebellion, the regulation of public land sales, the establishment of banks, the subsidizing of internal improvements, the enactment of Indian policy laws, and the adoption of tariffs were of vital concern. All of these drew clear expressions of western or frontier sentiment.

No institutional issue was to become more intertwined with western expansion than slavery: first in the discussions in the committee formulating the Ordinance of 1787, and subsequently in the Missouri statehood debate, the Wilmot Proviso and the administration of territories acquired by the treaty of Guadeloupe-Hildalgo, the admission of California, the Kansas-Nebraska controversy, and the Dred Scott decision. The subsequent Lincoln-Douglas debates reflected eloquent summary of the intensity of western sectional feelings.

In a more general way sectional influences had tremendous weight in congressional debates and actions, and in the shaping of a significant body of statute law. Equally as important, the operational organization of the national legislative body revealed a response to sectional forces. Thus the influence of the frontier must be measured overwhelmingly in terms of almost a century of shaping legislation, rather than in terms of spectacular innovation, the generation of original political theories and concepts, or in the willing acceptances of frequent institutional changes.

Measured by dependable standards, the American backwoodsman, turned yeoman farmer and journeyman, was politically, socially, and religiously a conservative individual. Territorial officials appointed by successive presidents continually renewed the thrust of federalism or nationalism under administrative instructions and legal mandates. At the grass roots, however, the onrushing settler carried with him only the skeletal forms of older American society whether it was the rounds and calls of the folk dance, the wedding infare, the revival meeting, the magistrate's court with its general folk assembly of court day, the courthouse ring, or a pride in a specific locality. He was an image worshipper, often translating his political loyalties into terms of adulation for the "old hero" who could best relate himself to the mainstream of everyday earthy experiences.

No clearer folk declaration has ever been made than the

determination of frontiersmen to observe established tradition by the transfer of beloved older place names from one island of territorial settlement to another. One has only to call the roll of the Bostons, Lexingtons, Lancasters, Philadelphias, Richmonds, Raleighs, Washingtons, Nashvilles, Jeffersonvilles, Hamiltons, Frankforts, and Louisvilles to appreciate this fact. In the same manner church names were carried west with equal fidelity wherever communicants of the old Bethels, Cavalries, Wesley Chapels, Shilohs, and Mount Moriahs lingered long enough to "hold preachings" at stated intervals.

Thus far the history of the American frontier has been discussed largely in the context of its political and institutional development. In the advance of the American people across this continent there were few, and perhaps no times or places, in which the movement progressed along a regular or orderly line. Nor was there at any time really a single frontier.

From the moment the settlement line thrust itself against the eastern Appalachian wall in the South in the first half of the eighteenth century, and later against the lakes and international barriers of the North, there was fragmentation of the forward advance. At these points the frontier began to fall into such sectional parts as the Shenandoah Valley, the lower Mississippi basin, the Old Northwest, and later west of the Mississippi, the Rockies, and the Far West. In the latter region there were several well-defined regional designations, each one exhibiting a distinct geographical or social personality.

Besides the regional islands in the general frontier advance there were the exciting topographical ones such as the flatboat river drama, the mining frontier in upper Missouri, and always the Indian enclaves, the fur trader epoch, the Santa Fe trade, the explorer's frontier, the great immigrant trails, the subsequent mineral rushes, the cattle and sheep drives, the military border lands, the railroad extensions, and the plains farmer's frontier. All of these, of course, were part and parcel of the greater westward movement, but each one within its particular character was a distinct entity, and so it must be considered and related to the national experience.

Had the westward movement been only a repetition of older patterns it would have become a historically boring chapter in American history of continental proportions. Quite to the contrary, almost all of the topical frontiers were glorified in time by being elevated to saga status. Mention of three of these is sufficient to illustrate this fact. The history of the fur trade in the Rockies with its rugged and free-for-all mountain men added a broader and more substantial dimension to that of the old Appalachian long hunters. Some mountain men, like the Sublette brothers, were direct blood descendants of the old generation of trail-breakers. The story of the rugged conquest of an unrelenting mountain empire with its Indian and fur trading rivalries became as heroic as the mountain peaks forming natural backdrops for the pageant.

This mountain drama had scarcely rung down the final curtain before an even more melodramatic movement was advancing across the land in the long snaking trails of immigrant covered wagons which in turn were followed by that incessant march to the Far West, and, hopefully, to fortunes documented in terms of gold. This latter moving frontier had one distinct characteristic. It crossed a vast scope of virgin territory in such a remarkably short time it neither had a direct influence on the intervening country nor, except for the drastic hardships of travel, was deeply influenced by it. These wagon trains transported across the continent to California and the Far Northwest intact the forms of older American borderland society, including the unified family and home. There perhaps has never been a more highly domesticated movement of people over such expanse of territory as this one. The drama of this venture rested largely on the fact that a majority of the immigrants lived to reach their destinations; they carried with them established forms of pioneering born of the latter decades of the eighteenth century.

Following the Civil War, which had its own western aspects, the cattle drives were started out of southwest Texas in search of grazing grounds and railway transportation. These drives and the spread of a residual ranching industry brought into full bloom the most colorful frontier character of all—the cowboy. This man on horseback became a highly captivating folk figure who had no real counterpart in history unless it be the nomadic tribesmen of the near eastern deserts. Certainly the Texas cattle driver would have disdained comparison with those patient, onion-eating footmen who stood father-protectors over goat and sheep herds in the rock-strewn lands of Greece and Macedonia.

The cowboy, his horse, and his herd were only part of the cattle frontier cast; there were the railroad towns, the saloons, girls, marshals, gamblers, bankers and cattlemen, and innocent, naive settlers with their starveling churches and agrarian-rural codes of social decorum. Most of these burgeoning communities in the early stages formed islands of para-civilization. All of these characters with their colorful setting and amoral natures supplied material for the great American story which has been presented in dime thrillers, novels, personal accounts, serious scholarly studies, and in almost countless moving pictures. The "Western" was long ago established as much an indigenous part of American literature as the writings of the New England poets, or those of William Dean Howells, Hamlin Garland, Edgar Lee Masters, and Mark Twain. Owen Wister, Zane Grey, Harold Bell Wright, and dozens of others all but removed the bitter sting of reality from this part of the raw frontier.

A. B. Guthrie, Jr., in two powerful novels about the moving frontier, glorified first the mountain man and then the sojourner on the covered wagon trail. He gave even greater depth and humanity to the adventures along the great trail than did Francis Parkman or Edwin Bryant. The saga of the gold rush produced an unknown number of accounts of pioneering on this new kind of frontier which in the past half century had fed the printing presses with fresh materials. Where the novelists, the narrative writers, and the personal reminiscers have created shelves of books, the most industrious authors, however, have been those who filled the state historical magazines with an ever-increasing flow of special articles. There has been no letup in the publication of this material, and each new issue of a western state historical society quarterly adds a new cubic to an understanding of the westward movement.

In a modern and serious vein, a new kind of historical approach is made to the study of western history. Never did so many people venturing into a virgin country come directly into association with such abundant natural resources. It was the exploitation of these that in time was to create issues of both sectional and national proportions. It no doubt would be within the realm of fact to say that never did modern man treat so blithely the resources that he found in a new land. He abused the soils, either by faulty methods of culivation and land uses, or by disregarding the balances of nature. He destroyed forest resources right and left so that by 1890 this virginal asset on the frontier was as much in danger of disappearance as the frontier line itself. The great lumber operations butchered stands of timber in statewide proportions, and the profligate despoilers made no effort to replant or reforest gutted areas. The story was the same from Maine to California and from Minnesota to Mississippi. One of the unhappiest words coined in the advance of the frontier was "cutover."

The mineral exploiters did no better by the land. In many places mining operations spoiled the country by passing the tracts of soil through mining machines which completely destroyed the natural layers of top soil. In others, land was laid waste by improper reclamation procedures. The same thing happened to streams which were choked by silt and debris. Cattle and sheep grazers failed to use caution in their struggle to make profits from their undertakings and so did farmers who broke the sod and defied nature in arid areas. All of these negative facts are as vital parts of the history of the westward movement as personal heroics and nostalgic color, and all must be reckoned with in an appraisal of the long-range significance of the frontier in American history.

The application of the federal system itself was one of the most successful accomplishments of the westward movement. There were innovations, of course, such as the development of mining laws, general laws governing grazing lands, the liberality toward woman suffrage in Wyoming and Utah, and ultimately in other western states. The rise of the land-grant college, with strong emphases upon scientific agriculture and with the main heartbeat being the United States Department of Agriculture, was definitely a successful venture. Not so successful was the Homestead Law, the various reclamation laws, and the many attempts to develop an Indian policy; but these actions by the federal government were not seriously questioned in principle and intent. In the Far West there was much less question of public subsidy of internal improvements than on the early eastern frontier. There were, however, responses on all the frontiers, and in all periods, to the federal monetary policies. The issues on the older frontier centered around private versus state banking, and those of the post-Civil War frontier about terms of credit, the nature of currency, and the place of the precious metals of the West in formulation of national monetary policies.

In the latter decades of the existence of the frontier it was difficult to determine at what point a state or a community ceased to be a part of the pioneering age and became a definite part of the urban-industrial society which generated its own peculiar personality, economics, and social traits. Like the great outward thrust of the virginal westward movement itself, there was no established line or chronological moment when the frontier era ended and a new one began. This also occurred in islands of change rather than along an identifiable line of progress. In 1890 the superintendent of the United States Census spoke only of the closing of a statistical frontier, not a physical one. There has never been a closing of the nostalgic and historical part of the westward movement, and perhaps never will be so long as historians continue to dredge the great volumes of virginal source materials in search of new perspectives and meanings of American history itself.

The Great American Frontier

A Story of Western Pioneering

I

Trailbreaking

The most exciting aspect of American pioneering was the breaking of trail into virgin territory. Spanish explorers had pushed deeply into the North American continent in the sixteenth century; but it was at the opening of the seventeenth century with John Smith and his fellow Jamestown adventurers that English pioneering, the movement that truly opened the continent, began. It was on the eighteenth-century frontier that George Croghan and other early Indian traders, both English and French, penetrated the Ohio Valley. In mid-century, Dr. Thomas Walker and Christopher Gist explored large blocks of Ohio Valley lands for companies of land speculators; both of them kept interesting journals describing what, at the time, was believed to have been largely fruitless explorations.

In a sense, Walker and Gist opened the great gates of the Cumberlands and the headwaters of the Ohio. They learned what the topography of the immediate western mountain valleys was like. Behind them came hundreds of pioneers who pushed the trail westward a little deeper into the interior. Lewis and Clark took up where the old trailbreakers had turned back and opened a path across the continent. It remained for others to explore more thoroughly the rest of the great West.

Mountain men opened trails into forbidding ridges and valleys in the Great Rockies. They discovered river passes, Indian tribes, furs, and new lands to be settled. On their heels came settlers to open land in Oregon and California. John C. Frémont headed an official exploring party, and his published experiences to a large extent removed much of the mystery of western exploration if not the thrill of pioneering in fresh country. Finally the railroad age of trailbreaking was to have its own color.

1.   The Expanding Frontier

The settler, the land scout and often even the explorer were preceded into the woods by the hunter and the trapper. The French
botanist, Francois A. Michaux, was greatly impressed by a frontier
hunter whom he overtook in the neighborhood of Marietta, Ohio.
The Frenchman seemed to understand something of the restlessness
that stirred the American backwoodsman and to sense also that
although the hunter set out to take beaver and other fur-bearers his
long thoughts turned from time to time to the civilization that
would follow him. He sensed that the fertile land in the Ohio
Valley and the great river channel would be prime movers in the
development of an American civilization which would become imbued with a sense of restless progress and that one phase of life
would be succeeded immediately by another.

Before arriving at Marietta, we met with one of these settlers,
who resided in the environs of Wheeling, and who being likewise on his way down the Ohio, we travelled with him for ten
days. He was alone in a canoe about eighteen or twenty feet
long, by twelve or fifteen inches wide, and was going to visit
the banks of the Missouri, which are inhabited by Americans,
about a hundred and fifty miles from its mouth. The excellent
quality of the land, which is reckoned more fertile than that on
the Ohio, and which the Spanish Government then caused
to be distributed gratis, together with the multitude of beavers,
elks, and particularly of bisons, were the motives that induced
him to emigrate to those distant countries, whence, after finding a convenient spot for his residence, he intended to return
to the Ohio to fetch his family, and by which his voyage would
amount to fourteen or fifteen hundred miles. His costume, like
that of all the American hunters, consisted of a round jacket
with sleeves, a pair of pantaloons, and a large woollen belt of

F. A. Michaux, *Travels to the Westward of the Alleghany Mountains, in
the States of Ohio, Kentucky, and Tennessee in the Year 1802* (London:
Richard Phillips, 1805, 52, 53.

a red or yellow colour: his hunting-implements were a carbine, a tomahawk or small hatchet, which the Indians use for cutting wood, or killing their enemies, two snares for beavers, and a large dirk hanging from his belt; a cloak or coverlet was all his baggage. Every evening he landed on the banks of the river, where he made a fire, and passed the night; and when he thought the place favourable for hunting. he went into the woods for several days together: the produce of the chace afforded him the means of subsistence, and by the sale of the skins he procured supplies of ammunition. Such were the first inhabitants of Kentucky and Tennessee, of which only a few now remain. It was they who began to cultivate these fertile regions, after taking them from the savages, who disputed their possession of them with the most sanguinary violence for a period of five or six years; but their long familiarity with a wandering and idle life, prevented the new comers from enjoying the fruit of their labours in profiting by the extraordinary price which those lands soon attained; they emigrated into countries still more distant, where they formed new establishments.

The same conduct will, probably, be pursued by those who now reside on the banks of the Ohio; for the same propensity which led them thither will cause them to emigrate still farther. These will be succeeded by new emigrants from the Atlantic States, who will also abandon their lands to go in search of a milder temperature and a more fertile soil. The last comers, instead of log houses with which the present residents are contented, will probably build their residences of planks, cultivate a greater quantity of land, and by perseverance render their new possessions more valuable by raising maize, wheat, tobacco, and hemp: the peaceable enjoyment of their property will be secured by their numerous population; they will rear abundance of cattle in their rich meadows, while an advantageous sale for the products of the country, will always arise from their conveyance by the Ohio.

The situation of this river being the best of any in the United States, must cause it to be considered as the centre of commerce between the United and the Western States, as it is by its means that the latter receive the manufactured articles with which Europe, India, and the Antilles, supply the former; while it is the only medium of communication that is opened to the ocean, for exporting the goods afforded by the vast and fertile part of the United States comprised between the Alleghany mountains, the lakes, and the left bank of the Mississippi.

2.   Up the Great Missouri

One of the greatest of frontier adventures was the expedition of Meriwether Lewis and William Clark up the Missouri and across the mountain divide to the Pacific Coast. No one knew in May 1804 what lay ahead of this small party of explorers. Between them and their goal lay a broad expanse of land and water—but what of the natural barriers, of animals, and, most important of all, of Indians? Their ascent began on the fourteenth of May. Preparation for this great venture bore kinship to modern man's exploration of space. So far as the leaders knew they were on a sacrificial mission from which they might not return. Yet it was the pressure of American adventure and rising nationalism that drove them westward.

All the preparations being completed, we left our encampment on Monday, May 14th, 1804. This spot is at the mouth of Wood river, a small stream which empties itself into the Mississippi, opposite to the entrance of the Missouri. It is situated in latitude 38° 55' 19" 6/10 north, and longitude from Greenwich, 89° 57' 45". On both sides of the Mississippi the land for two or three miles is rich and level, but gradually swells into a high pleasant country, with less timber on the western than on the eastern side, but all susceptible of cultivation. The point which separates the two rivers on the north, extends for fifteen or

"Journal of Lewis and Clark," John Bach McMaster, ed., *History of the Expedition under the Command of Captains Lewis and Clark,* 3 vols. (New York: Allerton Book, 1902), vol. I, pp. 37–39.

twenty miles, the greater part of which is an open level plain, in which the people of the neighborhood cultivate what little grain they raise. Not being able to set sail before four o'clock P. M., we did not make more than four miles, and encamped on the first island opposite a small creek called Cold Water.

May 15. The rain, which had continued yesterday and last night, ceased this morning. We then proceeded, and after passing two small islands about ten miles further, stopped for the night at Piper's landing, opposite another island. The water is here very rapid and the banks falling in. We found that our boat was too heavily laden in the stern, in consequence of which she ran on logs three times to-day. It became necessary to throw the greatest weight on the bow of the boat, a precaution very necessary in ascending both the Missouri and Mississippi rivers, in the beds of which, there lie great quantities of concealed timber.

The next morning we set sail at five o'clock. At the distance of a few miles, we passed a remarkably large coal hill on the north side, called by the French LaCharbonniere, and arrived at the town of St. Charles. Here we remained a few days.

St. Charles is a small town on the north bank of the Missouri, about twenty-one miles from its confluence with the Mississippi. It is situated in a narrow plain, sufficiently high to protect it from the annual risings of the river in the month of June, and at the foot of a range of small hills, which have occasioned its being called Petite Cote, a name by which it is more known to the French than by that of St. Charles. One principal street, about a mile in length and running parallel with the river, divides the town, which is composed of nearly one hundred small wooden houses, besides a chapel. The inhabitants, about four hundred and fifty in number, are chiefly descendants from the French of Canada; and, in their manners, they unite all the careless gayety, and the amiable hospitality of the best times of France: yet, like most of their countrymen in America, they are but ill qualified for the rude life of a frontier; not that they are without talent, for they possess much natural genius and vivacity; nor that they are destitute of enterprise, for their hunting excursions are long, laborious, and hazardous: but their exertions are all desultory; their industry is without system, and without perseverance. The surrounding country, therefore, though rich, is not, in general, well cultivated; the inhabitants chiefly subsisting by hunting and trade with the Indians, and confine their culture to gardening, in which they excel.

Being joined by Captain Lewis, who had been detained by business at St. Louis, we again set sail on Monday, May 21st, in the afternoon, but were prevented by wind and rain from going more than about three miles, when we encamped on the upper point of an island, nearly opposite a creek which falls in on the south side.

3.   Nature's Empire

As the Lewis and Clark Expedition moved up the Missouri River, every crossing of a hill or rounding of a bend revealed new wonders. None was more impressive than the changing animal life. The expedition had little or no difficulty in carrying out Thomas Jefferson's instructions regarding the fauna, changing geography, and climate. Everywhere there was evidence of an abundant nature pouring forth its offerings of animals, plants, and natural formations. To forest born and conditioned men the opening plains of the upper Missouri became a veritable wonderland.

Monday, September 16.– Whilst some of the party were engaged in the same way as yesterday, others were employed in examining the surrounding country. About a quarter of a mile behind our camp, and at an elevation of twenty feet above it, a plain extends nearly three miles parallel to the river, and about a mile back to the hills, towards which it gradually ascends. Here we saw a grove of plum-trees loaded with fruit, now ripe, and differing in nothing from those of the Atlantic

"Journal of Lewis and Clark," *ibid.*, pp. 121–123.

states, except that the tree is smaller and more thickly set. The ground of the plain is occupied by the burrows of multitudes of barking squirrels, who entice hither the wolves of a small kind, hawks, and polecats, all of which animals we saw, and presumed that they fed on the squirrel. This plain is intersected nearly in its whole extent by deep ravines and steep irregular rising grounds from one to two hundred feet. On ascending the range of hills which border the plain, we saw a second high level plain stretching to the south as far as the eye could reach. To the westward, a high range of hills about twenty miles distant runs nearly north and south, but not to any great extent, as their rise and termination is embraced by one view, and they seemed covered with a verdure similar to that of the plains. The same view extended over the irregular hills which border the northern side of the Missouri: all around the country had been recently burnt, and a young green grass about four inches high covered the ground, which was enlivened by herds of antelopes and buffalo; the last of which were in such multitudes, that we cannot exaggerate in saying that at a single glance we saw three thousand of them before us. Of all the animals we had seen the antelope seems to possess the most wonderful fleetness: shy and timorous they generally repose only on the ridges, which command a view of all the approaches of an enemy: the acuteness of their sight distinguishes the most distant danger, the delicate sensibility of their smell defeats the precautions of concealment, and when alarmed their rapid career seems more like the flight of birds than the movements of an earthly being. After many unsuccessful attempts, Captain Lewis at last, by winding around the ridges, approached a party of seven, which were on an eminence, towards which the wind was unfortunately blowing. The only male of the party frequently encircled the summit of the hill, as if to announce any danger to the females, who were formed in a group at the top. Although they did not see Captain Lewis, the smell alarmed them, and they fled when he was at the distance of two hundred yards: he immediately ran to the spot where they had been, a ravine concealed them from him, but the next moment they appeared on a second ridge at the distance of three miles. He doubted whether it could be the same, but their number and the extreme rapidity with which they continued their course, convinced him that they must have gone with a speed equal to that of the most distinguished racehorse.

4.   End of the Long Trail

On November 7, 1806 Lewis and Clark reached the Pacific. The latter part of their journey had involved them in the greatest hardships of the whole venture. Near the mouth of the Columbia they found rough terrain, bothersome Indians, fleas, and no signs of the ship they hoped to meet.

Tuesday, 5.– Our choice of a camp had been very unfortunate; for on the sand island opposite to us were immense numbers of geese, swan-ducks, and other wild fowl, who, during the whole night, serenaded us with a confusion of noises which completely prevented our sleeping. During the latter part of the night it rained, and we therefore willingly left our encampment at an early hour. We passed at three miles a small prairie, where the river is only three quarters of a mile in width, and soon after two houses on the left, half a mile distant from each other; from one of which three men came in a canoe merely to look at us, and having done so returned home. At eight miles we came to the lower point of an island, separated from the right side by a narrow channel on which, a short distance above the end of the island, is situated a large village: it is built more compactly than the generality of the Indian villages, and the front has fourteen houses, which are ranged for a quarter of a mile along the channel. As soon as we were discovered seven canoes came out to see us, and after some traffic, during which they seemed well-disposed and orderly, accompanied us a

"Journal of Lewis and Clark," *ibid.,* vol. II, pp. 251–259.

short distance below. The river here again widens to the space of a mile and a half. As we descended we soon observed, behind a sharp point of rocks, a channel a quarter of a mile wide, which we suppose must be the one taken by the canoes yesterday on leaving Image-canoe island. A mile below the channel are some low cliffs of rocks near which is a large island on the right side, and two small islands a little further on. Here we met two canoes ascending the river. At this place the shore on the right becomes bold and rocky, and the bank is bordered by a range of high hills covered with a thick growth of pine: on the other side is an extensive low island, separated from the left side by a narrow channel. Here we stopped to dine, and found the island open, with an abundance of grass, and a number of ponds well supplied with fowls; and at the lower extremity are the remains of an old village. We procured a swan, several ducks, and a brant, and saw some deer on the island. Besides this island, the lower extremity of which is seventeen miles from the channel just mentioned, we passed two or three smaller in the same distance. Here the hills on the right retire from the river, leaving a high plain, between which, on the left bank, a range of high hills running southeast and covered with pines forms a bold and rocky shore. At the distance of six miles, however, these hills again return and close the river on both sides. We proceeded on, and at four miles reached a creek on the right, about twenty yards in width, immediately below which is an old village. Three miles further, and at the distance of thirty-two miles from our camp of last night, we halted under a point of highland, with thick pine-trees on the left bank of the river. Before landing we met two canoes, the largest of which had at the bow the image of a bear, and that of a man on the stern: there were twenty-six Indians on board, but they all proceeded upwards, and we were left, for the first time since we reached the waters of the Columbia, without any of the natives with us during the night. Besides the game already mentioned, we killed a grouse much larger than the common size, and observed along the shore a number of striped snakes. The river here is deep, and about a mile and a half in width. Here too the ridge of the low mountains running northwest and southeast, cross the river, and form the western boundary of the plain through which we have just passed. This great plain or valley begins above the mouth of Quicksand River, and is about sixty miles wide in a straight line, while on the right and left it extends to a great distance: it is a fertile and delightful country, shaded by thick groves of tall timber, watered by small ponds, and running on both sides of the river. The soil is rich, and capable of any species of culture; but in the present condition of the Indians, its chief production is the wappatoo root, which grows spontaneously and exclusively in this region. Sheltered as it is on both sides, the temperature is much milder than that of the surrounding country; for even at this season of the year we observe very little appearance of frost. During its whole extent it is inhabited by numerous tribes of Indians, who either reside in it permanently, or visit its waters in quest of fish and wappatoo roots: we gave it the name of Columbia valley.

Wednesday, 6.– The morning was cool, wet, and rainy. We proceeded at an early hour between the high hills on both sides of the river, till at the distance of four miles we came to two tents of Indians in a small plain on the left, where the hills on the right recede a few miles from the river, and a long narrow island stretches along the right shore. Behind this island is the mouth of a large river a hundred and fifty yards wide, and called by the Indians, Coweliske. We halted for dinner on the island, but the red wood and green briars are so interwoven with pine, alder, ash, a species of beech, and other trees, that the woods form a thicket, which our hunters could not penetrate. Below the mouth of the Coweliske a very remarkable knob rises from the water's edge to the height of eighty feet, being two hundred paces round the base; and as it is in a low part of the island, and some distance from the high grounds, the appearance is very singular. On setting out after dinner we overtook two canoes going down to trade: one of the Indians, who spoke a few words of English, mentioned, that the principle person who traded with them was a Mr. Haley, and he showed a bow of iron and several other things which he said Mr. Haley had given him. Nine miles below that river is a creek on the same; and between them three smaller islands; one on the left shore, the other about the middle of the river; and a third near the lower end of the long narrow island, and opposite a high cliff of black rocks on the left, sixteen miles from our camp. Here we were overtaken by the Indians from the two tents we passed in the morning, from whom we now purchased wappatoo roots, salmon, trout, and two beaver skins, for which we gave five small fish hooks. At these cliffs the mountains, which had continued high and rugged on the left, retired from the river, and as the hills on the other side had left the water at the Coweliske, a beautiful extensive plain now presented itself before us: for a few miles we passed along side of an island a mile in width and three miles long, below which is a smaller island, where the high rugged hills, thickly covered with timber, border the right bank of the river, and terminate the low grounds: these were supplied with common rushes, grass, and nettles; in the moister parts with bullrushes and flags, and along the water's edge some willows. Here also were two ancient villages, now abandoned by their inhabitants, of whom no vestige remains except two small dogs almost starved, and a prodigious quantity of fleas. After crossing the plain and making five miles, we proceeded through the hills for eight miles. The river is about a mile in width, and the hills so steep that we could not for several miles find a place sufficiently level to suffer us to sleep in a level position: at length, by removing the large stones, we cleared a place fit for our purpose above the reach of the tide, and after a journey of twenty-nine miles slept among the smaller stones under the mountain to the right. The weather was rainy during the whole day; we therefore made large fires to dry our bedding and to kill fleas, who have accumulated upon us at every village we have passed.

Thursday, 7.– The morning was rainy and the fog so thick that we could not see across the river. We observed however, opposite to our camp, the upper point of an island, between which and the steep hills on the right we proceeded for five miles. Three miles lower is the beginning of an island separated from the right shore by a narrow channel; down this we proceeded under the direction of some Indians whom we had just met going up the river, and who returned in order to show us their village. It consists of four houses only, situated on this channel behind several marshy islands formed by two small creeks. On our arrival they gave us some fish, and we afterwards purchased wappatoo roots, fish, three dogs, and two otter skins, for which we gave fish hooks chiefly, that being an article of which they are very fond.

These people seem to be of a different nation from those we have just passed: they are low in stature, ill shaped, and all have heads flattened. They call themselves Wahkiacum, and their language differs from that of the tribes above, with whom they trade for wappatoo roots. The houses too are built in a different style, being raised entirely above the ground, with the eaves about five feet high, and the door at the corner. Near the end opposite to this door is a single fireplace, round which are the beds, raised four feet from the floor of earth; over the fire are hung the fresh fish, and when dried they are stowed away with the wappatoo roots under the beds. The dress of the men is like that of the people above, but the women are clad in a peculiar manner, the robe not reaching lower than the hip, and the body being covered in cold weather by a sort of corset of fur, curiously plaited, and reaching from the arms to the hip: added to this is a sort of petticoat, or rather tissue of white cedar bark, bruised or broken into small strands, and woven into a girdle by several cords of the same material. Being tied round the middle, these strands hang down as low as the knee in front, and to midleg behind, and are of sufficient thickness to answer the purpose of concealment whilst the female stands in an erect position, but in any other attitude is but very ineffectual defence. Sometimes the tissue is strings of silk grass, twisted and knotted at the end.

After remaining with them about an hour, we proceeded down the channel with an Indian dressed in a sailor's jacket for our pilot, and on reaching the main channel were visited by some Indians who have a temporary residence on a marshy island in the middle of the river, where is a great abundance of water fowl. Here the mountainous country again approaches the river on the left, and a higher mountain is distinguished towards the southwest. At a distance of twenty miles from our camp we halted at a village of Wahkiacums, consisting of seven ill-looking houses, built in the same form with those above, and situated at the foot of the high hills on the right, behind two small marshy islands. We merely stopped to purchase some food and two beaver skins, and then proceeded. Opposite to these islands the hills on the left retire, and the river widens into a kind of bay crowded with low islands, subject to be overflowed occasionally by the tide. We had not gone far from this village when the fog cleared off, and we enjoyed the delightful prospect of the ocean; that ocean, the object of all our labors, the reward of all our anxieties. This cheering view exhilarated the spirits of all of the party, who were still more delighted on hearing the distant roar of the breakers.

5. The Far Reaches of the Mississippi

In 1805 when explorers of the United States were seeking out the far reaches of the great Louisiana Purchase, Zebulon Montgomery Pike was chosen to locate the headwaters of the Mississippi. His objectives were geographical and political. First, he was to find the very head of the central stream artery, and then he was to determine the trader activities in the region. As Pike wrote, "I had no gentleman to aid me, and I literally performed the duties (as far as my limited abilities permitted) of astronomer, surveyor, command-

Major Zebulon M. Pike, *An Account of Expeditions to the Sources of the Mississippi, and through the Western Parts of Louisiana to the Sources of the Arkansaw, Kans. La Platte, and Pierre Jaun Rivers* (Philadelphia: C & A. Conrad, 1810), 64–67.

ing officer, clerk, spy, guide, and hunter; frequently preceding the
party for miles, in order to reconnoitre, and returning in the evening, hungry and fatigued, to sit down in the open air, by fire light,
to copy the notes and plot the courses of the day." This expedition
left St. Louis, August 9, at 4:00 P.M. This was late in the season to
begin exploration of the frigid Minnesota country. The expedition
succeeded in its central purpose.

27th January, Monday.– My Indian rose early, mended his
mockinsons, then expressed by signs something about his son
and the Frenchman we met yesterday. Conceiving he wished
to send some message to his family, I suffered him to depart.
After his departure I felt the curse of solitude, although he
truly was no company. Boley arrived at about 10 o'clock. He
said that he had followed us until some time in the night, when
believing that he could not overtake us, he stopt and made a
fire, but having no axe to cut wood, he was near freezing. He
met the Indians, who made him signs to go on. I spent the day
putting my gun in order, mending my mockinsons, &c. Provided plenty of wood, still found it cold, with but one blanket. I
can only account for the gentlemen of the N. W. company,
contending themselves in this wilderness for 10, 15, and some
of them 20 years, by the attachment they contract for the Indian women. It appears to me, that the wealth of nations
would not induce me to remain secluded from the society of
civilized mankind, surrounded by a savage and unproductive
wilderness, without books or other sources of intellectual enjoyment, or being blessed with the cultivated and feeling mind,
of a civilized fair.

28th January, Tuesday.– Left our encampment at a good
hour; unable to find any trail, passed through one of the most
dismal cypress swamps I ever saw, and struck the Mississippi
at a small lake. Observed Mr. Grant's tracks going through it;
found his mark of a cut off, (agreed on between us) took it,
and proceeded very well, until we came to a small lake, where
the trail was entirely hid; but after some search on the other
side, found it; when we passed through a dismal swamp, on
the other side of which, found a large lake; at which I was en-

tirely at a loss; no trail to be seen. Struck for a point 3 miles, where we found a Chipeway lodge of one man, his wife, and five children, and one old woman. They received us with every mark, that distinguishes their barbarity, such as setting their dogs on ours, trying to thrust their hands into our pockets, &c. but we convinced them that we were not afraid, and let them know, we were Chewockomen; (Americans) when they used us more civilly. After we had arranged a camp, as well as possible, I went into the lodge; they presented me with a plate of dried meat. I ordered Miller to bring about two gills of liquor, which made us all good friends, The old squaw gave me more meat, and offered me tobacco, which not using, I did not take. I gave her an order upon my corporal, for one knife and a half carrot of tobacco. . . . Heaven clothes the lilies and feeds the raven, and the same almighty Providence protects and preserves these creatures. After I had gone out to my fire, the old man came out and proposed to trade beaver skins, for whiskey; meeting with a refusal, he left me; when presently the old woman came out with a beaver skin, she also being refused, he again returned to the charge, with a quantity of dried meat, (this or any other I should have been glad to have had) when I gave him a peremptory refusal; then all further application ceased. It really appeared, that with one quart of whiskey, I might have bought all they possessed of. Night remarkably cold, was obliged to sit up nearly the whole of it. Suffered much cold and from want of sleep.

31st January, Friday.– Took my clothes in the Indian's lodge to dress, and was received very coolly, but by giving him a dram (unasked) and his wife a little salt, I received from them directions for my route. Passed the lake or morass, and opened on meadows, (through which the Mississippi winds its course) of nearly 15 miles long. Took a straight course through them, to the head; when I found we had missed the river; made a turn of about two miles, and regained it. Passed a fork which I supposed to be Lake Winnipie, making the course N. W. Passed a very large meadow or prairie, course west; the Mississippi only fifteen yards wide. Encamped one mile below the traverse of the meadow. Saw a very large animal, which, from its leaps, I supposed to have been a panther; but if so, it was twice as large as those on the lower Mississippi. He evinced some disposition to approach. I lay down (Miller being in the rear) in order to entice him to come near, but he would not. The night remarkably cold. Some spirits, which I had in a small keg, congealed to the consistency of honey.

1st February, Saturday.– Left our camp pretty early. Passed a continued train of prairie, and arrived at Lake La Sang Sue at half past two o'clock. I will not attempt to describe my feelings, on the accomplishment of my voyage, for this is the main source of the Mississippi. The Lake Winnipie branch is navigable, from thence to Red Cedar lake, for the distance of five leagues, which is the extremity of the navigation. Crossed the lake 12 miles to the establishment of the N. W. company; where we arrived, about 3 o'clock; found all the gates locked, but upon knocking were admitted, and received with marked attention and hospitality by Mr. Hugh M'Gillis. Had a good dish of coffee, biscuit, butter, and cheese for supper.

2nd February, Sunday.– Remained all day within doors. In the evening sent an invitation to Mr. Anderson, who was agent of Dickson, and also for some young Indians, at his house, to come over and breakfast in the morning.

3rd February, Tuesday.– Spent the day in reading Volney's Egypt; proposing some queries to Mr. Anderson, and preparing my young man to return, with a supply of provisions, to my party.

6.   Up the Arkansaw

Pike arrived back in St. Louis on Wednesday, April 30, 1806. He hardly had time to thaw out his system and overcome the shock of one of the most tedious journeys in American frontier exploration

Pike, *An Account of Expeditions* . . . , pp. 186–189.

before General James Wilkinson made known to him plans to explore the upper reaches of the "Arkansaw." On his new assignment Pike was to perform at least three tasks: deliver a group of Osage Indians safely to their homeland, make peace between the Kansas and Osage nations, and establish "good understanding" with the Yanctons, Tetaus, or Commanches. In the course of these herculean enterprises, Pike was to keep his eye out for the geography of the country, the activities of the Spanish, and make full field notes.

No one in St. Louis could have predicted on July 13, 1806, when the Pike expedition departed at 3 o'clock P.M. that it would meet with so many adventures and suffer so much tragedy. All of this took place between that date and the following first of July when the little band was returned to the United States at Nachitoches, Louisiana.

Jan. 19th. We again took the field, and after crawling about one mile in the snow, got to shoot eight times among a gang of buffalo; we could plainly perceive two or three to be badly wounded, but by accident they took the wind of us, and to our great mortification all were able to run off. By this time I had become extremely weak and faint, it being the fourth day since we had received sustenance, all of which we were marching hard, and the last night had scarcely closed our eyes to sleep. We were inclining our course to a point of woods, determined to remain absent and die by ourselves rather than return to our camp and behold the misery of our poor lads, when we discovered a gang of buffalo coming along at some distance. With great exertions I made out to run and place myself behind some cedars. By the greatest of luck, the first shot stopped one, which we killed in three more shots; and by the dusk had cut each of us a heavy load, with which we determined immediately to proceed to the camp, in order to relieve the anxiety of our men and carry the poor fellows some food.

We arrived there about twelve o'clock, and when I threw my load down, it was with difficulty I prevented myself from falling; I was attacked with a giddiness of the head, which lasted for some minutes. On the countenances of the men was not a frown, nor a desponding eye; all seemed happy to hail their

officer and companions, yet not a mouthful had they eaten for
four days. On demanding what were their thoughts, the sergeant replied that on the morrow the most robust had determined to set out in search of us and not return unless they
found us, or killed something to preserve the lives of their
starving companions.

Jan. 20th. The doctor and all the men able to march; returned to the buffalo to bring in the balance of the meat. On
examining the feet of those who were frozen we found it impossible for two of them [Sparks and Dougherty] to proceed, and
two others only without loads, by the help of a stick. One of the
former was my waiter, a promising young lad of twenty, whose
feet were so badly frozen as to present every probability of
losing them. The doctor and party returned toward evening,
loaded with the buffalo meat.

Jan. 21st. This day we separated the four loads which we
intended to leave, and took them some distance from camp,
where we secured them. I went up to the foot of the mountain
to see what prospect there was of being able to cross it, but
had not more than fairly arrived at its base when I found the
snow four or five feet deep; this obliged me to determine to
proceed and *cotoyer* the mountain [keep alongside the base
of the Sangre de Cristo range] to the south, where it appeared
lower, until we found a place where we could cross.

Jan. 22d. I furnished the two poor lads who were to remain
with ammunition, made use of every argument in my power
to encourage them to have fortitude to resist their fate, and
gave them assurance of my sending relief as soon as possible.
We parted, but not without tears.

We pursued our march, taking merely sufficient provisions
for one meal, in order to leave as much as possible for the two
poor fellows who remained. They were John Sparks and Thomas
Dougherty. We went on eight miles and encamped on a little
creek, which came down from the mountains. At three o'clock
went out to hunt, but killed nothing. Little snow.

After showing the sergeant a point to steer for, the doctor
and myself proceeded on ahead in hopes to kill something, as

we were again without victuals. About one o'clock it commenced snowing very hard; we retreated to a small copse of pine, where we constructed a camp to shelter us; and, as it was time the party should arrive, we sallied forth to search for them. We separated, and had not marched more than one or two miles, when I found it impossible to keep any course without the compass continually in my hand, and then was not able to see more than 10 yards. I began to perceive the difficulty even of finding the way back to our camp; and I can scarcely conceive a more dreadful idea than remaining on the wild, where inevitable death must have ensued. It was with great pleasure I again reached the camp, where I found the doctor had arrived before me. We lay down and strove to dissipate the ideas of hunger and misery by thoughts of our far distant homes and relatives. Distance eight miles.

7. Up the Wide Missouri

John Bradbury, a Scotch botanist, accompanying an American fur company party up the Missouri led by Wilson Price Hunt, was fascinated by three lonely frontiersmen his party came upon. His travel account, along with the published works of Thomas Nuttall, constitute intimate glimpses of the tasks of breaking trail in a raw country where nature, animals, and natives all took their toll. The men they met along the way attested this fact.

Whilst at breakfast in a beautiful part of the river, we observed two canoes descending on the opposite side. In one, by the help of our glasses, we ascertained there were two white men, and in the other only one. A gun was discharged, when they discovered us, and crossed over. We found them to be three men belonging to Kentucky, whose names were Robin-

John Bradbury, *Travels in the Interior of America* (Liverpool: Smith and Galway, 1817), 77, 78.

son, Hauberk, and Reesoner. They had been several years hunting on and beyond the Rocky Mountains, until they *imagined* they were tired of the hunting life; and having families and good plantations in Kentucky, were returning to them; but on seeing us, families, plantations, and all vanished; they agreed to join us, and turned their canoes adrift. We were glad of this addition to our number, as the Poncars had confirmed all that we had heard respecting the hostile disposition of the Nodowessies, or Sioux, towards us, with the additional information, that five nations or tribes had already assembled, with a determination to cut us off. Robinson was sixty-six years of age, and was one of the first settlers in Kentucky. He had been in several engagements with the Indians there, who really made it to the first settlers, what its name imports. "The Bloody Ground." In one of these engagements he had been scalped, and was obliged to wear a handkerchief on his head to protect the part. As the wind was fair, we this day made considerable progress, and had many fine views of the bluffs, along which, from the L'Eau qui Court, we had observed excellent roads, made by the buffaloes. These roads I had frequent opportunities of examining, and am of the opinion that no engineer could have laid them out more judiciously.

8. Exploring the Upper Mississippi River Country

The headwaters of the Mississippi remained a mystery to Americans for a surprisingly long time. Relevant to the question of its precise location were issues of international boundaries, the control of the Indian trade, and the nature of the river's origins. Henry Rowe Schoolcraft, Indian agent, territorial official, and hardy explorer, enjoyed the great adventure of traveling in the region at the head

Henry Rowe Schoolcraft, *Discovery and Sources of the Mississippi River* (Philadelphia: Lippincott, 1855), 139–141.

of the mighty stream. With scientific preciseness he recorded his observations in a voluminous report. Schoolcraft's explorations covered a longer period of time than Pike's, and his information on the region is more comprehensive.

No attempt has heretofore been made to determine the elevation of that part of the American continent which gives rise to the Mississippi River. From the observations made on the expedition, the elevation is confessedly less than would *a priori* be supposed. If it is not, like the Nile, cradled among mountains, whose very altitude and position are unknown, there is enough of the unknown about its origin to wish for more information. Originating on a vast continental plateau, or watershed, the superabundance of its waters are drained off by the three greatest rivers of North America, namely, the St. Lawrence, the Nelson's rivers of Hudson's Bay, and the Mississippi. Yet the apex of this height of land is moderate, although its distance from the sea at either point is immense. From the best data at command, I have endeavored to come at the probable altitude of this plateau, availing myself at the same time of the judgment of the several members of the expedition. Taking the elevation of Lake Erie above tide-water, as instrumentally determined, in the New York surveys, as a basis, we find Lake Superior lying at an altitude of six hundred and forty-one feet above the Atlantic. From thence, through the valley of the St. Louis, and across the Savanna summit, to the Mississippi, at the confluence of the Sandy Lake River, estimates noted on the route, indicate an aggregate rise of four hundred and ninety feet. The ascent of the river, from this point to Cass Lake, is estimated to be one hundred and sixty-two feet; giving this lake an aggregate elevation of thirteen hundred and ninety-three feet above the Atlantic. Barometrical admeasurements made in 1836, by Mr. Nicollet, in the service of the United States Topographical Bureau, place the elevation of this lake at fourteen hundred and two feet above the Gulf of Mexico, being just twelve feet above these early estimates. The same authority estimates its length from the Balize, at twenty-seven hundred and fifty miles. Its velocity below Cass Lake may be estimated to result from a mean descent of a fraction over five inches per mile.

The name of the Mississippi River is derived from the Algonquin language, through the medium of the French. The term appears first in the early missionary letters from the west end of Lake Superior about 1660. Sippi, agreeably to the early French annotation of the word, signifies a river. The prefixed word Missi is an adjective denoting all, and, when applies to various waters, means the collected or assembled mass of them. The compound term is then, properly speaking, an adverb. Thus, Missi-gago, means all things; Missi-gago-gidjetod, He who has made all things—the Creator. It is a superlative expression, of which great river simply would be a most lean, impracticable and inadequate expression. It is only symbolically that it can be called the father of American rivers, unless such sense occurs in the other Indian tongues.

Finding it impracticable to proceed higher in the search of the remote sources of the river at this time, a return from this point was determined on. The vicinity had been carefully scanned for its drift specimens, and fresh-water conchology. Wishing to carry along some further memorial of the visit, members of the party cut walking-canes in the adjoining thickets, and tied them carefully together; and at five o'clock in the afternoon (21st July) we embarked on our descent. An hour's voyage over the surface of this wide lake, with its refreshing views of northern scenery, brought us to the point where the Mississippi issues from it. Never did men ply their paddles with greater animation; and having the descent now in their favor, they proceeded eighteen miles before they sought for a spot to encamp. Twilight still served, with almost the clearness of daylight, while we spread our tents on a handsome eminence on the right-hand shore. Daylight had not yet dawned the next morning, when we resumed the descent. It was eight o'clock A.M. when we reached the border of Lake Winnipek. This name, by the way, is derived from a term heretofore given, which, having the Chippewa inflection of nouns in *ish*, graphically describe that peculiarity of its waters created by the disturbance of a clay bottom. The winds were high and adverse, which caused the canoemen to toil two hours in crossing. After reaching the river again, we passed its sedgy borders, to, and through Rush Lake, or the Little Winnipek; then by the inlet of Leech Lake River, and through the contortions of its channel, to within a few miles of the spot of our encampment at Deer River, on the 20th.

The great savannas, through which the Mississippi winds itself above the Pakagama, are called collectively, the Gatchi Betobeeg, Great Morasses, or bog meadows.

While descending the river, we encountered nine canoes filled with Chippewa Indians and their families. They were freighted with heavy rolls of birch-bark, such as their canoes are made from; together with bundles of rushes designed for mats. The annoyance suffered from mosquitos on this great plateau, was almost past endurance. We embarked again at a quarter past four, and reached the Falls of Pakagama at five o'clock. Just forty minutes were spent in making the portage. The rock at this spot is quartzite. The day was cloudy, with some rain. As night approached an animal, judged to be the wolverine, was seen swimming across the stream. The efforts of the men to overtake it were unavailing; it nimbly eluded pursuit, and dashed away into the thickets. In some queries sent to me by the New York Lyceum, this animal is alluded to as a species of the glutton. The Indians said there was no animal in their country deserving this name; the only animal they knew deserving of it, was the horse; which was eating all the time. We encamped on an abrupt sandy bank, where, however, sleep was impossible. Between the humidity of the atmosphere and the denseness of the foliage around us, the insect world seemed to have been wakened into unusual activity. Besides, we encamped so late, and were so jaded by a long day's travel, that the mosquito-nets were neglected. To get up and stand before a camp-fire at midnight and switch off the mosquitos, requires as much philosophy as to write a book; and at any rate, ours completely failed.

II

The Act of Pioneering

There were many phases to pioneering in the American backwoods. People were uprooted from their homes in older communities, or in the Old World. They had to dispose of most of their implements and household goods in order to travel as lightly as possible to distant places on the frontier. There were limited vehicles, few roads, and no streams within reach for the great horde that moved westward. The art of adaptation to new conditions began at the moment a family decided to move.

On the frontier the American pioneer made the most elementary beginnings, building the meagerest sort of a home, preparing his food in the most primitive type vessels, sleeping in a makeshift bed, and dressing himself in the roughest of clothing. Food was gathered from natural resources, prepared and served in the simplest and frequently in the most unrefined forms; health needs were served in the same way.

The biggest challenge, however, was that of cutting enough of a hole in the woods, or breaking enough sod on the plains, to plant a crop and to make a beginning of a farm. Beyond this there was the matter of establishing communities, counties, and even states. Western society developed out of the pioneering experience with certain definite traits. No one experience or no one set of conditions served to mould the frontier American personality; it was the product of the whole process of bringing virgin territory under exploitation by a westward moving Anglo-American civilization.

9. The Great Emigration

Pioneering involved not only the movement of men, but of their families, livestock, farming equipment, and meager household goods. Setting out from one of the settlements, as the family discussed here did from Carlisle, Pennsylvania, was closely akin to the wanderings of the Children of Israel in the Exodus. Building a cabin, clearing the land, planting the first crops, and fighting off the Indians required a tremendous amount of fortitude. Women and children suffered fears and hardships that have seldom been duplicated by other Americans. The movement of a pioneering family was, however, the planting of the seed of civilization in the western woods. Once a family planted itself on the land, it developed tremendous tenacity to remain there.

My father's family was one of twenty that emigrated from Carlisle, and the neighboring country, to western Pennsylvania, in the spring of 1784. Our arrangements for the journey would, with little variation, be descriptive of those of the whole caravan. Our family consisted of my father, mother, and three children (the eldest one five, the youngest less than one year old), and a bound boy of fourteen. The road to be traveled in crossing the mountains, was scarcely, if at all, practicable for wagons. Pack horses were the only means of transportation then, and for years after. We were provided with three horses, on one of which my mother rode carrying her infant, with all the table furniture and cooking utensils. On another were packed the stores of provisions, the plough irons, and other agricultural tools. The third horse was rigged out with a pack saddle, and two large creels, made of hickory widths in the fashion of a crate, one over each side, in which were stowed the beds and bedding, and the wearing apparel of the family. In the centre of these creels there was an aperture prepared for myself and sister, and the top was well se-

G. Wilkeson, "Early Recollections of the West," *The American Pioneer,* 2 vols. (Cincinnati: P. B. Brooks, Printer, 1843), vol. II, pp. 139–143.

cured by lacing, to keep us in our places, so that only our heads appeared above. Each family was supplied with one or more cows, which was an indispensable provision for the journey. Their milk furnished the morning and evening meal for the children, and the surplus was carried in canteens for use during the day.

Thus equipped, the company set out on their journey. Many of the men being unacquainted with the management of horses, or the business of packing, little progress was made the first day or two. When the caravan reached the mountains, the road was found to be hardly passable for loaded horses. In many places the path lay along the edge of a precipice, where, if the horse had stumbled, or lost his balance, he would have precipitated several hundred feet below. The path was crossed by many streams raised by the melting snow and spring rains, and running with rapid current in deep ravines. Most of these had to be forded, as there were no bridges, and but few ferries. For many successive days, hairbreadth escapes were continually occurring; sometimes horses falling, others carried away by the current, and the women and children with difficulty saved from drowning. Sometimes in ascending steep acclivities, the lashing of the creels would give way, both creels and children tumble to the ground, and roll down the steep, until arrested by some traveler of the company. In crossing streams, or passing places of more than ordinary difficulty in the road, mothers were often separated from some of their children for many hours. The journey was made in April, when the nights were cold. The men who had been inured to the hardships of war, could with cheerfulness endure the fatigues of the journey. It was the mothers who suffered; they could not, after the toils of the day, enjoy the rest they so needed at night. The wants of their suffering children must be attended to. After preparing their simple meal, they lay down with scanty covering in a miserable cabin, or as it sometimes happened, in the open air, and often unrefreshed, were obliged to rise early, to encounter the fatigues and dangers of another day.

As the company approached the Monongahela, they began
to separate. Some settled down near to friends and acquaintances who had preceded them. About half of the company
crossed the Monongahela, and settled on Chartier's creek, a
few miles south of Pittsburgh, in a hilly country, well watered
and heavily timbered. Settlers' rights to land were obtained
on easy terms. My father exchanged one of his horses for a
tract (bounded by certain brooks and marked trees), which
was found on being surveyed several years after, to contain
about two hundred acres. The new comers aided each other
in building cabins, which were made of round logs with a
slight covering of clapboards. The building of chimneys and
laying of floors, were postponed to a future day. As soon as
the families were all under shelter, the timber was girdled and
the necessary clearing made for planting corn, potatoes, and a
small patch of flax. Some of the party were despatched for
seed. Corn was obtained at Pittsburgh, but potatoes could not
be procured short of Legonier valley, distant three days' journey. The season was favorable for clearing, and by unremitted
labor, often continued through a part of the night, the women
laboring with their husbands, in burning brush and logs, their
planting was seasonably secured. But while families and neighbors were cheering each other on with the prospect of an abundant crop, one of the settlements was attacked by the Indians
and all of them were thrown into the greatest alarm. This was
a calamity which had not been anticipated. It had been confidently believed that peace with Great Britain would secure
peace with her Indian allies. The very name of Indian chilled
the blood of the late emigrants, but there was no retreat. If
they desired to recross the mountains they had not the provisions or means, and had nothing but poverty and suffering
to expect should they regain their former homes. They resolved
to stay.

The frontier settlements were kept in continual alarm. Murders were frequent, and many were taken prisoners. These
were more generally children, who were taken to Detroit
(which in violation of the treaty continued to be occupied

by the British), where they were sold. The attacks of the Indians were not confined to the extreme frontier. They often penetrated the settlement several miles, especially when the stealing of horses was a part of their object. Their depredation effected, they retreated precipitately across the Ohio. The settlers for many miles from the Ohio, during six months of the year, lived in daily fear of the Indians. Block houses were provided in several neighborhoods for the protection of the women and children, while the men carried on their farming operations, some standing guard while the others labored. The frequent calls on the settlers to pursue marauding parties, or perform tours of militia duty, greatly interrupted their attention to their crops and families, and increased the anxieties and sufferings of the women. The general government could grant no relief. They had neither money nor credit. Indeed there was little but the name in the old confederation. The state of Pennsylvania was unable to keep up a military force for the defence of her frontier. She had generously exhausted her resources in the struggle for national independence. Her legislature however, passed an act granting a bounty of one hundred dollars on Indian scalps. But an incident occurred which led to the repeal of this law before the termination of the war.

A party of Indian spies having entered a wigwam on French creek, supposed to be untenanted, discovered, while breakfasting, an Indian extended on a piece of bark over head. They took him prisoner, but reflecting that there was no bounty on prisoners, they shot him under circumstances which brought the party into disgrace, and the scalp-bounty law into disrepute.

The settlement was guarded, and in fact preserved from utter dispersion by a few brave men. Brave is a term not sufficiently expressive of the daring boldness of the Bradys, Sprouts, Poes, Lesnets, Wetzels, Caldwells, Crawfords, Williamsons, Pauls, Harrisons and Zanes, who for years encountered unheard of privations in the defence of the border settlements, and often carried the war successfully into the Indian country.

10. Man and the Raw Frontier

Felix Renick was an Ohio pioneer with a rich background of experience in the deep forest. In his discussion of the westward movement in its more primitive stages in the great Northwest Territory
he revealed much of the mode of early life in the region. He had
a vivid recollection of the trials, sorrows, and triumphs of the pioneers, whether it be eating the ruddy meats of a lonely old hunter,
or "re-civilizing" young boys captured by the Indians. Fortunately
he was literate enough to record a good story of the beginnings of
settlement above the Ohio River.

Here we also met with a man who had formerly resided on
the south branch, with whom we had a partial acquaintance;
he had left the branch some years previously, still keeping in
the front rank of the white settlement, supplying himself and
family with both food and raiment principally with his rifle.
He then occupied a small cabin on the West side of the river,
a small distance from the mouth of Licking, and as it was on
our intended route up the river, he insisted on our coming
and taking breakfast with him in the morning, observing that
he had made a good hunt that day and could give us plenty
of the best wild meat the country afforded, &c. We of course
could not well refuse his kind invitation, and accordingly
repaired there by times next morning. The breakfast, which
on our arrival was stewing over the log cabin fire, was soon
dished up, and we fell to. The meat looked very well, color
fair, taste not bad, but rather oily, and we thought not exactly
like any flesh we had ever tasted before. Our host had got into
an earnest and detailed account of his previous day's hunting
exploits, to which we were all in duty bound to listen. None
of us had room to ask what it was, or slip in a word of inquiry
on any subject whatever, and had our friend had patience to

Felix Renick, "A Trip to the West," *The American Pioneer*, 2 vols. (Cincinnati: R. P. Brooks, Printer, 1842), vol. I, pp. 75–80.

postpone the relation of his narrative until we had finished our meal, all would have went off, or rather down, well enough; but about the height of our meal he came to the great and hazardous engagement he and his faithful dog had with the largest, fattest and finest panther he had ever seen, part of whose carcass we were then, as he informed us, feasting on, pointing to a corner in the cabin where the balance was cut up and salted down on the green hide of the animal. He observed that this he considered the best part of his hunt, and the only part he had brought in, and that he must hurry off after the balance. Our meal was ended in pretty short order, and we being as willing to hurry off from the best of his hunt as he was to go after the worst, we soon parted, he after his game, and we on our journey.

We traveled up the river, exploring each side up to a small cluster of cabins, which I think was called Johnson's station, though I am not certain as to the name; it was situated in the Wapatomaka bottom, a small distance above the mouth of a creek of that name emptying into the Muskingum on the West side. Here we unexpectedly found an old widow lady by the name of Johnson, who, by intermarriage, was more or less connected with myself and both my traveling companions. She was also a sister to the wife of Mr. William Robinson, who was taken prisoner by Logan. As the suffering of this family is connected with the early settlement of western Virginia, I presume a short sketch of their history will not be altogether uninteresting to yourself or readers. I was taken unwell the night we got to Mrs. Johnson's, and was compelled to remain there, while my companions went up as far as the mouth of Walhonding, a principal branch of Muskingum, where Roscoe now stands. While they were gone the old lady gave me the history which I shall now relate.

The name of Mrs. Johnson's father was Frederick See, an uncle of my wife. He, with a brother-in-law and a few other families, had moved at an early day and settled on Greenbriar, a branch of the Great Kanawha, in the interval of peace between the Indians and whites. In those days, the Indians were

at war with each other. The war trace at that time, between
the northern and southern tribes, was along the south branch
of Potomac, and through the Greenbriar settlement. In a time
of peace between the whites and Indians, of those large war
parties, seventy or eighty in number, that had been in the habit
of traveling back and forth, came and encamped several days
on Mr. See's place, and appeared to be in a kind of frolic.
Mr. See, notwithstanding their pretended friendship, expressed
over and again to his family his fears of their evil design; and
to win their favor as much as possible, he killed a fine hog for
them, gave them bread and other things they wanted. His
kindness however availed nothing. When the preconcerted
time came for the blow to be struck, it fell first on his own
head; and as the common mode of Indians is to make the
declaration of war, not with the pen, but with the hatchet, so
it was done in this case. Mr. See had a large family; several
daughters grown, or nearly so, and one married, with a first
child at her breast. Several Indians one day entered the house
in a friendly manner as usual, and at a certain signal drove
their tomahawks into the heads of the old gentleman and his
son-in-law, and made prisoners of all the balance of the family.
The blood of the father fell on the head and face of a little
son, who was at the time fondling him. The Indians, not wishing to kill the boy, on seeing him so bloody, were fearful he
might be hurt, took him up, carried him to the creek, and
washed him, and found that he was safe. The Indians had
divided, and while this tragedy was going on many other families near by were sharing the same fate.

After committing what other depredations their savage
minds dictated, they gathered their prisoners and booty together and set out for their town. There were several women
among the prisoners who had young children at their breasts,
all of which, contrary to their common custom, the Indians
had spared. Mrs. Johnson said that her sister pressed her babe
to her breast, and bore her long and speedy march with great
fortitude; hoping, but as the sequel will show hoping in vain,
that fortune might yet favor her with a speedy exchange, or

with relief in some other way, and that she would still be blessed with a descendent of him most near and dear to her: but of this great blessing, the hope of which she had so fondly cherished, she had the excruciating mortification to be deprived. The day before they reached the Indian town, the Indians took all the young children and in the most barbarous manner killed them, leaving their bodies in the woods to be devoured by the first carnivorous animal that might find them. After this, Mrs. Johnson said, her sister's life appeared to be a burthen to her, and she did every thing in her power to provoke the Indians to kill her, making several attempts to kill some of them; but they kept so close a watch on her, that she never could effect it. She, however, lived through all this, and afterwards became the wife of William Robinson, before mentioned. Soon after getting to the towns, the prisoners were divided and put into different families, the women to hard drudging and the boys to run wild with the young Indians, to amuse themselves with bow and arrow, dabble in the water, or obey any other notion their wild natures might dictate. Having lost or misplaced a journal I kept at the time, I cannot remember the length of time these unfortunate families were detained as prisoners. It was, however, some years, when peace was again restored, and an exchange of prisoners took place. These families were collected by some of their friends, who were in attendance, and set out with them to their native homes.

11.   The Log Cabin Home

The log cabin was the home base of the American pioneer in the wooded areas of the westward movement. Hundreds of thousands of these crude structures were built across the land. So commonplace were they that few persons took the trouble to describe them

John S. Williams, "Our Cabin; or, Life in the Woods," *The American Pioneer*, vol. II, pp. 444, 445.

in detail. Not only could the cabin be built quickly from materials readily at hand, but it also served as a fortress of safety against surprise Indian raids, the elements, and prowling animals. It is not surprising, as John S. Williams, an Ohio pioneer, describes: certain fairly well established rules came to prevail in the location and construction of cabins.

In building our cabin it was set to front the north and south, my brother using my father's pocket compass on the occasion. We had no idea of living in a house that did not stand square with the earth itself. This argued our ignorance of the comforts and conveniences of a pioneer life. The position of the house, end to the hill, necessarily elevated the lower end, and the determination of having both a north and south door, added much to the airyness of the domicil, particularly after the green ash puncheons had shrunk so as to have cracks in the floor and doors from one to two inches wide. At both the doors we had high, unsteady, and sometimes icy steps, made by piling up the logs cut out of the wall. We had, as the reader will see, a window, if it could be called a *window,* when, perhaps, it was the largest spot in the top, bottom, or sides of the cabin at which the wind *could not* enter. It was made by sawing out a log, placing sticks across, and then, by pasting an old newspaper over the hole, and applying some hog's lard, we had a kind of glazing which shed a most beautiful and mellow light across the cabin when the sun shone on it. All other light entered at the doors, cracks, and chimney.

Our cabin was twenty-four by eighteen. The west end was occupied by two beds, the centre of each side by a door, and here our symmetry had to stop, for on the side opposite the window, made of clapboards, supported on pins driven into the logs, were our shelves. Upon these shelves my sister displayed, in ample order, a host of pewter plates, basins, and the dishes, and spoons, scoured and bright. It was none of your new-fangled pewter made of lead, but the best of London pewter, which our father himself bought of Townsend, the manufacturer. These were the plates upon which you could hold your meat so as to cut it without slipping and without dulling your knife. But, alas! the days of pewter plates and sharp dinner knives had passed away never to return. To return to our internal arrangements. A ladder of five rounds occupied the corner near the window. By this, when we got a floor above, we could ascend. Our chimney occupied most of the east end; pots and kettles opposite the window under the shelves, a gun on hooks over the north door, four split-bottom chairs, three three-legged stools, and a small eight by ten looking-glass sloped from the wall over a large towel and combcase. These, with a clumsy shovel and a pair of tongs, made in Frederick, with one shank straight, as the best manufacture of pinches and blood blisters, completed our furniture, except a spinning-wheel and such things as were necessary to work with. It was absolutely necessary to have *three-legged* stools, as four legs of any thing could not touch the floor at the same time.

The completion of our cabin went on slowly. The season was inclement, we were weak-handed and weak-pocketed, in fact laborers were not to be had. We got our chimney up breast high as soon as we could, and got our cabin daubed as high as the joists outside. It never was daubed on the inside, for my sister, who was very nice, could not consent to "live right next to the mud." My impression now is, that the window was not constructed till spring, for until the sticks and clay was put on the chimney we could possibly have no need for a window; for the flood of light which always poured into the cabin from the fireplace would have extinguished our paper window, and rendered it as useless as the moon at noonday. We got a floor laid over head as soon as possible, perhaps in a month; but when it *was* laid, the reader will readily conceive of its imperviousness to wind or weather, when we mention that it was laid of loose clapboards split from a red oak, the stump of which may be seen beyond the cabin. That tree grew in the night, and so twisting that each board laid on two diagonally opposite corners, and a cat might have shook every board on our ceiling.

It may be well to inform the unlearned reader that clapboards are such lumber as pioneers split with a frow, and re-
semble barrel staves before they are shaved, but are split
longer, wider, and thinner; of such our roof and ceiling were
composed. Puncheons were planks made by splitting logs to
about two and a half or three inches in thickness, and hewing
them on one or both sides with the broad-axe. Of such our
floor, doors, tables, and stools were manufactured. The eave-
bearers are those end logs which project over to receive the
butting poles, against which the lower tier of clapboards rest
in forming the roof. The trapping is the roof timbers, compos-
ing the gable end and the ribs, the ends of which appear in
the drawing, being those logs upon which the clapboards lie.
The trap logs are those of unequal length above the eve bearers, which form the gable ends, and upon which the ribs rest.
The weight poles are those small logs laid on the roof, which
weigh down the course of clapboards on which they lie, and
against which the next course above is placed. The knees are
pieces of heart timber placed above the butting poles, successively, to prevent the weight poles from rolling off.

12.   The Impermanent Frontier

Repeatedly travelers to the United States in the first half of the
nineteenth century commented on the lack of permanence of
homes, towns, and even roads in the country. Everything gave
the appearance of being temporary. Especially was this true the
nearer to the frontier one traveled. Timothy Flint, the well-known
frontier missionary, not only sensed this lack of permanence, but
he also fathomed the human spirit behind it. "New Country" was
a favorite topic of conversation, and thousands of individuals were
drawn on westward by its appeal. At times American backwoodsmen came into competition with the Spanish settlers, and occasion-

Timothy Flint, *Recollections of the Last Ten Years* (Boston: Cummings,
Hillard, and Company, 1826), 204–209.

ally a backwoods hunter found himself in the clutches of arbitrary officials who clung tenaciously to their uncertain foothold in the West.

I have spoken of the moveable part of the community, and unfortunately for the western country, it constitutes too great a proportion of the whole community. The general inclination here, is too much like that of the Tartars. Next to hunting, Indian wars, and the wonderful exuberance of Kentucky, the favourite topic is new countries. They talk of them. They are attached to the associations connected with such conversations. They have a fatal effect upon their exertions. They have no motive, in consonance with these feelings, to build with old Cato, "for posterity and the immortal gods." They only make such improvements as they can leave without reluctance and without loss. I have every where noted the operation of this impediment in the way of those permanent and noble improvements which grow out of a love for that appropriated spot where we were born, and where we expect to die. There are noble and most tender prejudices of this kind, which in the best minds are the strongest, and which make every thing dear in that cradle of our affections. There is a fund of virtuous habits, arising out of these permanent establishments, which give to our patriotism "a local habitation and a name." But neither do I at all believe the eloquent but perverse representation that Talleyrand has given of these same moving people, who have no affection for one spot more than another, and whose home is in the wild woods, or the boundless prairies, or wherever their dogs, their cattle, and their servants, are about them. They lose, no doubt, some of the noble prejudices which are transmitted with durable mansions through successive generations. But they in their turn, have virtues, that are called into exercise by the peculiarities of their case and character, which are equally unknown. But whatever may be the effect of the stationary or the moving life upon the parties respectively, there can be no doubt about the result of this spirit upon the face of the country. Durable houses of brick or of

stone, which are pecularly called for, on account of the scarcity of timber,—fences of hedge and ditch,—barns and gra-
naries of the more durable kind,— the establishment of the
coarser manufactories, so necessary in a country like this,—
the planting of artificial forests, which on the wide prairies
would be beautiful and useful,—all that accumulation of
labour, industry, taste, and wealth, that unite to beautify a
family residence, to be transmitted as a proud and useful
memento of the family,—these improvements, which seem to
be so naturally called for on these fertile plains, will not become general for many years. Scarcely has a family fixed
itself, and enclosed a plantation with the universal fence,—
split rails, laid in the worm-trail, or what is known in the north
by the name of Virginia fence,—reared a suitable number of
log buildings, in short, achieved the first rough improvements,
that appertain to the most absolute necessity, than the assembled family about the winter fire begin to talk about the
prevailing theme,—some country that has become the rage,
as a point of immigration. They offer their farm for sale, and
move away.

Some go a step farther than this, and plant an orchard; and
no where do the trees grow so thriftily or rapidly. In the space
of two or three years from the time of planting, they become
loaded with fruit. But even this delightful appendage to a
permanent establishment, an orchard, which, with its trees,
so thrifty, and of the colour of young willows, looks, on these
plains, so regular and beautiful,—even this does not constitute
a sufficiently permanent motive of residence. It is true there
are places in Ohio, Kentucky, and Tennessee, that are substantial and beautiful, and on the noble models of the German establishments in the centre of Pennsylvania; and they show to
such singular advantage, that they only make us regret that
they are not more common. In the generations to come, when
the tide of immigration shall have reached the western sea, and
the recoil shall begin to fix the people of these open plains in
Illinois and Missouri, on their prairies, then they will plant these
naked, but level and rich tracts; then they will rear substantial

mansions of brick or stone; then they will discover the strata
of coal; then they will draw the hedge and ditch for leagues
together in a right line, and beautiful plantations will arise,
where now there are nothing but naked wastes of prairie, far
from wood and water.

The two states of Missouri and Illinois, had long had French
establishments in them. Kaskaskia, in Illinois, is said to date its
commencement farther back than Philadelphia. The early
history of these states, their being considerable establishments
many years ago, and their having on an emergency sent vast
quantities of flour to New Orleans, are facts well known. Some
of the establishments on the west bank of the Mississippi, as
at St. Genevieve and St. Louis, are ancient, in comparison with
the rest of the country. But under the French and Spanish
regime, they had existed as straggling French boating, hunting,
and fur establishments,—in manners, in pursuits, and character, as different from American establishments as can be imagined. They were in a manner neglected by the Spanish and
French governments. Nothing could sit easier on the shoulders
of an indolent race of hunters, who led a half savage life in the
woods, than did this regime. There was little to tempt the
avarice, or stimulate the ambition or jealousy of the commandants. Every married man with a family went to the commandant of the district, and for a very trifling *douceur* obtained a
settlement-right, amounting to an American section; and these,
although the owners at the time, probably, had no anticipations
of their ultimate value under another order of things, were of
course selected in the best possible positions. Favourites of the
commandant obtained one, two, or three leagues square, called
Spanish concessions. The commandant, a priest, a file of soldiers, and a *calaboza* made up the engine of government. The
priest was generally a Nimrod of a hunter, a card-player, and,
as far as the means could be obtained, a wine-bibber. The
commandant, an ignorant and despotic man, whose legislation
and execution all centered in his cane. Afraid of the Indians,
and still more afraid of the Anglo-Americans, who were in
those days a furious set of outlaws, and who were deemed by

the Spanish to be a compound of Atheist, drunkard, and boxer; they were glad to let the wheels of government go on as smoothly as possible. When the commandant was raised in his temper, the object of his resentment was immediately brought before him, tried on the spot, and if found guilty, was sent straight to the *calaboza*. But to blunt the acuteness of his feelings, and render the reflections of his first hours as little bitter as possible, a suitable provision of whiskey was sent to the unhappy culprit, who would become very drunk; and after the long sleep that followed, was over, and he became clamorous for more whiskey, the commandant generally stipulated that the prisoner upon liberation should be gone, and then he was liberated. They were all summoned as a kind of militia, not to fight or prepare for it, but to report themselves, and to appear before the commandant once a year. And this, together with the restriction of having no public Protestant preaching, was the whole burden. When we add, that the maintaining these military posts was very expensive, and that the commandants spent all the money in their respective districts, we shall easily see whence it happens that the old settlers look back to the French and Spanish times, as the golden age. It is curious to observe with how much ardour they recur to the recollections of those happy days. And these recollections are the cause, that those people and their descendants have still a strong predilection for the French and Spanish governments, and one great reason of their wish to emigrate to Texas.

But, however happy these hunters, left unmolested in the wilderness, may have been, the country made no advances towards actual civilization and improvement under them. Like the English mariners on the sea, their home was in boats and canoes, along these interminable rivers, or in the forests hunting with the Indians. The laborious and municipal life, and the agricultural and permanent industry of the Americans, their complex system of roads, bridges, trainings, militia, trials by jury, and above all, their taxes, were as hostile to the feelings of the greater portion of the inhabitants, when we purchased

Louisiana, as the fixed home and labour of a Russian are said to be to a Tartar.

13. A Cotton Country Hegira

In the spring of the year, in the first decade of the nineteenth century, the Williams family moved from near Raleigh, North Carolina, across the mountains to western Tennessee. The stream of emigration from North Carolina ran flush in these years, and the Tennessee frontier was being settled rapidly by families who were on the trail of cotton lands. They came bringing slaves, household goods, and livestock. In 1872 Joseph H. Williams described not only the journey of his family, but also the rise of communities around their wilderness homestead.

On the banks of the beautiful creek, north of the Big Hatchie River, in the early March days, little less than three-score years ago, my father pitched his tent, and called it home. There the abode of civilization was first planted in the trackless wilderness. Then but a lad of less than twelve summers, the haunts of the countless wild beasts which filled the land are freshly mapped out as if it were but yesterday. The frightful howl of the wolf, and the sharp, startling scream of the panther, became as familiar as household words.

> Twas there in childhood I played;
> In the untrod wilderness I strayed;
> Land of my youth, whose memories last,
> Linking the present with the past.

Thither my father moved from the lands of the old settled part of Mississippi, south of latitude °32, a distance of more

Joseph H. Williams, *Old Times in West Tennessee. Reminiscences-Semi-Historic-of Pioneer Life and the Early Emigrant Settlers in the Big Hatchie Country, By a descent of one of the First Settlers* (Memphis: W. G. Cheney, 1873), 7–37.

than three hundred miles, through a trackless, savage territory. The fatigue and peril of moving a large family of white and black, through a savage wilderness, with all the paraphernalia of comfortable living, in those days of rude travel, was an undertaking requiring almost super-human endurance and inflexible will, but my father proved himself equal to it.

In January 1818 through the lonely vistas of the pine woods, was seen a long train of movers. In front rode my father, on his faithful and sure-footed dapple-gray mare, with heavy holsters swinging across the pommel of his saddle, with their black bear-skin covering. Stern, thoughtful and reticent, with indomitable will, he had resolved to convoy his charge through whatever peril or difficulty that should menace him. Following close behind was a large black carryall, containing mother, grandmother and the young children. The carryall (ambulance it would be called now-a-days) my father had made in North Carolina, with an eye single to its usefulness as a sleeping apartment, as well as traveling vehicle; long and broad, deep sides and high back, with heavy leather curtains, lined with thick green baize, when closely buttoned down, and bed made up in it, was comfortable enough for an emperor's wife. It was the traveling and sleeping apartment of my mother, grandmother and three young sisters.

Provident in arrangement, my father had gone to Mobile and purchased a year's supply of everything requisite to a comfortable living in the wilds of the Big Hatchie—coffee, tea, rice, sugar, flour, spices, and medicines, cards, cotton, and spinning wheels, every variety and kind of seeds, implements of husbandry, carpenter and blacksmith tools, and assorted nails, not forgetting an ample stock of powder, lead and shot, selecting twenty head of choice milch cows with their calves and yearlings, and about the same number of stock hogs. My mother contributed her share in the necessary preparation for the journey; every one, both black and white, were properly and comfortably clad in homespun clothes—stout overcoats for the men and long jackets for the women. The seats and knees of her boy's pants she padded with dressed buckskin (this economic measure is appreciated by all who have made long journeys, camping out every night). The train, when in motion, presented an imposing appearance. The weather being favorable, the country open pinewoods, now and then a few miles of neighborhood road, which happened to lay in our course, we reached the Choctaw territory at nightfall of the fifth day. There we remained over until Monday. My father considered it necessary to communicate with the chief, and obtain safe conduct through his territory. These little diplomatic arrangements completed, and the services of a guide or pilot, secured, word was given to *gear up!* The second week opened upon us leading slowly through the Choctaw Nation, rumbling over roots and such undergrowth as did not impede travel. We made some days as much as ten miles, oftener, however, not more than six or eight. We were not unfrequently delayed for several days when difficult crossings of streams were to be made. Often it was found impracticable to construct bridges, when floats (pontoons) were made, and the wagons unloaded and taken apart, and everything packed across by hand. All these difficulties were met and overcome with a hearty goodwill, and songs of good cheer. Marvelous had been the stories told by Negroes of the good things in store for them in the Big Hatchie country. That it was literally a land flowing with milk and honey; so rich in soil that you only had to make a hole in the ground with your heel, drop the corn into it, and it would grow without work; the forest hanging with the most delicious fruits, and the ground covered with strawberries; even to fat pigs, ready roasted, and running about with knife and fork in their backs, much of which they wrought in song.

We found the Choctaws friendly and well disposed. My father did not, however, relax his vigil in having a close watch kept upon the stock during the night. The cows and hogs were belled, so as to give alarm when in the slightest disturbed. The camp was infested with Indians every night, bringing in every variety of game, with other eatables, asking to trade. My father had supplied himself with a good stock of beads and red things. A lively trade was carried on most every night. Venison and wild turkeys were in abundance, with beautiful bead baskets, and every variety of bead-work. A few loads of powder or a red cotton handkerchief would pay for a fat gobbler or a saddle of venison. We fared sumptuously.

Reaching the Chickasaw territory, the Choctaw guide was relieved, my father making him many presents for his faithful services, sending presents to his chief. A Chickasaw guide was engaged, and the course of travel decided upon. To avoid the broken country along the head waters of the numerous streams flowing westwardly, a more easterly direction was advised.

Leaving the lazy and proverbially filthy Choctaw, we entered the Chickasaw nation—noble race of the red man, first to resist the iron heel of the white man, famed for their bravery and ferocious bearing in war, and among the first to make a generous and lasting peace, and cultivate the arts of civilization. The country through which we traveled was slightly rolling, wood principally oak and hickory, devoid of tangled undergrowth. Traveling for days without incident or difficulty worthy of mention, we reached the thickly settled portion of the nation, in the vicinity of which was situated the principal village, at which the chief resided. It was on a Friday; man and beast needed rest, and the order was given that we would lay over till Monday. No travel was done on the Sabbath. My father, a strict old-side Presbyterian, was true to his faith in "observing the Sabbath, to keep it holy," and required of his family, both black and white, that they should do the same.

The tents were pitched upon a lovely spot, on the margin of a gentle slope overlooking the beautiful prairie to the east, a clear running brook close by. When the bright morning sun rose, chasing the gray mist over the broad expanse of the lovely prairie to the east and northeast, numerous Indian settlements, or villages were seen in the distance. The village at which the chief resided lay to the northwest of us some six miles. Orders were given to prepare for washing—to Jack and Jim to get out the big kettle and swing it, the washtubs, and stretch the clothesline, the cattle and hogs to be driven over the prairie, and a close watch kept upon them.

During the day the chief, accompanied by several of his braves and his interpreter, visited the camp. The interpreter was a Negro slave, and belonged to the chief, who owned many slaves. The object of his visit was to invite my father to visit him, extending the hospitalities of the village to the whole camp. A reciprocal trade was carried on during the day. The squaws brought a large basket of corn and pumpkins, some with rice and hominy, others with hickory-nut kernels, carefully picked-out, many of them without being broken. The trade was interrupted by the boys coming into camp, delighted with their findings while roaming over the prairie. Everybody's curiosity was excited to see what; from a dozen voices at one, "Let me see!" "Let me see!" "*O, do let me see!*" The objects of so much curious interest were several white flint arrow heads and a large corroded leaden ball. Such was the marvel at what had been picked up on the prairie that the chief and his braves, who had been standing seemingly unconcerned, were applied to for something of their history. They certainly had a history; relics of art, of the white and red man, found side by side in the wilds of a savage country, excite the curious to know something of them. The chief, a huge mass of fat, with a jolly, good natured face, and an intelligent, laughing eye, shook his big sides with a grunt and spoke through his interpreter thus: "Long, long ago," pointing in the direction from which the boys came running, "on yonder hill a big battle was fought between the red man and the white man. The red men killed all the white men, since which time the red man has been at peace with the white man." This was the only information obtained to the numerous inquiries as to when, and who were the white men engaged in such deadly conflict with the red men. The rock from which the arrow-head was cut did not exist in this region. The size of the leaden ball differed from the ordinary rifle bullet then in use, and its corroded state excited interest as to its antiquity. My father, thinking he could throw some light upon the subject, spoke, addressing himself to the chief, who had settled himself upon the ground, with his fat legs crossed under him: "that more than two hundred and eighty years ago, Spain, a powerful nation across the big water, sent a great many big ships, with men, arms and ammunition, and fine horses, to take possession of this country; that they landed somewhere on the coast of Florida, under the command of a great man called Fernando De Soto; that De Soto, landing his men, guns and horses, marched up through the territory of the Alabamas, then, turning west, crossed the Tombigbee somewhere near the Chickasaw village, passing through their territory, crossing the Mississippi at the Chickasaw bluffs; that the Chickasaws were offended with the strangers for entering their territory without asking their big chief to smoke the *calumet*, gave them battle, killing a great number. . . ."

Leaving our beautiful camping-ground on the margin of the prairie, my father directed his course toward the village to redeem his promise—to eat with the chief. The country was an open hickory barren, and but few obstructions were found to impede travel. We arrived at the village by noon. The chief, with his escort, met my father at the edge of the village, conducting him and the entire train in front of his place of dwelling, which was on a broad street running through the center of the village east and west, studded on each side with antiquated looking china-trees, giving quite the appearance of civilized life. A big dinner had been prepared, and everybody, black as well as white, participated in the great chief's regal hospitality.

The chief and his braves talked much about the Big Hatchie country, calling it their hunting ground, exhibiting many bear and panther skins procured in that region. The chief showed my father great kindness, sending several of his best hunters along with us to kill game and pilot the best route to Bolivar, then an Indian trading post. Leaving the village an hour before nightfall, we camped at a fine spring. Resuming travel the next morning, it was continued without interruption, our Indian guides bringing in a venison or fat gobbler every day, arriving at Bolivar the last week in February, having been in the wilderness forty days and nights.

14. Frontiersmen at Home

Though historians of the American frontier have long considered the land as a central theme of national history, in the long run they may well be proved wrong by a deeper study of population problems. Generally the American people took delight in their expanding population, and, in a sense, each decade after the United States Government began taking the census brought them the feeling of triumph. The missionary, and Harvard graduate, Timothy Flint took notice of the western population after the 1830 census was published. He looked not so much at the empirical statistics as at the people in flesh and blood. He was able to present a picture of human beings marching across the land. Some of them were robust and strong, others succumbed to disease and hardships. In a way those who succumbed were noble pioneers because their passing emphasized the potency of disease and hardship in the history of a nation.

The following synoptical view will show, in a few words, the astonishing advance of this population. In 1790, the population of this valley, exclusive of the country west of the Mississippi, and of Florida, which were not then within our territorial limits, was estimated, by enumeration, at little more than 100,000. In 1800, it was something short of 380,000. In 1810, it was short of a million. In 1820, including the population west of the Mississippi, rating the population of Florida at 20,000, and that of the parts of Pennsylvania and Virginia included in this valley at 300,000, and it will give the population of 1820 at 2,500,000. It will be perceived, that this is an increase, in more than a duplicate ratio, in ten years.

Some considerable allowance must be made, of course, for the flood of immigration, which can not reasonably be expected to set this way, for the future, as strongly as it has for

Timothy Flint, *A Condensed Geography and History of the Western States, or the Mississippi Valley*, 2 vols. (Cincinnati: E. H. Flint, 1828), vol. I, pp. 198–202.

the past. There is no doubt, however, that Ohio, with the
largest and most dense population of any of the western states,
will have double the number of inhabitants, by the census of
1830, which she had by that of 1820.—During that interval,
her gain by immigration will not equal her loss by emigration;
and, of course, will be simply that of natural increase. In the
rapidity of this increase, we believe, this state not only exceeds any other in the West, but in the world. It is the good
natured jest of all, who travel through the western states, that,
however productive in other harvests, they are still more so in
an unequalled crop of flaxen headed children; and that 'this is
the nobler growth our realms supply.' The population of this
valley at the next census, will no doubt, exceed four millions.
It will have by a million, more inhabitants, than the thirteen
good old United States, when, at the commencement of the
revolutionary war, they threw down the gauntlet in the face
of the parent country, then the most powerful empire on the
globe.

Notwithstanding the impression, so generally entertained in
the Atlantic country, that this valley is universally unhealthy,
and notwithstanding the necessary admission, that fever and
ague is prevalent to a great and an annoying degree, the stub-
born facts, above stated, demonstrate, beyond all possibility of
denial, that no country is more propitious to increase by natural population. Wherever the means of easy, free and ample
subsistence are provided, it is in the nature and order of human things, that population should increase rapidly. In such a
country, though some parts of it should prove sickly, perseverance will ultimately triumph over even this impediment,
the most formidable of all. In the fertile region, for the insalu-
brious districts are almost invariably those of the highest fertility, immigrants will arrive, become sickly, and discouraged;
and, perhaps, return with an evil report of the country. In the
productive and sickly sections of the south, allured by its rich
products, and its exemption from winter, adventurers will successively arrive, fix themselves, become sickly, and it may be,
they will die. Others, lusting for gain, and with that reckless-

ness to the future, for wise ends awarded us by Providence, and undismayed by the fate of those who have preceded them, will replace them. By culture, draining, the feeding of cattle, and the opening the country to the fever-banishing breeze, the atmosphere is found gradually to meliorate. The inhabitants, taught by experience and suffering, come by degrees to learn the climate, the diseases, and preventatives; and a race will finally stand, which will possess the adaptation to the country, which results from acclimation: and even these sections are found, in time, to have a degree of natural increase of population with the rest. Such has proved to be the steady advance of things in the sickliest parts of the south. The rapidity of our increase in numbers multiplies the difficulties of subsistence, and stimulates and sharpens the swarming faculties and propensities in the parent hive, and will cause, that in due lapse of time and progress of things, every fertile quarter section in this valley will sustain its family.

15. The Mark of the Frontier

During the first half of the nineteenth century there were literally hundreds of travelers who visited the expanding area of the American frontier. The writing of travel guides was for some authors a satisfying if not profitable venture. The Reverend Robert Baird was such an author and compiler. His *View of the Valley of the Mississippi* is such a book. Baird not only introduced the traveler to land and water routes, but he gave him also a sense of the kind of people he would see on the way. He sensed the fact that there had come into existence not only a new type of American, but in large measure a new nationalism as well.

. . . I shall only give a general description of the character, manners and pursuits of the people of the West, avoiding details as much as possible.

Robert Baird, *View of the Valley of the Mississippi, or the Emigrants and Traveler's Guide to the West* (Philadelphia: H. S. Tanner, 1834), 99–103.

The population of the Valley of the Mississippi is exceedingly heterogeneous, if we regard the very great variety of nations of which it is composed. There is not a country in Europe which has not furnished some portion of its population. But by far the greater proportion of the European population, is from Great Britain and Ireland. Of course, emigrants from these portions of Europe, speaking our own language, and having so many of the elements of character and manners homogeneous with our own, produce no influence, worthy of notice, on the lineaments of the national character of the West, especially after their amalgamation with us, which is effected by a short period of residence. The emigrants from France, however, possessing traits of character very diverse from our own, speaking a very dissimilar language, and still more, grouped together as they almost invariably are, produce a very great diversity in the general character and manners of the West, as far as that sort of population prevails. But inasmuch as it is confined almost entirely to Louisiana, and some isolated portions of Illinois, Missouri, and Michigan, and has little or no influence upon the other parts of this vast country, but little notice will be taken of it, in this general description of the character and manners of the people of the West.

As it regards the emigrants from the other countries of Europe, the smallness of their numbers, compared with the entire population, and their dispersion throughout the country, render their influence too inconsiderable an element to be taken into account in a description of the national character and manners of the West. We must look to those causes and circumstances which exist amongst themselves, and which have a chief influence in moulding the character of the population of the Valley of the Mississippi, unless indeed we mean to speak of the West, not as it is, but as it exists in our imagination.

The great difficulty in describing the character and manners of the West, taken in the general, arises from the fact that they do not *essentially* differ from those of the population of the Atlantic states. The shades of difference,—and they are only shades,—are such as have been created by causes and circumstances existing in the West alone. Every one who has seen much of the West, at once perceives these shades; but they are too attenuated and impalpable to admit of being very distinctly portrayed. I shall, however, endeavour to indicate some of the traits of difference, after having made the remarks which I am about to make, with regard to the mode in which the West has been peopled from the Atlantic states.

In travelling over the various states and territories of the West, I have been struck with a fact which is somewhat remarkable. It is the manner in which that country has been colonized. The emigration to the Valley of the Mississippi seems to have gone on in columns, moving from the East almost due West, from the respective states from which they originated. From New-England the emigrating column advanced through New-York, peopling the middle and western parts of that state in its progress; but still continuing, it reached the northern part of Ohio, then Indiana, and finally Illinois. A part of the same column from New-England and New-York is diverging into Michigan. It is true also, that straggling companies, as it were, diverge to a more southerly direction, and scatter over the middle and southern parts of the Valley, and are to be found in every state, in every county and town, in greater or less numbers. The Pennsylvania and New Jersey column advanced within the parallels of latitude of those states into West Pennsylvania, and still continuing, advanced into the middle and southern parts of Ohio, extends even into the middle parts of Indiana and Illinois. The Virginia column advanced first into the western part of that state and Kentucky,—which was long a constituent part of it,—thence into the southern parts of Indiana and Illinois, until it has spread over almost the whole of Missouri. The North Carolina column advanced first into East Tennessee, thence into West Tennessee, and also into Missouri. And the South Carolina and Georgia column has moved upon the extensive and fertile lands of Alabama, and has in some degree peopled Mississippi. Louisiana was a foreign colony. The American part of it is composed of emigrants from the upper part of the Valley, and from the southern and eastern states. The same remark is true of the small population of the state of Mississippi. In Arkansas the emigrating columns of Kentucky and Tennessee predominate. As was remarked of the New-England column, it may be said that straggling parties from all the others have wandered from the main bodies, and have taken a more northerly or southerly direction. A hundred considerations of business or affinity, have operated to occasion this divergency.

The above mentioned fact furnishes a better key than any other that I know of, to furnish a correct knowledge of the diversities of customs and manners which prevail in the Valley of the Mississippi. For if one knows what are the peculiarities of the several states east of the Allegheny Mountains, he may expect to find them, with some shades of difference, occasioned by local circumstances, in the corresponding parallels in the West. Slavery keeps nearly within the same parallels. And so does every other peculiarity. The New-England column is intelligent, industrious, economical, enterprising, moral, and fond of institutions for the promotion of knowledge and religion. The Pennsylvania column of Scotch, Irish, Germans, &c. partakes of all the characteristics of those worthy nations. The southern columns have a great degree of similarity, and are distinguished by high-mindedness, generosity, liberality, hospitality, indolence, and, too often, dissipation. The southern character, however, is a noble one, when moulded by good influences.

The peculiarities, or, to speak more properly, the developments of character, which may be said to distinguish the population of the West, may be readily enumerated; and they are all created by the peculiar circumstances in which the people have been placed in that new world. They are,

1. *A spirit of adventurous enterprise:* a willingness to go through any hardship or danger to accomplish an object. It was the spirit of enterprise which led to the settlement of that country. The western people think nothing of making a long journey, of encountering fatigue, and of enduring every species

of hardship. The great highways of the West—its long rivers —are familiar to very many of them, who have been led by trade to visit remote parts of the Valley.

2. *Independence of thought and action.*—They have felt the influence of this principle from their childhood. Men who can endure any thing: that have lived almost without restraint, free as the mountain air, or as the deer and the buffalo of their forests—and who know that they are Americans all—will act out this principle during the whole of life. I do not mean that they have such an amount of it as to render them *really* regardless alike of the opinions and the feelings of every one else. But I have seen many who have the virtue of independence greatly perverted or degenerated, and who were not pleasant members of a society, which is a state requiring a compromising spirit of mutual co-operation in all, and a determination to bear and forbear.

3. *An apparent roughness,* which some would deem *rudeness of manners.*

These traits characterize, especially, the agricultural portions of the country, and also in some degree the new towns and villages. They are not so much the offspring of ignorance and barbarism, (as some would suppose), as the results of the circumstances of a people thrown together in a new country, often for a long time in thin settlements; where, of course, acquaintances for many miles around are soon, of necessity, made and valued from few adventitious causes. Where there is perfect equality in a neighbourhood of people who know but little about each other's previous history or ancestry—but where each is lord of the soil which he cultivates. Where a log cabin is all that the best of families can expect to have for years, and of course can possess few of the external decorations which have so much influence in creating a diversity of rank in society. These circumstances, have laid the foundation for that equality of intercourse, simplicity of manners, want of deference, want of reserve, great readiness to make acquaintances, freedom of speech, indisposition to brook real or imaginary insults, which one witnesses among the people of the West.

The character and manners of the traders and merchants who inhabit the principal cities and towns of the West, do not differ greatly from those of the same class in the Atlantic states.

16.   Western Humanity

Whatever may have been the Reverend Timothy Flint's theological capabilities, he was a good sociologist, geographer, and commentator upon contemporary frontier society. He viewed the humanity of the frontier in attempts to make moral and spiritual assessments of its conditions. Fortunately he visited a wide scope of territory and remained long enough in many places to make seasoned appraisals of his neighbors. He recognized the various differences which prevailed among the people from several sections of the United States. Added to this were mature observations on the adaptations made by the European immigrants. Basically he searched for the changes which frontier environment had wrought on the people who lived in it for most of their lives.

We shall remark upon the character of the French part of our population in describing Louisiana and Missouri, where the greater portion of that people is found. We shall remark upon the distinctive character of the people of Kentucky, in giving the geography of that state. We only wish to catch here, if possible, the slight, but perceptible peculiarities of national character, which our peculiar circumstances and conditions have imposed upon us.

The people of this valley are as thorough a combination and mixture of the people of all nations, characters, languages, conditions and opinions, as can well be imagined. Scarcely a state in the Union, or a nation in Europe, but what has furnished us immigrants. Philosophers and noblemen have visited us from beyond the seas; some to study our natural history, or to contemplate a new people rising from the freshness of nature, over the fertile ruins of a once submerged world; or deluded here by the pastoral dreams of Rousseau, or Chateaubriand; or, in the sample of the savages, to study man in a state of nature.

The much greater proportion of the immigrants from Europe are of the poorer classes, who come here from hunger, poverty, oppression, and the grinding vassalage of crowded and miserable tenants of an aristocratic race, born to the inheritance of the soil, and all the comforts and hopes of present existence. They find themselves here with the joy of shipwrecked mariners, cast on the untenanted woods, and instantly become cheered with the nerving hope of being able to build up a family and fortune from new elements. 'The north has given to us, and the south has not kept back.' The puritan and the planter, the German and the Irishman, the Briton and the Frenchman, each with their peculiar prejudices and local attachments, and all the complicated and inwoven tissue of sentiments, feelings and thoughts, that country, and kindred, and home, indelibly combine with the web of our youthful existence, have here set down beside each other. The merchant, mechanic and farmer, each with their peculiar prejudices and jealousies, have found themselves placed by necessity in the same society. Mr. [Robert] Owen's grand engine of circumstances begins to play upon them. Men must cleave to their kind, and must be dependent upon each other. Pride and jealousy give way to the natural yearnings of the human heart for society. They begin to rub off mutual prejudices. One takes a step, and then the other. They meet half way, and embrace; and the society, thus newly organized and constituted, is more liberal, enlarged, unprejudiced, and of course more affectionate and pleasant, than a society of people of unique birth and character, who bring all their early prejudices, as a common stock, to be transmitted as an inheritance in perpetuity.

The rough, sturdy and simple habits of the backwoods men, living in that plenty, which depends only on God and nature, and being the preponderating cast of character in the western country, have laid the stamina of independent thought and feeling deep in the breasts of this people. A man accustomed only to the fascinating, but hollow intercourse of the polished circles in the Atlantic cities, at first feels a painful revulsion, when mingled with this more simple race. But he soon becomes accustomed to the new order of things, and if he have a heart to admire simplicity, truth and nature, begins to be pleased with it. He respects a people, where a poor, but honest man enters the most aristocratic mansion with a feeling of ease and equality.

It may readily be supposed, that among such an infinite variety of people, so recently thrown together, and scarcely yet amalgamated into one people, and in a country, where the institutions are almost as fresh and simple as the log houses, any very distinctive national character could hardly yet be predicated of the inhabitants. Every attentive observer, however, discriminates the immigrants from the different nations, and even from the different states of our own country. The people of Ohio and Indiana, for example, have a character somewhat distinct from that of the other western states. That of the former, especially, is modelled, as a very fair sample of the New England and New Jersey patterns. In the latter this character is blended, not merged with the manners, opinions and dialect of Kentucky. Illinois, though a free state, has a clear preponderance of Kentucky nationality. Kentucky, Tennessee, Missouri, the upper part of Alabama, and all Arkansas, have distinct manners, in which the nationality of Kentucky is the ground color. The country still more south, peopled with large planters of cotton and sugar cane, with numerous gangs of slaves, have the peculiar manners, that have naturally grown out of their condition. On these states, too, especially on Louisiana, we begin to discern the distinct impress and influence of French temperament and manners. These shades of difference are very distinctly visible to persons, who have been long and intimately acquainted with the people of the different regions where they are marked.

But young as the country is, variously constituted and combined, as are the elements of its population, there is already marked, and it is every year more fully developed, a distinctive character of the western people. A traveller from the Atlantic cities, and used only to their manners, descending from Pittsburg, or Wheeling, the Ohio and the Mississippi in a steam boat of the larger class, will find on board, what may be considered fair samples of all classes in our country, except the farmers. To become acquainted with the younger representatives of the yeomanry, he must acquaint himself with the crews of the descending flat boats. Sufficiently copious specimens of the merchants and traders, the artizans, the large planters, the speculators, and last, though not least, the ladies, will be seen on board the different steam boats descending to New Orleans or on their return voyage. The manners, so ascertained, will strike such a traveller as we have supposed, with as much of novelty, distinctness, and we may add, if he be not bigotted and fastidious, with as much pleasure, saving the language, as though he had visited a country beyond the seas. The dialect is different. The enunciation is different. The peculiar and proverbial colloquy is different. The figures and illustrations, used in common parlance, are strikingly different. We regret, that fidelity to our picture, that frankness and truth compel us to admit, that the frequency of profanity and strange curses is ordinarily an unpleasant element in the conversation. The speaking is more rapid. The manner has more appearance of earnestness and abruptness. The common comparisons and analogies are drawn from different views and relations of things. Of course he is every moment reminded, that he is a stranger among a people, whose modes of existence and ways of thinking are of a widely different character from those in the midst of which he was reared.

Although we have so often been described to this traveller, as backwoods men, gougers, ruffians, demi-savages, a repulsive mixture, in the slang phrase, of the 'horse and the alligator,' we confidently hazard the opinion, that when a little accustomed to the manners of the better class of people among us, he will institute a comparison between our people and his own, not unfavorable to us. There is evidently more ease and frankness, more readiness to meet a wish to form an acquaintance, sufficient tact, when to advance, and how far, and where to pause in this effort, less holding back, less distrust, less feeling as if the address of a stranger were an insult, or a degradation. There is inculcated and practised on board the steam boats a courtesy to ladies, which is delightful in its proper extent; but which is here, sometimes, apt to overstep the modesty of nature, in the affectation of a chivalrous deference, which would be considered misplaced, or ridiculous, on the Atlantic shores. A series of acquaintances are readily and naturally formed between fellow passengers, in their long descents to New Orleans, very unlike the cold, constrained, and almost repelling and hostile deportment of fellow passengers in the short stage and steam boat passages in the Atlantic country. They are very different from the intimacies of fellow passengers in crossing the Atlantic, and infinitely more pleasant. Putting out of the question ennui, sea sickness, and the constant rolling of the vessel, circumstances so unpropitious to the desire of pleasant intercourse, custom has prescribed a state and distance on shipboard, which cause, that cabin passengers often cross the ocean together, without acquiring any thing more than speaking intimacy at the end of the voyage. Not so on these passages, where the boat glides steadily and swiftly along the verge of the fragrant willows. The green shores are always seen with the same coup d'œil, that takes in the magnificent and broad wave of the Mississippi. Refreshments come in from the shore. The passengers every day have their promenade. The claims of prescriptions on the score of wealth, family, office, and adventitious distinctions of every sort, are laid aside, or pass for nothing. The estimation, the worth and interest of a person are naturally tried on his simple merits, his powers of conversation, his innate civility, his capacities to amuse, and his good feelings.

The distinctive character of the western people may be traced in its minuter shades to a thousands causes, among which are not only their new modes of existence, the solitary lives which they, who are not inhabitants of towns, lead in remote and detached habitations, for the greater part of the time, and the greater aptitude and zest, which they will naturally have, when thus brought together, as we have described above, to enjoy society; but it chiefly results from the unchangeable physical formation of the country. For instance, it has been remarked, that the inhabitants of the western country, when thrown upon the blue water, are sailors almost at once. Their long inland water courses, at once the channels of conveyance and communication, place them in primary nautical schools, train them to familiar acquaintance with all the methods of managing and propelling water crafts, and naturally conduct their thoughts from their interior forests, and their rural and secluded abodes, down to the ocean. The skill and facility, thus acquired, in being familiar with the movements of the canoe, the periogue and skiff, almost from the days of infancy, give them the same dexterity and daring on the ocean, when they are at length wafted down to its tempestuous bosom, with those who were reared on the shores of the element. But an inhabitant of the Atlantic shore can have but a faint conception of the sublime emotions with which a young man, reared in the silence and seclusion of the western forests, first beholds the illimitable extent of the 'broad, flat sea.' Every intelligent and gifted son of the West will be a poet for the first few hours of his sailing on the ocean, if sea sickness does not banish the visitings of the muse.

Their forests and prairies concur with their inclinations and abundant leisure, to give them the spirit-stirring and adventurous habits of the chase. Their early training to leave the endearments and the maternal nursing of home, for an absence of three or four months, on voyages of constant exposure, and often of a length of more than five hundred leagues, will naturally tend to create a character, widely unlike the more shrinking, stationary and regular habits of the people of the older country. Multitudes, perhaps the majority of those in the middle walks of life in the Atlantic country, never extend their travels beyond their metropolis, or their chief mart. Every part of the middle and northern states is traversed in every direction by fine roads, on which are continually passing great numbers of stage coaches. In the West, all this is entirely different. There are roads, indeed, some of which nature, and but a very few, art, has rendered tolerably passable. But the passing on them, even in the most populous districts is very limited. The passages are seldom more than from village to village, settlement to settlement, and for the most part subservient to arriving at the real roads, the great turnpikes of the West, her long rivers.

These rivers, which bound or intersect every state in the West, are of a character entirely unlike most of those which flow east of the mountains. They are narrow, deep, and to a person used only to the rivers of the East, and judging them by comparison and by their width, of an inconceivable length of course. Their depth of water resulting from the narrowness of their channels, and the level and alluvial country, through which for the most part they flow, render them almost universally susceptible of steam boat, or at least boat navigation. The instance of a young man of enterprize and standing, as a merchant, trader, planter, or even farmer, who has not made at least one trip to New Orleans, is uncommon. From the upper and even middle western states, before the invention of steam boats, it was a voyage of long duration, and we may add, of more peril, than a voyage across the Atlantic. These rivers are still descended, as before that invention, in boats of every description. In making the descent from Pittsburg to Natchez, last autumn, in an uncommonly low stage of the waters, we noted between two and three hundred descending boats, of different descriptions, and of the larger class. The greater portion, however, were flat and keel boats. Almost all the crews, that descend on these boats, return on steam boats. An ascending steam boat carries from one to three hundred passengers; and the average trip from New Orleans to Louisville, or St. Louis, may be twelve days, and to Cincinnati thirteen. Every principal farmer, along the great water courses, builds, and sends to New Orleans the produce of his farm in a flat boat.—

Thus a great proportion of the males of the West, of a relative standing and situation in life, to be most likely to impress their opinions and manners upon society, have made this passage to New Orleans. They have passed through different states and regions, have been more or less conversant with men of different nations, languages and manners. They have experienced that expansion of mind, which can not fail to be produced by traversing long distances of country, and viewing different forms of nature and society. Every boat, that has descended from Pittsburg, or the Missouri, to New Orleans, could publish a journal of no inconsiderable interest. The descent, if in autumn, has probably occupied fifty days. Until the boatmen had passed the mouth of the Ohio, they must have been in some sense amphibious animals, continually getting into the water, to work their boat off from shoals and sandbars. The remainder of the descent was amidst all the dangers of sawyers, sandbars, snags, storms, points of islands, wreck heaps, difficulty and danger of landing, and a great many anomalous trials and dangers. The whole voyage is a scene of anxiety, exposure and labor.

17. The Early Mormon Frontier

Sections of this chapter have discussed the process of pioneering by the general population. There were also groups of people like the Shakers, the Rappites, and even some of the more cohesive Protestant denominations who played important pioneering roles. There was no more cohesive group than the Mormons who moved westward, sometimes in advance of the settlement line, to establish new communities. In 1839, after harrassment by neighbors in northern Ohio and in Missouri, a large Mormon group took refuge in Illinois at a town they named Nauvoo, on the Mississippi. Here their flamboyant and sometimes bellicose leader, Joseph Smith, felt

Thomas Ford, *A History of Illinois* (Chicago: S. C. Griggs and Company, 1854), 223–230.

secure. The Mormons involved themselves in a fractious frontier political situation and reaped trouble. Dissidents of the community were antagonized further by Joseph Smith's vision authorizing the practice of polygamy and established a newspaper, *The Nauvoo Expositor,* which Smith partisans wrecked. Internecine upheaval resulted in Smith's arrest, and the murder by a mob of Smith and his brother while they were incarcerated in prison. During the imprisonment of the brothers, Governor Thomas Ford, in June 1844, went to the scene of the trouble and made a report on what he thought really occurred in the town of Nauvoo. This incident represented much of the frontiersman's prejudice against religious unorthodoxy or social deviations.

The Mormons themselves published the proceedings of the council in the trial and destruction of the heretical press; from which it does not appear that any one was tried, or that the editor or any of the owners of the property had notice of the trial, or were permitted to defend in any particular. The proceeding was an ex parte proceeding, partly civil and partly ecclesiastical, against the press itself. No jury was called or sworn, nor were the witnesses required to give their evidence upon oath. The councillors stood up one after another, and some of them several times, and related what they pretended to know. In this mode it was abundantly proved that the owners of the proscribed press were sinners, whoremasters, thieves, swindlers, counterfeiters and robbers; the evidence of which is reported in the trial at full length. It was altogether the most curious and irregular trial that ever was recorded in any civilized country; and one finds difficulty in determining whether the proceedings of the council were more the result of insanity or depravity. The trial resulted in the conviction of the press as a public nuisance. The Major was ordered to see it abated as such, and if necessary, to call the legion to his assistance. The Mayor issued his warrant to the city marshal, who, aided by a portion of the legion, proceeded to the obnoxious printing office and destroyed the press and scattered the types and other materials.

After this it became too hot for the seceding and rejected

Mormons to remain in the holy city. They retired to Carthage, the county seat of Hancock county; and took out warrants for the mayor and members of the common council and others engaged in the outrage, for a riot. Some of these were arrested, but were immediately taken before the municipal court of the city on habeas corpus, and discharged from custody. The residue of this history of the Mormons, up to the time of the death of the Smiths, will be taken, with such corrections as time has shown to be necessary, from my report to the legislature, made on the 23d of December, 1844.

On the seventeenth day of June following, a committee of a meeting of the citizens of Carthage presented themselves to me, with a request that the militia might be ordered out to assist in executing process in the city of Nauvoo. I determined to visit in person that section of country, and examine for myself the truth and nature of their complaints. No order for the militia was made; and I arrived at Carthage on the morning of the twenty-first day of the same month.

Upon my arrival, I found an armed force assembled and hourly increasing under the summons and direction of the constables of the county, to serve as a posse comitatus to assist in the execution of process. The general of the brigade had also called for the militia, en masse, of the counties of Mc-Donough and Schuyler, for a similar purpose. Another assemblage to a considerable number had been made at Warsaw, under military command of Col. Levi Williams.

The first thing which I did on my arrival was to place all the militia then assembled, and which were expected to assemble, under military command of their proper officers.

I next dispatched a messenger to Nauvoo, informing the mayor and common council of the nature of the complaint made against them; and requested that persons might be sent to me to lay their side of the question before me. A committee was accordingly sent, who made such acknowledgments that I had no difficulty in concluding what were the facts.

It appeared clearly both from the complaints of the citizens and the acknowledgments of the Mormon committee that the whole proceedings of the mayor, the common council, and the municipal court, were irregular and illegal, and not to be endured in a free country; though perhaps some apology might be made for the court, as it had been repeatedly assured by some of the best lawyers in the State who had been candidates for office before that people, that it had full and competent power to issue writs of habeas corpus in all cases whatever. The common council violated the law in assuming the exercise of judicial power; in proceeding ex parte without notice to the owners of the property; in proceeding against the property in rem; in not calling a jury; in not swearing all the witnesses; in not giving the owners of the property, accused of being a nuisance, in consequence of being libelous, an opportunity of giving the truth in evidence; and in fact, by not proceeding by civil suit or indictment, as in other cases of libel. The mayor violated the law in ordering this erroneous and absurd judgment of the common council to be executed. And the municipal court erred in discharging them from arrest.

As this proceeding touched the liberty of the press, which is justly dear to any republican people, it was well calculated to raise a great flame of excitement. And it may well be questioned whether years of misrepresentation by the most profligate newspaper could have engendered such a feeling as was produced by the destruction of this one press. It is apparent that the Mormon leaders but little understood, and regarded less the true principles of civil liberty. A free press well conducted is a great blessing to a free people; a profligate one is likely soon to deprive itself of all credit and influence by the multitude of falsehoods put forth by it. But let this be as it may, there is more lost to rational liberty by a censorship of the press by supressing information proper to be known to the people, than can be lost to an individual now and then by a temporary injury to his character and influence by the utmost licentiousness.

There were other causes to heighten the excitement. These people had undertaken to innovate upon the established systems of religion. Their legal right to do so, no one will question. But all history bears testimony that innovations upon religion have always been attended by a hostility in the public mind, which sometimes has produced the most desolating wars; always more or less of persecution. Even the innocent Quakers, the unoffending Shakers, and the quiet and orderly Methodists in their origin, and until the world got used to them, had enough of persecution to encounter. But if either of these sects had congregated together in one city where the world could never get to know them; could never ascertain by personal acquaintance the truth or falsity of many reports which are always circulated to the prejudice of such innovators; and moreover, if they had armed themselves and organized into a military legion as the citizens of Nauvoo, and had been guilty of high-handed proceedings carried on against the heretical press, the public animosity and their persecutions must have greatly increased in rancor and severity.

In addition to these causes of excitement, there were a great many reports in circulation, and generally believed by the people. These reports I have already alluded to, and they had much influence in swelling the public excitement.

It was asserted that Joe Smith, the founder and head of the Mormon church, had caused himself to be crowned and anointed king of the Mormons; that he had embodied a band of his followers called "Danties," who were sworn to obey him as God, and to do his commands, murder and treason not excepted; that he had instituted an order in the church, whereby those who composed it were pretended to be sealed up to eternal life against all crimes, save the shedding of innocent blood or consenting thereto. That this order was instructed that no blood was innocent blood, except that of the members of the church; and that these two orders were made the ministers of his vengeance, and the instruments of an intolerable tyranny which he had established over his people, and which he was about to extend over the neighboring country. The people affected to believe that with this power in the hands of an unscrupulous leader, there was no safety for the lives or property of any one who should oppose him. They affected likewise to believe that Smith inculcated the legality of perjury, or any other crime in defence, or to advance the interests of true believers; and that himself had set them the example by swearing to a false accusation against a certain person, for the crime of murder. It was likewise asserted to be a fundamental article of the Mormon faith, that God had given the world and all it contained to them as his saints; that they secretly believed in their right to all the goodly lands, farms, and property in the country; that at present they were kept out of their rightful inheritance by force; that consequently there was no moral offence in anticipating God's good time to put them in possession by stealing, if opportunity offered; that in fact the whole church was a community of murderers, thieves, robbers, and outlaws; that Joseph Smith had established a bogus factory in Nauvoo, for the manufacture of counterfeit money; and that he maintained about his person a tribe of swindlers, blacklegs, and counterfeiters, to make it and put it into circulation.

It was also believed that he had announced a revelation from heaven, sanctioning polygamy, by a kind of spiritual wife system, whereby a man was allowed one wife in pursuance of the laws of the country, and an indefinite number of others, to be enjoyed in some mystical and spiritual mode; and that he himself, and many of his followers, had practiced upon the precepts of this revelation by seducing a large number of women.

It was also asserted that he was in alliance with the Indians of the western territories, and had obtained over them such a control, that in case of a war he could command their assistance to murder his enemies.

Upon the whole, if one-half of these reports had been true, the Mormon community must have been the most intolerable collection of rogues ever assembled; or, if one-half of them were false, they were the most maligned and abused.

Fortunately for the purposes of those who were active in creating excitement, there were many known truths which gave countenance to some of these accusations. It was sufficiently proved in a proceeding at Carthage, whilst I was there, that Joe Smith had sent a band of his followers to Missouri, to kidnap two men, who were witnesses against a member of his church, then in jail, and about to be tried on a charge of larceny. It was also a notorious fact, that he had assaulted and severely beaten an officer of the county, for an alleged non-performance of his duty, at a time when that officer was just recovering from severe illness. It is a fact also, that he stood indicted for the crime of perjury, as was alleged, in swearing to an accusation for murder, in order to drive a man out of Nauvoo, who had been engaged in buying and selling lots and land, and thus interfering with the monopoly of the prophet as a speculator. It is a fact also, that his municipal court, of which he was chief justice, by writ of habeas corpus had frequently discharged individuals accused of high crimes and offences against the laws of the State; and on one occasion had discharged a person accused of swindling the government of the United States, and who had been arrested by process of the federal courts; thereby giving countenance to the report, that he obstructed the administration of justice, and had set up a government at Nauvoo independent of the laws and government of the State. This idea was further corroborated in the minds of the people, by the fact that the people of Nauvoo had petitioned Congress for a territorial government to be established there, and to be independent of the State government. It was a fact also, that some larcenies and robberies had been committed, and that Mormons had been convicted of the crimes, and that other larcenies had been committed by persons unknown, but suspected to be Mormons. Justice, however, requires me here to say, that upon such investigation as I then could make, the charge of promiscuous stealing appeared to be exaggerated.

Another cause of excitement, was a report industriously circulated, and generally believed, that Hiram Smith, another leader of the Mormon church, had offered a reward for the destruction of the press of the "Warsaw Signal," a newspaper published in the county, and the organ of the opposition to the Mormons. It was also asserted, that the Mormons scattered through the settlements of the county, had threatened all persons who turned out to assist the constables, with the destruction of their property and the murder of their families, in the absence of their fathers, brothers, and husbands. A Mormon woman in M'Donough county was imprisoned for threatening to poison the wells of the people who turned out in the posse; and a Morman in Warsaw publicly avowed that he was bound by his religion to obey all orders of the prophet, even to commit murder if so commanded.

But the great cause of popular fury was, that the Mormons at several preceding elections, had cast their vote as a unit; thereby making the fact apparent, that no one could aspire to the honors or offices of the country within the sphere of their influence, without their approbation and votes. It appears to be one of the principles by which they insist upon being governed as a community, to act as a unit in all matters of government and religion. They express themselves to be fearful that if division should be encouraged in politics, it would soon extend to their religion, and rend their church with schism and into sects.

III

The Course of Life
on the Log Cabin Frontier

Life in the early West was not without its vagaries. Some of it was as serious as a nerve-shattering Indian raid, but a good part was human if not lighthearted and casual. This was bound to have been true, because many thousands followed the rainbow of promise westward. It may be that they were as much captivated by the search for a new-world Eden as they were by the availability of fresh, cheap land.

Slashing through the woods and prairies they pushed communities and settlements beyond reasonable lines of social intercourse, and settlers were driven to devise their own amusements. Sometimes they did this in breakdown dances, play-party games, rifle matches, and learned debates on abstruse subjects. Whatever they did there was about it a touch of rich but heavy-handed humor. The frontier may have produced a bounteous crop of heroes; it also produced a generous supply of greenhorns. The western bumpkin was a thoroughly delightful person, because he was the one American who was as free of inhibitions as a human could be.

In spite of the casualness of the frontiersmen and their whimsical sense of humor, there was a deep-seated feeling of national importance. Long before the spirit of manifest destiny was formalized into a phrase, frontiersmen were conscious that they bore a burden of national destiny on their shoulders.

18.   The Long Rifle

The long rifle was a symbol of pioneering. Fabulous stories were
told of the abilities of marksmen to hit almost impossible targets.
Daniel Boone was said to be a crack shot, so were Simon Kenton,
Davy Crockett, and hundreds of other woodsmen. Men took pride
in their weapons, and their performance was a mark of prestige
for gun as well as man. Shooting at targets broke the tedium of
backwoods life, kept the aiming eye sharp, and the trigger finger
supple. Sometimes, according to Robert Carlton (Baynard Hall,
a Presbyterian minister and first professor in Indiana University),
it was the means of fetching home valuable prizes and a family's
meat supply.

Let none think we western people follow rifle shooting, however, for mere sport; that would be nearly as ignoble as shot
gun idleness! The rifle procures, at certain seasons, the only
meat we ever taste; it defends our homes from wild animals
and saves our cornfields from squirrels and our hen roosts
from foxes, owls, opossums and other "varmints." With it we
kill our beeves and our hogs, and cut off our fowl's heads; do
all things in fact, of the sort with it, where others use an axe,
or a knife, or that far east *savagism*, the thumb and finger.
The rifle is a woodman's lasso. He carries it everywhere as—
a very degrading comparison for the gun, but none other occurs—a dandy a cane. All, then, who came to our tannery or
store came thus armed; and rarely did a customer go, till his
rifle had been tried at a mark, living or dead, and we had listened to achievements it had done and could do again. No
wonder, in these circumstances, if I should practice; especially
when it needed but the flash of a rifle-pan to set off our in-bred
magazine of tendencies towards bullet moulds and horn load-
ers! No wonder, that, after many failures, even in hitting a

Robert Carlton [Baynard Rush Hall], *The New Purchase; Early Years in
the Far West* (New Albany, Ind.: J. R. Numacher, 1855), 103–107.

tree, Mr. Carlton could be seen in his glory at last, standing within the lines of beholders right and left, and forty-five yards off-hand planting bullet after bullet into the same augur hole! Reader, may you live a thousand years; but if you *must* die, unless somebody will save your life by splitting an apple on your head—William Tell size—at fifty yards off-hand with a rifle ball send for me—shut your eyes for fear of flinching— and at the crack—go, your life is your own!

Old Dick is one hobby mounted literally and maybe now too often, metaphorically; the rifle is my other. But with *this* by no means must we bore you: and, therefore, after narrating my famous shots in behalf of the Temperance Society, we shall for the present put the gun on the rack over the fireplace.

Glenville and myself were once, on some mercantile affairs, traveling in an *adjoining* county, when we came suddenly on a party preparing to shoot at a mark; and from the energy of words and gestures it was plain enough a prize of unusual importance was proposed. We halted a moment, and found the stake to be a half-barrel of whiskey. If ever, then and there was to be sharp-shooting; and without question, then and there was present every chap in the settlements that could split a bullet on his knife blade or take the rag off the bush. "Glenville," said I, seized with a sudden whim, "lend me fifty cents; I mean to shoot."

"Nonsense Carlton; you *can't* win here; and if you could, what does the president of a temperance society want with a barrel of whiskey?"

"John, if I can find a gun here anything like my own, I *can* win. And although I have never before won or lost a penny, I shall risk half a dollar now for the fun of the thing, and to have the satisfaction of knocking yonder barrel in the head and letting out the stuff into the branch here."

After some further discussion Glenville acquiesced, and we drew near the party; where dismounting, I made the following speech and proposal:

"Well, gentlemen, I think I can outshoot any man on the ground, if you will let us come in and any neighbor here will allow me to shoot his gun, in case I can find one to my notion; and here's my fifty cents for the chance. But, gentlemen and fellow-citizens, I intend to be right out and out like a back-woodsman; and so you must all know we are cold water men, and don't believe in whiskey; and so, in case we win, the barrel is, you know, ours, and then I shall knock the article in the head. But then we are willing to pay either in money or temperance tracts the amount of treat every gentleman will get if anybody else wins."

To this a fine, hardy-looking farmer, apparently some sixty years old, and evidently the patriarch of the settlement, replied;

"Well, stranger, come on; you're a powerful honest man anyhow; and here's my hand to it; if you win, which will be sort a tough on you though, you may knock the stingo in the head. And stranger, you kin have this here gun of mine, or Long Jake's there; or any one you have a notion on. How do you shoot?"

"Off-hand, neighbour; any allowance?"

"Yes; one hundred yards with a rest; eighty-five yards off-hand."

"Agreed."

"Agreed."

1st. A place level as possible was selected and cleared of all intervening brushes, twigs, etc. 2d. A large tree was chosen. Against this the target shingles were to be set, and from its roots, or rather trunk, were measured off towards the upper end of the cleared level, the two distances, eighty-five and one hundred yards. A pair of very fine natural dividers were used on this occasion; viz: a tall young chap's legs, who stepped with an elastic jerk, counting every step a yard; a profitable measure if one was *buying* broadcloth; but here the little surplusses on the yards were equally to the advantage of all. 3d. Cross lines at each distance, eighty-five and one hundred yards, were drawn on the measured line; and on the first the marksman stood who fired off-hand, while on the second the rests were placed or constructed. Rests depended on taste and fancy; some made their own—some used their comrades'—and some rested the rifle against the side of a tree on the line: and of all the rests this is the best, if one is careful to place the barrel, near its muzzle, against the tree, and not to press hard upon the barrel. Some drive in two forked stakes, and place on them a horizontal piece; and some take a chair, and then seated on the ground, they have the front of the chair towards them, and its legs between their feet, resting the whole gun upon the seat of the chair. Again, many set a small log or stone before them, then lying down flat on their—hem! they place the muzzle on the rest, and the butt of the gun on the ground near their face; and then the rifle seems as moveless as if screwed in a vice. In this way Indians and woodsmen often lie in ambuscade for deer at the licks, or enemies in war.

4th. Every man prepared a separate target. This was a poplar shingle, having near its middle a spot blackened with powder or charcoal as a ground; and, on this ground was nailed at its four corners, a piece of white paper about an inch square, and its center formed by a diamond hole; two corners being perpendicularly up and down. From the interior angles of the diamond were scratched with a knife point two diagonals, and at their intersection was the true center. With a radius of four inches from this centre was then circumscribed a circle: if beyond this circumference any *one* of the allotted shots struck, but a hair's breath, all other shots, even if in the very centre, were nugatory—the unlucky marksman lost.

5th. Each man had three shots. And provided the three were *within* the circle, each was to be measured by a line from the centre of the diamond to the near edge of the bullet-hole— except a ball grazed the centre, and then the line went to the centre of the hole—and then, the three separate lengths added were estimated as one string or line, the shortest securing the prize. This is called line shooting.

6th. Each one fixed his target against the tree as he pleased; and then, each man was to fire his three shots in succession, without being hurried or retarded. We occupied, on an average, today every man, about fifteen minutes.

19.   The Axe

As an effective instrument for opening the westward way, the rifle has been eloquently immortalized. However, the axe was a more powerful force. Because it was an undramatic, utilitarian tool it seldom, if ever, caught the eye of the contemporary historian. Occasionally a man bragged of his prowess at chopping, or a traveler described the havoc wrought with an axe. Dr. Daniel Drake opened a tiny hole in the Kentucky wilderness in 1788, and he lived to see the Ohio Valley brought out of the woods by men wielding the instrument he described as "noble."

When we arrived at Mr. May's deer lick, in the autumn of 1788, there were no inhabitants in that part of the country. But immigration, like that of the Western Reserve when you were an infant, was a constant, not a mere wet weather stream. Within the six years that elapsed, the number of settlers had increased to such an extent that one could not wander a mile in any direction, without meeting with a clearing of two to ten acres, often enclosed with a brush fence, and designated as a human residence by a one story unhewed log cabin, with the latch string always out. The usual number of ragged children was around the door, or playing in warm weather, under the shade of some shellbark hickory or venerable sugar tree, which might perchance have escaped the axe of the destroyer. By the way, it is remarkable that it should have remained for [Alexis] De Tocqueville, at a very late period, to pronounce an eulogy on the power of that noble instrument, without which the forests of the West could never have been subdued and made the abode of civilized man. An axe weighed from 3 to 4½ lbs. avoirdupois, according to the strength of him who was to wield it. The helve was invariably made of shellbark hickory,

Daniel Drake, *Pioneer Life in Kentucky* (Cincinnati: Robert Clark and Co., 1870), 41–43.

of an ovate shape, about two feet four inches in length, and having always scratched upon it a one & two feet measure for the purpose of measuring off the "rail cuts" or the cabin logs. Grindstones were scarce, but every house was provided with a whetstone, and when the instrument was newly sharpened, woe be to the boys or the women who might dull it against a stone or turn its edge by cutting the bone of a gammon of bacon. The lower part of the helve was always made smaller than the upper, so as to give it a slight degree of elasticity which not only increased the power of the instrument, but saved the hand from a jar in using it. Finally, it was a rule, never to be violated, to warm the blade or edge in winter before proceeding to chop hard wood; otherwise it might break. To this moment it is wonderful to me that so many different things could be done with this simple instrument—that it could be made to perform the functions of so many others— and that a single man in a single day could, by its aid alone, destroy so many trees.

20. Getting Married

There was no set formula for marriage and its formalities on the frontier. Anything counted from a common law union to a highly formalized community wedding with all of the legal and religious rites administered in high style. The main objective of a union of contracting parties was to form a new home and start a family, and often neither of these tasks could wait for favorable time and circumstance.

Will you have a description of a western wedding in the quaint old days of pioneer life?

Early on a fine morning, there rides up to the door of a log cabin, one of our Young American friends, about eighteen

William Henry Milburn, *The Rifle, Axe, and Sadd ags, and Other Lectures* (New York: Derby and Jackson, 1857), 45--10 years of age, on his father's best horse and best saddle—if that worthy gentleman own a saddle—the likelihood is that it is nothing but a blanket. In the door stands a blithe and buxom lassie of fifteen summers, but fully grown and finely moulded. Saluting her frankly, he presents his horse fair to her. Without recourse to block or stile, she lays one hand confidingly on his knee, the other on the horse's rump, and throws herself gracefully into the pillion behind him. Thus riding double, they start for the parson's, three or four of his male friends bearing them company. There are no roads except bridle-paths, and they therefore ride in Indian file. The old fighting times have taught them one good lesson, to hold their tongues unless they have something to say; hence the party is a silent one. Half a dozen or a dozen miles are passed, when a clearing in the woods is gained, in the centre of which stands a lowly cabin. In its door you shall see one, two, three, four—as it were, a series of short steps—of tow-headed urchins, who announce to the inmates the approach of the company. The foremost rider gives the customary hail, "Hillo, the house there." In obedience to this summons there appears upon the threshold a large, raw-boned gentleman, not in cassock, bands and surplice, not even in clerical black, but in a linsey-woolsey or buckskin hunting-shirt. Seeing the strangers, he courteously invites them to alight and come in. Before this invitation is complied with, however, the candidate for matrimonial honors inquires, is the parson at home? His interlocutor responds that he is that person. Whereupon the young man announces, "You see, this young woman and me have come here to git married; kin you do it?"

"Well, I reckon."

"Well, we're in a great hurry, kin you do it quick?"

"Certainly."

The ceremony is proceeded with as regularly as if it were in a cathedral. The young people's hands are joined, and the good man's benediction is given as he pronounces them man and wife. The new husband asks,

"Is that all, parson?"

"That's all I can do for you."

Straightening to his full height with great dignity, the young man inquires,

"Well, parson, what's the damage?"

Parsons are modest men. With a blush and a stammer, our clerical friend intimates that the less said upon that subject the better.

"Oh, no, parson," responds the young backwoodsman. "I wish you to understand that I don't choose to begin life on tick."

Simple folk that they were, they held that a wife who was not worth paying the parson for, was not worth having. Thus urged, the clergyman signifies,

"Anything that is pleasant to you is agreeable to me."

Whereupon the young husband requests one of his friends "to fetch it in off the horse's neck."

Doubtless, the wisest of you, if you have never lived upon the frontier, would be puzzled to tell what that is on the horse's neck. It turns out to be a *corn-shuck horse-collar.* This is the parson's fee, and right glad he is to get it.

The bridal train return as they have come, until within a half mile of the bride's father's cabin, when all the young men of the party, save the one with the lady behind, start at a helter-skelter gallop through the woods, dodging the limbs, jumping the fallen trees, yelling and screaming as if they were crazy. This is what they call the bottle race. In the door of the cabin stands a gentleman, his arm uplifted, grasping in his fist a great black bottle, which he is shaking desperately, as if to incite the racers to greater speed. Up rushes the foremost of the horsemen, clutches "black Betty," gives her one triumphant wave around his head in token of his victory, applies her mouth to his mouth, imbibing the consequences, and then returns to our young couple, that they may drink their own health and happiness, in the best bald-face whisky the settlement furnishes.

And now here are assembled all the neighbors from miles around—men, women, children and dogs. The men have been amusing themselves with the usual athletic sports of the border, flinging the rail, hurling the tomahawk, pitching quoits, wrestling, running foot and horse races, and shooting at a mark. The women are mostly busied about the barbecue. A trench has been dug, in one end of which you will see the flames blazing, in another the coals smouldering. Here the meats are being prepared for mastication.

But it is now high noon, dinner-time the world over, so think our simple-minded farmers. The grand repast is served beneath a rustic arbor, formed by leafy branches. Here, upon the puncheon slabs, are served bear meat, buffalo meat, venison, wild turkey, and as the daintiest of all the delicacies, baked 'possum. For side dishes, you have "big hominy," pyramids of corn dodgers, with plenty of milk and butter, if the country be far enough advanced for cows. If not, bear's oil must take the place. It is used as a sop for bread, as gravy for meat, and is pronounced wonderful by those who like it. The men draw their hunting-knives from their belts, commence the business of carving, using their fingers for forks. Every mother's skirt is clutched by her brood of little ones, begging for dodger and gravy, while around every hunter, fawn and leap his hounds, begging for their share of the repast.

21. Spiritual Outpouring

The camp meeting was, for large numbers of people across the frontier, the most exciting annual event in their lives. At these meetings they heard vivid and emotional preaching, they were frightened within a narrow margin of their lives, and they came to view the worldly course of life with awe. The meetings, however, were not too emotionally frightening for people to have a rich, social visit with their neighbors. Cane Ridge, in Bourbon County, Kentucky in 1801 was the first camp meeting to attract widespread attention, and it was to become a historical landmark in religious

John F. Wright, *Sketches of Life and Labors of James Quinn* (Cincinnati: Methodist Book Concern, 1851), 106–109, 112–114.

history. In the 1840s James Quinn, a Methodist circuit rider, recalled the meeting.

The most celebrated of all the meetings was the one held at
Cane Ridge, seven miles from Paris, Ky., which commenced
on the 6th of August, and continued a week. The number attending this was estimated at twenty thousand, and it was supposed that three thousand fell to the ground under the mighty
power of God. Here the drunkard, the Deist, the nominal professor, indeed, all classes of sinners, were prostrated on the
earth together, and confessed with equal frankness that they
had not the true knowledge of God. And many arose released
from the burden of sin, and, being made new creatures in
Christ, they mingled their voices together in praise to God for
pardoning mercy. Some of the subjects of this glorious revival
still linger on earth; but many of them, both Methodists and
Presbyterians, have long since passed away, to their home in
heaven.

When held on every circuit, the time was usually fixed to
suit the quarterly visitations of the elder during the warm
season. If a *new* ground was selected, a day was appointed,
some time previous to the meeting, when all might come together to do the public work for the accommodation of the
congregation. The ground was usually laid off to the best advantage, so as to secure the best shade, etc. Reference was had,
in the selection, to a supply of good spring water, and a running brook for the use of horses—a good grove, accessible
from various roads, and in a central position for the circuit.
The stand was usually elevated some four feet from the
ground, and in front of the preachers' tent. The seats were
arranged, separated by aisles, into different sections, that they
might be easy of access. A broad aisle was in front of the stand,
extending the whole distance of the seats. On one side of this
aisle, the seats were appropriated *exclusively* to the females,
and on the other to the males. The inner circle of tents was
arranged so as to furnish room within for the congregation at

its largest size; but the space was frequently found insufficient, and on the Sabbath preachers were often called to serve congregations without who could not hear from the principal stand. Sometimes there were many circles of tents divided by narrow streets and alleys, allowing room for the vast multitudes to pass, and space for small fires for the purpose of cooking. Hours were fixed upon, at which it was expected that all the families would breakfast, dine, and sup simultaneously. The whole system of rules was designed to promote the convenience, harmony, and enjoyment of all in attendance, as well as the good order of the meeting. The sound of the trumpet around the encampment, a short time after daylight, was the signal for all to arise and prepare for family devotions. After a sufficient time was allowed, another signal of the trumpet was given for prayer in each tent, preceded by singing two or three verses of a hymn. A short time after sunrise the trumpet was again sounded for prayer meeting at the stand, at which many attended, while breakfast was being prepared. It was usual to have preaching and exhortation at eight and eleven, A.M., and at three and candle-lighting P.M. The intervals were often occupied with prayer-meetings at the stand, or in several tents, where the mourners, or earnest seekers of salvation were embraced in praying circles. . . . At night the whole scene was awfully sublime. The ranges of tents, the fires reflecting light amidst the branches of the forest trees; the candles and lamps illuminating the ground; hundreds moving to and fro with torches like Gideon's army; the sound of exhortation, singing, praying, and rejoicing rushing from various parts of the encampment, was enough to enlist the feelings of the heart and absorb all powers of thought.

The labors performed at those camp meetings were well calculated to wear out preachers. Their efforts in the pulpit, in the open air, sometimes affected them unkindly; but their labors in the crowded praying circle, and in hot tents, did them far greater injury. When we have witnessed the astonishing preservation of the health of the ministers while exposed to the night air, a damp atmosphere, wet ground, and often having to lie on damp beds at those meetings we have been ready to say, truly "they are immortal till their work is done."

The singing, though not scientific, was devotional and strictly congregational, so that the mingled voices of the many reverberated through the shady bowers like the roar of a mighty cataract, and were solemnly impressive. After prayer and praise we heard a common-place discourse, of barely sufficient interest to secure respectful attention. When the speaker had taken his seat, another of very different appearance rose up in the open stand, from whose remarks on the arrangements of the meeting we soon learned that he was the presiding officer of the district. His features were comely, his form was symmetrical, and his movements were graceful. He was in the vigor of life, of medium height, slightly corpulent; wore a loose, flowing robe; his countenance indicated heavenly serenity, and, taken altogether, made an appearance at once imposing and attractive. Having finished his brief and well-timed announcements, he referred to the master-builder, and explaining the use of each, he assumed the style of exhortation, earnestly persuading the people to embrace and practice what they had heard. The slowly-measured but full-toned accents of his manly voice fell like heavenly music upon the ears and hearts of the enchained auditors, while the message of salvation as borne by him came to them as waters to a thirsty soul, and as good news from a far country. As he progressed he became inspired with his theme, and rising from one point of interest to another, carried the whole assembly with him. Among the motives urged to leave off sinning and commence praying, was that of avoiding future misery and securing heavenly bliss. Of the contrast between the final end of saint and sinner, he furnished Scriptural example, which, though familiar to all, was so presented as to appear new, and fix a powerful impression. Without circumlocution he recited the history of the rich man and Lazarus. While portraying the sufferings of the beggar, his manner was plaintive and moving;

but when introducing him by the ministry of angels to the society of redeemed and glorified spirits in the abodes of bliss,
he became animating and inspiring, as if he saw the light of
heaven, heard the music of angels, and felt the streams of
consolation from the river of life. But suddenly he recalled
himself and hearers to attend the case of the once wealthy
and pompous, but now deceased and lost sinner: 'The rich
man also died, and was buried.' Reciting these solemn words,
the countenance and manner of the speaker were changed
from joyful to sad; his trembling accents expressed the weight
of anguish which pressed his heart; his eyes which had just
glowed with delight now looked terrible things, as he saw
the lost soul taking its downward plunge to endless perdition.
Then elevating his voice to its utmost extent, throwing his
whole soul into his subject, and at the same time bringing his
foot with all his might down upon the floor of the stand, he
exclaimed, with fearful energy: 'And in hell he lifted up his
eyes, being in torment, and seeth Abraham afar off, and Lazarus in his bosom.' Cold chills ran over us, the hair seemed to
rise up on our heads, and the flesh to crawl upon our bones,
while groans of pity and shrieks of horror commingled around
us, like the startling tones of a sweeping tempest, attended
with a shock of Divine power as sensibly felt as it had been
the tread of an earthquake.

22.   The Lawyers' Circuits

Circuit riding on the frontier included lawyers and judges as well
as preachers, and it may have been a toss-up as to which endured
the most hardships—the preachers or the lawyers. The lawyers, no
doubt, had the most fun, because they rode in packs and had fewer
inhibitions. The circuit judge led his band of lawyers from one

Oliver Hampton Smith, *Early Indiana Trials* (Cincinnati: Moore, Wil-
stach, Keys and Co., 1885), 168, 169.

courthouse to the next. Lawyers who fought bitterly with an opponent in behalf of their clients during the day, drank, joked, and slept with the opposition at night. This was the kind of circuit that Abraham Lincoln rode with so much merriment and political success. Oliver Hampton Smith, later United States senator from Indiana, recalled the days on the Hoosier circuit when he sat as presiding judge.

The fall term of the Circuit Courts, 1825, found Judge Eggleston and myself well mounted, once more on the Circuit. The Judge upon his pacing Indian pony, the same that I afterward rode through an electioneering Congressional campaign; I then rode my gray "fox." We were joined at Centerville by James Rariden, mounted on "Old Gray," one of the finest animals I have ever seen. Our Court was to be held on the next Monday at Fort Wayne. We reached Winchester late in the evening and took lodgings at the hotel of Paul W. Way, but no newspaper heralded the arrival. How different was a circumstance that occurred when I was in the Senate of the United States. Silas Wright, Thomas H.. Benton and James Buchanan, for recreation, ran up to Philadelphia; the next day the *Pennsylvanian* announced that Senators Benton and Buchanan had arrived in that city and taken lodging at the United States Hotel. A few days after the three distinguished Senators were in their seats. I sat at the time in the next seat to Gov. Silas Wright; turning to the gov., "I see by the papers that Mr. Benton and Mr. Buchanan have been in Philadelphia and taken lodgings at the United States Hotel; how did it happen that your name was not announced, as you were with them?" "I did not send *my* name to the printer." So it was with us.

After early breakfast we were once more upon our horses, with one hundred miles through the wilderness before us. There were two Indian paths that led to Fort Wayne, the one by chief Francis Godfroy's on the Salamonia river, the other in a more easterly direction, crossing the Mississenawa higher up and striking the "Quaker trace" from Richmond to Fort

Wayne, south of the head waters of the Wabash river. After
a moment's consultation, Mr. Rariden, who was our guide,
turned the head of "Old Gray" to the eastern path, and off
we started, at a brisk traveling gait in high spirits. The day
passed away; it was very hot, and there was no water to be
had for ourselves or horses. About one o'clock we came to the
Wabash River, nearly dried up, but there was grass upon the
bank for our horses, and we dismounted, took off the saddles,
blankets and saddle-bags, when the question arose, should we
hold the horses while they graze, tie them to bushes, spancel
them, or turn them loose? We agreed that the latter was the
best for the horses and easiest for us, but I raised the question
of safety, and brought up the old adage, "Safe bind safe find."
Mr. Rariden.—"You could not drive Old Gray away from me."
Judge Eggleston.—"My Indian pony will never leave me." I
made no promises for my "Gray Fox." The bridles were taken
off, and the horses turned loose to graze. A moment after, Old
Gray stuck up his head, turned to the path we had just come,
and bounded off at a full gallop swarming with flies, followed
by the pacing pony of the Judge, at his highest speed. Fox
lingered behind, but soon became infected with the bad example of his associates, and away they all went, leaving us sitting
under the shade of a tree that stood for years afterward on the
bank of the Wabash. Our horses were, a week afterward, taken
up at Fort Defiance, in Ohio, and brought to us at Winchester
on our return. It took us but a moment to decide what to do.
Ten miles would take us to Thompson's on Townsend's Prairie.
Our saddles and blankets were hung up above the reach of the
wolves. Each took his saddle-bags on his back, and we started
at a quick step—Rariden in the lead, Judge Eggleston in the
center, and I brought up the rear. The heat was intense. None
of us had been much used to walking. I am satisfied we must
all have broken down, but most fortunately there had fallen
the night before a light rain, and the water lay in the shade
in the horse tracks. We were soon on our knees, with our
mouths to the water.—Tell me not of your Croton, ye New
Yorkers, nor of your Fairmount, ye Philadelphians, here was

water "what *was* water." Near night we reached the prairie worn down with heat and fatigue. The thunders were roaring and the lightnings flashing from the black clouds in the west. A storm was coming up on the wings of a hurricane, and ten minutes after we arrived at Mr. Thompson's it broke upon us in all its fury, and continued raining in torrents during the night. We were in a low, one story log cabin, about twenty feet square, no floor above, with a clapboard roof. Supper, to us dinner, was soon ready. Three articles of diet only on the plain walnut table, corn-dodgers, boiled squirrels, and sassa-fras tea.—Epicures at the 5 o'clock table of the Astor, St. Nicholas, Metropolitan and Revere, how do you like the bill of fare? To us it was sumptuous and thankfully received. Supper over, we soon turned in, and such a night of sweet sleep I never had before or since. The next morning our saddles and blankets were brought to us from the Wabash. The landlord provided us with ponies and we set forward at full speed, arrived at Fort Wayne that night, and took lodgings at the hotel of William N. Hood. In the morning court met, Judge Eggleston, President, and side judges, Thompson and Cushman on the bench. Fort Wayne contained about two hundred inhabitants, and the county of Allen some fifty voters. There were no cases on the docket to try of a criminal character. Court adjourned early, and we all went up the St. Mary river, to Chief Richardville's to see an Indian horse race.

23. Yankee Peddlers

Expanding western settlements not only dispersed the American population over an ever-widening area, they also created markets for eastern goods. All sorts of things were sold across the frontier

G. W. Featherstonhaugh, *Excursion Through the Slave States from Washington on the Potomac to the Frontier of Mexico; with Sketches of Popular Manners and Geological notices*, 2 vols. (London: J. Murray, 1844), 91, 92.

from shoes to metal coffins. But no single item caught the fancy of the frontiersman as did the clock. The New England Yankee was also a curiosity. He was a fast talker, a sharp trader, and a courageous traveler. He was an excellent representative of the rising industrial East in which more and more ingeniously made Yankee goods were being put on the market. The clock brought to the backwoodsmen a bit of company by its monotonous ticking, but even more important was the fact that it brought to him a sense of the passage of time. The writer was an aristocratic Englishman who published two fairly significant books about his travels along the Mississippi and across the South.

These worthy people think, if you are not looking for land to settle, that you must be pedlars: there are no markets or shop-keepers in the country for them to go to, and therefore the markets come to them—pedlars to sell goods, and tailors to cut out and make their new clothes. As to the Yankee clock pedlars, they are everywhere, and have contrived, by an assurance and perseverance that have been unrivalled from the Maccabees down, to stick up a clock in every cabin in the western country. Wherever we have been, in Kentucky, in Indiana, in Illinois, in Missouri, and here in every dell of Arkansas, and in cabins where there was not a chair to sit on, there was sure to be a Connecticut clock. The clock pedlar is an irresistible person; he enters a log cabin, gets familiarly acquainted with its inmates in the shortest imaginable time, and then comes on business.

"I guess I shall have to sell you a clock before I go."

"I expect a clock's of no use here; besides, I ha'n't got no money to pay for one."

"Oh, a clock's fine company here in the woods; why you couldn't live without one after you'd had one awhile, and you can pay for it some other time."

"I calculate you'll find I ain't a going to take one."

The wife must now be acted upon.

"Well, mistress, your husband won't take a clock; it is most surprising: he hadn't ought to let you go without one. Why, every one of your neighbours is a going to git one. I suppose, however, you've no objection to my nailing one up here, till I come back in a month or so. I'm sure you'll take care of it, and I shall charge you nothing for the use of it at any rate."

No reasonable objection, of course, can be made to this. It is nailed up; he instructs her how to keep it in order, and takes leave. But what can equal their delight, when, with a bright, clear sound, it strikes the hours! "Well," they exclaim, "if that don't beat all! Sartin, it is most delightful, curous company!" The wife now teaches her husband to wind up the clock, and great care is taken of it, as it is a deposit, and must be restored in as good condition as it was received. Too soon, Jonathan, the wily tempter, returns, talks of taking the clock down: "it was the best clock he ever had, they are such nice people he almost wishes it was theirs." Such a friendly and disinterested proceeding throws down all the icy barriers that prudence had raised between them and the shrewd Yankee. Before morning the wife gets the husband's consent, and the clock becomes theirs for the mere formality of his giving a note, payable in six months, for some eighteen or twenty dollars, and then,

"If the clock shouldn't go well he can change it for another, to be sure he can; ha'n't he got to come that way in the spring?"

He comes sure enough to dun the poor creatures, bringing one clock along with him; and as all the clocks have stopped, as a matter of course, either because they were good for nothing, or because they have wound them up too often, he changes the clock at every place he stops, cobbling them up in succession as they come into his hands, and favouring every one of his customers with the bad clock of his neighbour. The denouement is not a very pleasant one; long after the clocks have ceased to strike, the constables come and wind up the whole concern, and mistress pays too often with her cows for the inconsiderate use of her conjugal influence.

24. The Road to Freedom in the Old Northwest

Long before Harriett Beecher Stowe, Theodore Weld, or any other anti-slavery crusader described conditions of slavery in Kentucky, James B. Finley, then only sixteen years of age, took a party of twelve emancipated Negroes into the freedom of the Northwest Territory. He moved them from central Kentucky to the mouth of the Scioto at Portsmouth on the Ohio.

. . . Twelve of the emancipated negroes were mounted on pack-horses, and started for Ohio. My father placed me in charge of the company, though I was but sixteen years of age. We carried with us clothes, bed-clothes, provisions, and cooking utensils. We were accompanied with parts of three families, with a great drove of hogs, cows, and sheep. After we crossed the Ohio river it became excessively cold; and, having no road but a path through the woods, we were not able to travel more than eight or ten miles per day. Some days we were under the necessity of lying by, it was so intensely cold. The colored people are, at best, a helpless race, and unable to stand the cold; and it was with difficulty that some of them were kept from freezing. After sixteen days of toil and hardship, we reached our place of destination on the bank of the Scioto below Chilicothe. Here we built our winter camps, making them as warm as we could. Our bread was made of pounded hominy and corn meal, and we lived on this together with what we could find in the woods. Fortunately for us, game was plenty, and we caught opossums by the score. The colored people lived well on this food, and were as sleek and black as the raven. In the spring my father and the rest of the family moved out, and,

W. P. Strickland, ed., *Pioneer Life of the West, the Autobiography of James B. Finley* (Cincinnati: Methodist Book Concern, 1854), 111–113.

as soon as we could erect a cabin, all hands went to work to put in a crop of corn.

It was necessary to fence in the prairie, and every one had to inclose with a fence as much ground as he had planted. The work of fencing fell to my lot. Myself and another lad built a camp, in which we lodged at night and cooked our provisions. We frequently killed turkeys and wild ducks, with which we supplied our larder, and with our johnny-cake, baked on a board before the fire, we had a good supply for a vigorous appetite.

After our corn was gathered and laid by, the immigrants came pouring into the country. From that time to the beginning of March I traveled over the trace from Chilicothe to Manchester sixteen times. On one of these visits my brother John accompanied me, father having sent us by that route to Kentucky for seed-wheat. We took three horses with us, and after having procured the seed, we started back. On our homeward journey we found considerable difficulty in loading our horses with the bags. We could take them off when we stopped for the night, without any difficulty, but how to replace them when we wished to start in the morning, was not so easy a matter. Necessity, however, which is the mother of invention, taught us a way by which the difficulty was obviated. It was this: when we wished to stop we would seek the largest logs, and unload upon them, by which means we had less difficulty in placing the bags on the backs of the horses. Thus we tugged our way through the wilderness, without seeing the face of a human being till we reached Paint creek. This wheat, I believe, was the first sown on the waters of the Scioto.

This year our horses ran away, and my father sent me in company with an Indian, whom he had employed for that purpose, to go and hunt them. We had not gone four miles from the settlement, before the Indian was bitten by a rattlesnake on the ankle, between his leggin and moccasin. It was one of the large, yellow kind, full of poison. As soon as the Indian killed his enemy, he took his knife, went a few paces, and dug up a root, the stalk of which resembled very much the stalk of flax, about nine inches long. The root was yellow and very slender, being no thicker than a knitting-needle. This root he chewed and swallowed. He then put more in his mouth, and after chewing it, put it upon the wound. Soon after he became deathly sick, and vomited. He repeated the dose three times, with the same result, and then putting some fresh root on the bite, we traveled on. The place where he was bitten after awhile became swollen, but it did not extend far, and soon subsided. This root is undoubtedly the most effectual cure for poison in the world—a specific antidote.

IV

Land, the Western Lodestar

Of all the western attractions, adventure, curiosity, romance, and escape from the problems of an older society, none was so appealing as the availability of virgin land. Whether it be land for the taking by "tomahawk right," taking up a Revolutionary War veteran's claim, purchasing a small tract from a land office, "booming," or squatting on a portion of the public domain, people relished the idea of owning land. This obsession was a part of the attitude of the little fellow and the big speculator alike.

Never in the history of mankind had so many persons tried to claim so large an area of land so quickly and to bring it under some kind of orderly control for protection of title. New Englanders made an orderly approach to their rather limited frontier, but in areas where the western territory bulged out in never ending stretches, the land systems became less orderly. In sharp contrast was the mode of platting land claims in the older states of Virginia and the Carolinas. By a system of metes and bounds a frontiersman staked off the amount of land he wished to claim. He set such perishable markers as trees, stumps, rocks, stream courses, and even buildings and changeable paths and roadways. That there was constant conflict over claims was to be assumed. Land boundaries criss-crossed, tracts overlapped, landmarks were destroyed or moved, and rascals entered the country to help further to confuse matters. Repeatedly after 1776 Virginia attempted to institute some order in her land-granting but failed. Pennsylvania and New York had no better luck on the frontier.

A second phase of the land question was the speculator who by some curious reasoning believed that shortly there would be an influx of settlers in sufficient numbers to insure him a profit on the resale of lands. Individuals and companies were engaged in the speculative business.

Once Virginia ceded its western lands to the control of the Confederation, the union of states entered a new era of administering the western domain. The Ordinance of 1785 brought reform to the system of surveys and land location, but it took an enormous amount of public pressure and legislation to bring about changes in the distributive system. From the passage of the Harrison Land Law in 1801 to the adoption of the Homestead Law in 1862 efforts were made to satisfy the little settler. This was the area where the most public pressure was being exerted on states and the United States Government. In time there were "Sooners" who rushed illegally onto Indian lands, "Boomers" who pressured distribution of large public areas, the squatters, the pre-emptioners, and scheming homesteaders.

It can hardly be said that the public land issue was ever settled. There still rages the arguments over the wilderness areas versus the conservationists, industrialists, cattle grazers, and other exploiters of the remaining public domain. But whatever the details of land history, and there are many, the greatest western attraction was land.

25.   Corn Patch and Cabin Right, 1776

In 1776 the Virginia General Assembly in trying to devise an orderly system of public land distribution dealt with a basic problem which would also beset the young nation. In its first land act were several provisions that would apply to future federal land policies. This act attempted to carry out what Thomas Jefferson would later call "the seeding of democracy" by providing that the little claimant could have the land if within ten years he had built a cabin and grown a crop of corn on his claim. In practice it made no actual difference how flimsy the cabin was, or how poorly tended the corn patch might have been, a gesture was sufficient proof of intent.

William Waller Henning, *The Statutes at Large; being a Collection of all the laws of Virginia, 1619–1792.* 10 vols. (New York: R. and W. Bartow, 1823), vol. X, 38–41.

That all surveys of waste and unappropriated lands made upon any of the western waters before the first day of January, in the year 1778, and upon any of the eastern waters before the end of the present session of assembly, by any county surveyor commissioned by the masters of William and Mary College, acting in conformity to the laws and rules of government then in force, and founded either upon charter, importation rights duly proved and certified according to ancient usage, as far as relates to indentured servants, and other persons not being convicted, upon treasury rights for money paid the receiver general duly authenticated upon entries on the western waters, regularly made before the 26th day of October, in the year 1763, on the eastern waters at any time before the end of this present assembly session, with the surveyor of the county for tracts of land not exceeding four hundred acres, or entry in council books, and made [official] . . .

IV. And whereas great numbers of people have settled in the country upon the western waters, upon waste and unappro-priated lands, for which they have been hitherto prevented from suing out patents or obtaining legal titles by the king of Great Britain's proclamations or instructions to his governours, or by the late change of government, and the present war hav-ing delayed until now, the opening of a land office, and the establishment of any certain terms for granting lands, and it is just that those settling under such circumstances should have some reasonable allowance for the charge and risk they have incurred, and that the property so acquired should be secured to them: *Be it therefore enacted,* That all persons who, at any time before the first day of January, in the year one thousand seven hundred and seventy eight, have really and bona fide settled themselves or their families, or at his, her, or their charge, have settled others upon any waste or unappropriated lands on the said western waters, to which no other person hath any legal right or claim, shall be allowed for every family so settled, four hundred acres of land, or such smaller quantity as the party chooses, to include such settlement. And where any such settler hath had any survey made for him or her, under any order of the former government, since the twenty sixth day of October, in the year one thousand seven hundred and sixty three, in consideration of such settlement for less than four hundred acres of land such settler, his or her heirs, may claim and be allowed as much adjoining waste and unappropriated land, as together with the land so surveyed will make up the quantity of four hundred acres.

V. And whereas several families for their greater safety have settled themselves in villages or townships, under some agreement between the inhabitants of laying off the same into town lots, to be divided among them, and have, from present necessity, cultivated a piece of ground adjoining thereto in common: *Be it enacted*, That six hundred and forty acres of land whereon such villages and towns are situate, and to which no other person hath a previous legal claim, shall not be entered for or surveyed, but shall be reserved for the use and benefit of the said inhabitants until a true representation of their case can be made to the general assembly, that right and justice may be done therein; and in the mean time there shall be allowed to every such family, in consideration of their settlement, the like quantity of land as is herein allowed to other settlers adjacent, or convenient to their respective village or town, and to which no other person hath, by this act, the right of preemption, for which said quantities to be adjusted, ascertained, and certified by the commissioners to be appointed by virtue of this act, in manner herein after directed. The proper claimants shall be respectively entitled to entries with the surveyor of the county wherein the land lies, upon producing to him certificates of their rights from the said commissioners of the county, duly attested, within twelve months next after the end of this present session of assembly, and not afterwards; which certificate the said surveyor shall record in his books, and then return them to the parties, and shall proceed to survey the lands so entered, according to law. And upon due return to the land office of the plats and certificates of survey, together with the certificates from the said commissioners of the rights, by settlement upon which the entries were founded, grants may and shall issue to them and their heirs or assigns, in manner before directed. And if any such settlers shall desire to take up a greater quantity of land than is herein allowed to them, they shall on payment to the treasurer of the consideration money, required from other purchasers be entitled to the preemption of any greater quantity of land adjoining to that allowed them in consideration of settlement, not exceeding one thousand acres, and to which no other person hath any legal right or claim. And to prevent doubts concerning settlements, *It is hereby declared,* That no family shall be entitled to the allowance granted to settlers by this act, *unless they have made a crop of corn in that country, or resided there at least one year* since the time of their settlement. All persons who, since the said first day of January, in the year one thousand seven hundred and seventy eight, have actually settled on any waste or unappropriated lands on the said western waters, to which no other person hath a just or legal right or claim, shall be entitled to the preemption of any quantity of land, not exceeding four hundred acres, to include such settlement at the state price to other purchasers. And all those who, before the said first day of January, in the year one thousand seven hundred and seventy eight, had marked out or chosen for themselves, any waste or unappropriated lands, and built any house or hut, or made other improvements thereon, shall also be entitled to the preemption upon the like terms, of any quantity of land, to which no other person hath any legal right or claim; but no person shall have the right of preemption for more than one such improvement provided they respectively demand and prove their right to such preemption, before the commissioners for the county, to be appointed by virtue of this act within eight months, pay the consideration money, produce the auditor's certificate for the treasurer's receipt for the same, take out their warrants from the register of the land office within ten months, and enter the same with the surveyor of the county, within twelve months next after the end of the present session of assembly; and thereafter duly comply with the rules and regulations of the land office.

26. The Rectilinear Survey on the Upper Ohio

Following Virginia's cession of its lands in the Northwest, active steps were taken for the administration of this vast empire of public lands. The Ordinance of 1785 grew out of several sources. First, it was an attempt of the special committee appointed to deal with the Northwest Territory to bring order out of land granting chaos. The southern states of the old colonial system had followed a haphazard plan of land claims and surveys with continuous chaos and confusion as a result. The New England colonies had adopted from the outset a more orderly procedure of land surveys and grants. Thus the Ordinance of 1785 reflects some of both experiences.

The rectilinear system of surveys, comprising ranges, townships, and sections, established a dependable measure of land which could be scientifically located and re-measured. A system of granting the public lands of the Northwest was established, and provisions were made for token support, at least, of a system of public schools. In many respects this was one of the most significant pieces of land legislation adopted in the United States. It basically established an orderly system of land surveys which was adhered to across the continent.

Be it ordained by the United States in Congress assembled, that the territory ceded by individual States to the United States, which has been purchased of the Indian inhabitants, shall be disposed of in the following manner:

A surveyor from each state shall be appointed by Congress or a committee of the States, who shall take an Oath for the faithful discharge of his duty, before the Geographer of the United States. . . .

J. C. Fitzpatrick, ed., *Journals of the Continental Congress* (Washington: Government Printing Office, 1931–1944), vol. XXVIII, pp. 375–380.

The Surveyors, as they are respectively qualified, shall proceed to divide the said territory into townships of six miles square, by lines running due north and south, and others crossing these at right angles, as near as may be, unless where the boundaries of the late Indian purchases may render the same impracticable . . . .

The first line, running north and south as aforesaid, shall begin on the river Ohio, at a point that shall be found to be due north from the western termination of a line, which has been run as the southern boundary of the state of Pennsylvania; and the first line, running east and west, shall begin at the same point, and shall extend throughout the whole territory. Provided, that nothing herein shall be construed, as fixing the western boundary of the state of Pennsylvania. The geographer shall designate the townships, or fractional parts of townships, by numbers progressively from south to north; always beginning each range with number one; and the ranges shall be distinguished by their progressive numbers to the westward. The first range, extending from the Ohio to the lake Erie, being marked number one. The Geographer shall personally attend to the running of the first east and west line; and shall take the latitude of the extremes of the first north and south line, and of the mouths of the principal rivers.

The lines shall be measured with a chain; shall be plainly marked by chops on the trees, and exactly described on a plat; whereon shall be noted by the surveyor, at their proper distances, all mines, salt springs, salt licks and mill seats, that shall come to his knowledge, and all water courses, mountains and other remarkable and permanent things, over and near which such lines shall pass, and also the quality of the lands.

The plats of the townships respectively, shall be marked by subdivisions into lots of one mile square, or 640 acres, in the same direction as the external lines, and numbered from 1 to 36; always beginning the succeeding range of the lots with the number next to that with which the preceding one concluded. . . .

. . . And the geographer shall make . . . returns, from time to time, of every seven ranges as they may be surveyed. The Secretary of War shall have recourse thereto, and shall take by lot therefrom, a number of townships . . . as will be equal to one seventh part of the whole of such seven ranges . . . for the use of the late continental army. . . .

The board of treasury shall transmit a copy of the original plats, previously noting thereon, the townships and fractional parts of townships, which shall have fallen to the several states, by the distribution aforesaid, to the Commissioners of the loan office of the several states, who, after giving notice . . . shall proceed to sell the townships or fractional parts of townships, at public vendue, in the following manner, viz: The township or fractional part of a township N 1, in the first range, shall be sold entire; and N 2, in the same range, by lots; and thus in alternate order through the whole of the first range. . . . provided, that none of the lands, within the said territory, be sold under the price of one dollar the acre, to be paid in specie, or loan office certificates, reduced to specie value, by the scale of depreciation, or certificates of liquidated debts of the United States, including interest, besides the expense of the survey and other charges thereon, which are hereby rated at thirty six dollars the township . . . on failure of which payment, the said lands shall again be offered for sale.

There shall be reserved for the United States out of every township, the four lots, being numbered 8, 11, 26, 29, and out of every fractional part of a township, so many lots of the same numbers as shall be found thereon, for future sale. There shall be reserved the lot N 16, of every township, for the maintenance of public schools, within the said township; also one third part of all gold, silver, lead and copper mines, to be sold, or otherwise disposed of as Congress shall hereafter direct. . . .

And whereas Congress . . . stipulated grants of land to certain officers and soldiers of the late continental army . . . for complying therefore with such engagements, Be it ordained, That the secretary of war . . . determine who are the objects of the above resolutions and engagements . . . and cause the townships, or fractional parts of townships, hereinbefore reserved for the use of the late continental army, to be drawn for in such manner as he shall deem expedient.

27. The Ordinance of 1787

There is no doubt that this was a major document in the Confederation history of the United States. In its outline of future state organization and the management of western territory, it has remained an influential force in our history. There has grown up about this document a considerable body of controversy. Those historians who have viewed it as basic to the expansion of the federalistic system of government have had high praise for its importance. On the other hand, historians have questioned its importance beyond the immediate assistance to land-hungry promoters who wished to move into the fertile public lands of the Ohio country. The Ordinance of 1787, however, goes far beyond the mere establishment of rules by which the immediate Northwest Territory should be governed. It contains provisions for the descent of property, for the establishment of police powers, a discussion of slavery expansion, and of religion. Most important of all, there was written into the document a prescription by which future states might be added to the confederation of states, a provision which actually settled the issue of whether or not there would be new states created from the vast western territory.

§1 Be it ordained by the United States in Congress assembled, That the said territory, for the purpose of temporary government, be one district, subject, however, to be divided into two districts, as future circumstances may, in the opinion of Congress, make it expedient.

§2 Be it ordained by the authority aforesaid, That the estates, both of resident and non-resident proprietors in the said territory, dying intestate, shall descend to, and be distributed among, their children and the descendants of a deceased

Documents Illustrative of the Formation of the Union of the American States (Washington: Government Printing Office), 47–56.

child, in equal parts, the descendants of a deceased child or grandchild to take the share of their deceased parent in equal parts among them; and where there shall be no children or descendants, then in equal parts to the next of kin, in equal degree; and among collaterals, the children of a deceased brother or sister of the intestate shall have, in equal parts among them, their deceased parent's share; and there shall, in no case, be a distinction between kindred of the whole and half blood; saving in all cases to the widow of the intestate, her third part of the real estate for life, and one-third part of the personal estate; and this law relative to descents and dower, shall remain in full force until altered by the legislature of the district. And until the governor and judges shall adopt laws as hereinafter mentioned, estates in the said territory may be devised or bequeathed by wills in writing, signed and sealed by him or her in whom the estate may be (being of full age,) and attested by three witnesses; and real estates may be conveyed by lease and release, or bargain and sale, signed, sealed, and delivered by the person, being of full age, in whom the estate may be, and attested by two witnesses, provided such wills be duly proved, and such conveyances be acknowledged, or the execution thereof duly proved, and be recorded within one year after proper magistrates, courts, and registers shall be appointed for that purpose; and personal property may be transferred by delivery; saving, however to the French and Canadian inhabitants, and other settlers of the Kaskaskies, Saint Vincents, and the neighboring villages, who have heretofore professed themselves citizens of Virginia, their laws and customs now in force among them, relative to the descent and conveyance of property.

§3 Be it ordained by the authority aforesaid, That there shall be appointed, from time to time, by Congress, a governor, whose commission shall continue in force for the term of three years, unless sooner revoked by Congress; he shall reside in the district, and have a freehold estate therein, in one thousand acres of land, while in the exercise of his office.

§4 There shall be appointed from time to time, by Congress, a secretary, whose commission shall continue in force for four years unless sooner revoked; he shall reside in the district, and have a freehold estate therein in five hundred acres of land, while in the exercise of his office. It shall be his duty to keep and preserve the acts and laws passed by the legislature, and the public records of the district, and the proceedings of the governor in his executive department, and transmit authentic copies of such acts and proceedings every six months to the Secretary of Congress. There shall also be appointed a court, to consist of three judges, any two of whom to form a court who shall have a common-law jurisdiction, and reside in the district, and have each therein a freehold estate in five hundred acres of land while in the exercise of their offices; and their commissions shall continue in force during good behavior.

§5 The governor and judges, or a majority of them, shall adopt and publish in the district such laws of the original States, criminal and civil, as may be necessary, and best suited to the circumstances of the district, and report to Congress from time to time, which laws shall be in force in the district until the organization of the general assembly therein, unless disapproved of by Congress; but afterwards the legislature shall have authority to alter them as they shall think fit.

§6 The governor, for the time being, shall be commander-in-chief of the militia, appoint and commission all officers in the same below the rank of general officers; all general officers shall be appointed and commissioned by Congress.

§7 Previous to the organization of the general assembly, the governor shall appoint such magistrates and other civil officers, in each county or township, as he shall find necessary for the preservation of the peace and good order in the same. After the general assembly shall be organized the powers and duties of magistrates and other civil officers shall be regulated and defined by the said assembly; but all magistrates and other civil officers, not herein otherwise directed, shall, during the continuance of this temporary government, be appointed by the governor.

§8 For the prevention of crimes and injuries, the laws to be adopted or made shall have force in all parts of the district, and for the execution of process, criminal and civil, the governor shall make proper divisions thereof; and he shall proceed from time to time as circumstances may require, to lay out the parts of the district in which the Indian titles shall have been extinguished, into counties and townships, subject, however, to such alterations as may thereafter be made by the legislature.

§9 So soon as there shall be five thousand free male inhabitants, of full age, in the district, upon giving proof thereof to the governor, they shall receive authority, with time and place, to elect representatives from their counties or townships, to represent them in the general assembly: Provided, That for every five hundred free male inhabitants there shall be one representative, and so on, progressively, with the number of free male inhabitants, shall the right of representation increase, until the number of representatives shall amount to twenty-five; after which the number and proportion of representatives shall be regulated by the legislature: Provided, That no person be eligible or qualified to act as a representative, unless he shall have been a citizen of one of the United States three years, and be a resident in the district, or unless he shall have resided in the district three years; and, in either case, shall likewise hold in his own right, in fee-simple, two hundred acres of land within the same: Provided, also, That a freehold in fifty acres of land in the district, having been a citizen of one of the United States, and being a resident in the district, or the like freehold and two years' residence in the district, shall be necessary to qualify a man as an elector or a representative.

§10 The representatives thus elected shall serve for the term of two years; and in case of the death of a representative, or removal from office, the governor shall issue a writ to the county or township, for which he was a member, to elect another in his stead, to serve for the residue of the term.

§11 The general assembly, or legislature, shall consist of the governor, legislatve council, and a house of representatives.

The legislative council shall consist of five members, to continue in office five years, unless sooner removed by Congress; any three of whom to be a quorum; and the members of the council shall be nominated and appointed in the following manner, to wit: As soon as representatives shall be elected, the governor shall appoint a time and place for them to meet together; and, when met they shall nominate ten persons, resident in the district, and each possessed of a freehold in five hundred acres of land, and return their names to Congress, five of whom Congress shall appoint and commission to serve as aforesaid; and whenever a vacancy shall happen in the council, by death or removal from office, the house of representatives shall nominate two persons, qualified as aforesaid, for each vacancy, and return their names to Congress, one of whom Congress shall appoint and commission for the residue of the term; and every five years, four months at least before the expiration of the time of service of the members of the council, the said house shall nominate ten persons, qualified as aforesaid, and return their names to Congress; five of whom Congress shall appoint and commission to serve as members of the council five years, unless sooner removed. And the governor, legislative council, and house of representatives, shall have authority to make laws in all cases for the good government of the district, not repugnant to the principles and articles in this ordinance established and declared. And all bills, having passed a majority in the house, and by a majority in the council, shall be referred to the governor for his assent; but no bill, or legislative act whatever, shall be of any force without his assent. The governor shall have power to convene, prorogue, and dissolve the general assembly, when, in his opinion, it shall be expedient.

§12 The governor, judges, legislative council, secretary, and such other officers as Congress shall appoint in the district, shall take an oath or affirmation of fidelity, and of office; the governor before the President of Congress, and all other officers before the governor. As soon as a legislature shall be formed in the district, the council and house assembled, in one

room, shall have authority, by joint ballot, to elect a delegate
to Congress, who shall have a seat in Congress, with a right of
debating but not of voting, during this temporary government.

§13   And for extending the fundamental principles of civil
and religious liberty, which form the basis whereon these re-
publics, their laws and constitutions, are erected; to fix and
establish those principles as the basis of all laws, constitutions,
and governments, which forever hereafter shall be formed in
the said territory; to provide, also, for the establishment of
States, and permanent government therein, and for their admission to a share in the Federal councils on an equal footing
with the original States, at as early periods as may be consistent with general interest:

§14   It is hereby ordained and declared, by the authority
aforesaid, that the following articles shall be considered as
articles of compact, between the original States and the people
and States in said territory, and forever remain unalterable,
unless by common consent, to wit:

ARTICLE I   No person, demeaning himself in a peaceable and
orderly manner, shall ever be molested on account of his mode
of worship, or religious sentiments, in said territory.

ARTICLE II   The inhabitants of the said territory shall always be entitled to the benefits of the writs of habeas corpus,
and of the trial by jury; of a proportionate representation of
the people in the legislature, and of judicial proceedings according to the course of the common law. All persons shall
be bailable, unless for capital offences, where the proof shall be
evident, or the presumption great. All fines shall be moderate;
and no cruel or unusual punishments shall be inflicted. No
man shall be deprived of his liberty or property, but by the
judgment of his peers, or the laws of the land, and should the
public exigencies make it necessary, for the common preservation, to take any person's property, or to demand his particular services, full compensation shall be made for the same.
And, in the just preservation of rights and property, it is understood and declared, that no law ought ever be made or
have force in the said territory, that shall, in any manner what-

ever, interfere with or affect private contracts, or engagements, bona fide, and without fraud previously formed.

ARTICLE III   Religion, morality, and knowledge being necessary to good government and the happiness of mankind, schools and the means of education shall forever be encouraged. The utmost good faith shall always be observed towards the Indians; their lands and property shall never be taken from them without their consent; and in their property, rights, and liberty, they never shall be invaded or disturbed, unless in just and lawful wars authorized by Congress; but laws founded in justice and humanity, shall, from time to time, be made, preventing wrongs being done to them, and for preserving peace and friendship with them.

ARTICLE IV   The said territory, and the States which may be formed therein, shall forever remain a part of this Confederacy of the United States of America, subject to the Articles of Confederation, and to such alterations therein as shall be constitutionally made; and to all such acts and ordinances of the United States in Congress assembled, conformable thereto. The inhabitants and settlers in the said territory shall be subject to pay a part of the Federal debts contracted or to be contracted, and a proportional part of the expenses of government to be apportioned on them by Congress according to the same common rule and measure by which apportionments thereof shall be made on the other States; and the taxes for paying their proportion shall be laid and levied by the authority and direction of the legislatures of the district or districts, or new States, as in the original States, within the time agreed upon by the United States in Congress assembled. The legislatures of those districts or new States, shall never interfere with the primary disposal of the soil by the United States in Congress assembled, nor with any regulations Congress may find necessary for securing the title in such soil to the bona fide purchasers. No tax shall be imposed on lands the property of the United States; and, in no case, shall non-resident proprietors be taxed higher than residents. The navigable waters leading into the Mississippi and Saint Lawrence, and the carrying places between the same, shall be common highways and forever free, as well to the inhabitants of the said territory as to the citizens of the United States, and those of any other States that may be admitted into the confederacy, without any tax, impost, or duty therefor.

ARTICLE V   There shall be formed in the said territory, not less than three nor more than five States; and the boundaries of the States, as soon as Virginia shall alter her act of cession and consent to the same, shall become fixed and established as follows, to wit: The western State in the said territory, shall be bounded by the Mississippi, the Ohio, and Wabash Rivers; a direct line drawn from the Wabash and Post Vincents, due north, to the territorial line between the United States and Canada; and, by the said territorial line to the Lake of the Woods and Mississippi. The middle State shall be bounded by the said direct line, the Wabash from Port Vincents to the Ohio, by the Ohio, by a direct line drawn due north from the mouth of the Great Miami to the said territorial line, and by the said territorial line. The eastern State shall be bounded by the last-mentioned direct line, the Ohio, Pennsylvania, and the said territorial line: Provided, however, And it is further understood and declared, that the boundaries of these three States shall be subject so far to be altered, that, if Congress shall hereafter find it expedient, they shall have authority to form one or two States in that part of the said territory which lies north of an east and west line drawn through the southerly bend or extreme of Lake Michigan. And, whenever any of the said States shall have sixty thousand free inhabitants therein, such State shall be admitted, by its delegates, into the Congress of the United States, on an equal footing with the original States, in all respects whatever, and shall be at liberty to form a permanent constitution and State government: Provided, The constitution and government so to be formed, shall be republican, and in conformity to the principles contained in these articles, and, so far as it can be consistent with the general interest of the confederacy, such admission shall be allowed at an earlier period, and when there may be a less number of free inhabitants in the State than sixty thousand.

ARTICLE VI   There shall neither be slavery nor involuntary servitude in the said territory, otherwise than in the punishment of crimes whereof the party shall have been duly convicted: Provided, always, That any person escaping into the same, from whom labor or service is lawfully claimed in any one of the original States, such fugitive may be lawfully reclaimed, and conveyed to the person claiming his or her labor or service as aforesaid.

Be it ordained by the authority aforesaid, That the resolutions of the 23d of April, 1784, relative to the subject of this ordinance, be, and the same are hereby, repealed, and declared null and void.

Done by the United States in Congress assembled, the 13th day of July, in the year of our Lord 1787, and of their sovereignty and independence the twelfth.

28.   Descriptive Deeds

A central fact in frontier expansion was litigation over land claims. The Old West was full of lawyers of varying professional capabilities. It took a numerous bar to straighten out all the confusion of land boundaries, ineffectively drawn deeds, and overlapping claims. Many of the issues arose from the carelessness of imprecise surveyors, ignorant landowners, and poorly established landmarks. All of these failures made it almost impossible to reestablish surveys after the lapse of time. No wonder the Federal Land Offices gave such specific instructions after years of experience as to how surveyors should locate and mark boundaries. To illustrate the differences in deeds between metes and bounds surveys and one for a

The first document is a private deed to property in Estill County, Kentucky, 1881. The second is an entry for the property of Ansel Smith, Winston County, Mississippi, 1890.

rectilinear survey, two documents were drawn at random. These deeds are on records in the counties and states indicated below.

A Kentucky Metes and Bounds Deed

This indenture made and entered into this 4th day of October [1881] between John Walker and Talitha his wife of the one part and Wallace E. McCreery and John Daniels of the other part all of Estill County and state of Kentucky: Witnesseth that for and in consideration of the sum of $100 to him in hand paid the receipt whereof doth hereby acknowledge hath granted, bargained and Sold and doth these presents grant bargain and Sell unto Said McCreery and Daniels a certain tract or parcel of land situate lying and being in the County of Estill and bounded as follows to wit, Beginning about fifty yards below the Pretty Springs at a Maple and Spanish Oak thence S 51 W 50 poles to a white oak thence N 53 W 12 poles to three black gums thence N 37 E 40 poles to a poplar and Spanish Oak thence N 78 E 58 poles to two poplars thence Same course continued to a Stake thence S 51 W 104 poles to Beginning containing a Survey of one hundred acres more or less together with all and Singular premises and appurtenances thereto or in any wise belonging To have and to hold the Said tract or parcel of land unto Said McCreery and Daniels and their heirs forever and the Said Walker and Wife doth and will forever warrant and defend the title.

A Mississippi Rectilinear Deed

Ansel Smith's property: beginning at the Southeast Corner of the Southeast quarter of the Northeast (SE¼ of NE¼) of Section Ten (10) Township of Fourteen (14) north of Range Eleven (11) east, being a point of beginning of lot conveyed: —Run thence North three and eighty-five one hundreths (3.85) chains; run thence West thirteen (13) chains; run thence South three and eight-five (3.85) chains; run thence East thirteen (13) chains to point of beginning, being five (5) acres, more or less lying and being in the SE¼ of NE¼ of

Section 10, Township 14 north of Range 11 East in Winston County, Mississippi.

29.   The Pre-emption Law, 1841

The very nature of the westward movement sent settlers out ahead of the established line of government itself and certainly out ahead of the government surveyors. Long before there was a plan of surveying western public lands, settlers were jumping ahead of political controls. Along the Ohio, there were the early claimants who entered the Indian lands before possession had been established by treaty, and either the Indians or militiamen had to force them back across the Ohio. In Iowa there were "sooners" in the "half breed" strip. Coupled with this problem was the issue of using public lands to finance internal improvements. Political pressures were great from squatters and the states themselves. The Pre-emption Law of 1841 reflected this fact.

An Act to appropriate the proceeds of the sales of the public lands and to grant pre-emption rights.

§8   That there shall be granted to each State . . . five hundred thousand acres of land for . . . internal improvement: Provided, that to each of the said States which has already received grants for said purposes, there is hereby no more than a quantity of land which shall together with the amount such State has already received . . . make five hundred thousand acres . . . .

§10   That from and after the passage of this act, every . . . man, over the age of twenty-one years, and being a citizen of the United States, or having filed his declaration of intention to become a citizen . . . who since the first day of June, A.D. eighteen hundred and forty, has made . . . a settlement in person on the public lands to which the Indian title had been

United States Statutes at Large, vol. V., pp. 455–457.

. . . extinguished, and which . . . shall have been surveyed prior thereto, and who shall inhabit and improve the same, and who . . . shall erect a dwelling thereon . . . is hereby, authorized to enter with . . . the land office . . . by legal subdivisions, any number of acres not exceeding one hundred and sixty, or a quarter section of land, to include the residence of such claimant, upon paying to the United States the minimum price of such land, subject, however, to the following limitations and exceptions: No person shall be entitled to more than one preemptive right by virtue of this act; no person who is the proprietor of three hundred and twenty acres of land in any State or Territory of the United States, and no person who shall quit or abandon his residence on his own land to reside on the public land in the same State or Territory, shall acquire any right of pre-emption under this act; no lands included in any reservation . . . no lands reserved for the support of schools, nor the lands . . . to which the title has been or may be extinguished by the United States at any time during the operation of this act; no sections of land reserved to the United States alternate to other sections granted to any of the States for the construction of any canal, railroad, or other public improvement; no section . . . included within the limits of any incorporated town; no . . . parcel or lot of land actually settled and occupied for the purpose of trade and not agriculture; and no lands on which are situated any known salines or mines, shall be liable to entry under and by virtue of the provisions of this act. . . .

§11   That when two or more persons shall have settled on the same quarter section of land, the right of pre-emption shall be in him or her who made the first settlement, provided such persons shall conform to the other provisions of this act; and all questions as to the right of pre-emption arising between different settlers shall be settled by the register and receiver of the district within which the land is situated, subject to an appeal to and a revision by the Secretary of the Treasury of the United States.

§12   That prior to any entries being made under and by

virtue of the provisions of this act, proof of the settlement and improvement thereby required, shall be made to the satisfaction of the register and receiver of the land district in which such lands may lie, agreeably to such rules as shall be prescribed by the Secretary of the Treasury, who shall be entitled to receive fifty cents from each applicant for his services, to be rendered as aforesaid; and all assignments and transfers of the right hereby secured, prior to the issuing of the patent, shall be null and void.

§13 That before any person claiming the benefit of this act shall be allowed to enter such lands, he or she shall make oath before the receiver or register of the land district in which the land is situated, (who are hereby authorized to administer the same,) that he or she has never had the benefit of any right of pre-emption under this act; that he or she is not the owner of three hundred and twenty acres of land in any State or Territory of the United States, nor hath he or she settled upon and improved said land to sell the same on speculation, but in good faith to appropriate it to his or her own exclusive use or benefit; and that he or she has not, directly or indirectly, made any agreement or contract, in any way or manner, with any person or persons whatsoever, by which the title which he or she might acquire from the Government of the United States, should enure in whole or in part, to the benefit of any person except himself or herself; and if any person taking such oath shall swear falsely in the premises, he or she shall be subject to all the pains and penalties of perjury, and shall forfeit the money which he or she may have paid for said land, and all right and title to the same; and any grant or conveyance which he or she may have made, except in the hands of bona fide purchasers, for a valuable consideration, shall be null and void. And it shall be the duty of the officer administering such oath to file a certificate thereof in the public land office of such district, and to transmit a duplicate copy to the General Land Office, either of which shall be good and sufficient evidence that such oath was administered according to law.

§14 That this act shall not delay the sale of any of the

public lands of the United States beyond the time which has been, or may be, appointed by the proclamation of the President, nor shall the provisions of this act be available to any person or persons who shall fail to make the proof and payment, and file the affidavit required before the day appointed for the commencement of the sales as aforesaid.

30. Starting Life at Ground Level on a Nebraska Homestead

Backers of a governmental land policy which would permit the distribution of public lands to the little home-seeking settler were at times pictured to Congress as boomers of western expansion. When finally the Homestead Act of May 1862, was passed no doubt thousands of land-hungry settlers themselves dreamed of settling in one of the western public land states and living their lives in some degree of ease and economic security. This hardly proved to be the case as was revealed in the foregoing letter of a homesteader in Nebraska in the 1870s. Tons of letters and journals described the raw experiences of homesteaders, most of whom were forced literally to start lives in their new homes in the arid West level with the ground. These letters contained stories of disappointment, frustration, and grief. The winds blew continuously, myriads of insects gnawed growing crops into failure, of necessity houses were small and crudely furnished, and there was biting loneliness which all but unsettled and defeated newcomers. Money was scarce, and the settler had to "make-do" with whatever materials were immediately at hand. This Nebraska homesteader's personal experiences almost sums up that of thousands of others. (Punctuation has been added to the letter.)

This afternoon I will try to write you a few lines. I do not remember when I wrote last but I believe it was in June; I don't

Martha V. and Uriah Oblinger to Uriah's Father, Mother, Brother, and Sister, August 8, 1876, Oblinger Papers, Nebraska State Historical Society, Lincoln, Nebraska.

think you have had a letter from Neb since the 4th. We have been very busy and most of the time without stamps and money. We have managed to keep ourselves in groceries such as we were compelled to have by selling butter and a few vegetables. We have had an abundance of Peas, Beans, Reddish, and other garden truck. It has kept us scraping and gathering pretty close to keep agoing, but we have managed so far not to go in debt one cent this summer. Uriah is going to town tomorrow afternoon and I want to send a little butter and Potatoes and corn and pickles to get some groceries. *Credit* is pretty hard for any one to get in Sutton and we have learned he is a poor customer to deal with and the least we have to do with him that much better off we are. Every inch of dry goods we have got this summer was 6½ yds of calico for the girls' dresses, but we will have to get some pretty soon or we will have to grease and go naked. We have 220 bushels of threshed barley 200 of it here in the house ready to sell when the market opens for it. We hear it is worth 35 cts in Carlton and one man near Grafton has engaged 900 bushels at 50 cts per bushel but the grain merchants do not want it yet for fear of it heating on their hands.

We had our barley threshed about two weeks ago thinking we could sell it right away so we could get us something and get a well. We need a well so bad it has been almost impossible to get along this summer without one, having two heads of horses and 4 head of cattle to water. I find it pretty hard to get along and take care of milk with little water but I have made butter to shorten and grease everything. I think they do well for common cows. I do not know what we would have done if we had not got them for we have not had a snip of meat in the house since last winter until the other day our neighbor (Geo Smith) killed a hog and we got 9 lbs to have for threshers & well diggers. I fried it and packed it down to keep until they come. I often think of your Pickel pork barrel and think of the nice sweet meat we use to fry and put on the table, but we would not eat it because it was not lean ham or shoulder. I have often wished this summer I could go to that barrel and pick out the fattest piece in it. *We could eat it here,* not because we are starving but because we are so healthy and have such good appetites we can eat anything.

The people here are about through with their grain. There has been an immense lot of grain raised here this season and it has been a favorable season to take care of grain; most all the grain is good. Some of the oats are not very good by being struck with rust. Uriah's oats are splendid they will yield 40 bushels per acre and are a splendid quality. Uriah has the brag crop of the neighborhood to take it all through it he did have to tend it with three year old colts. He took time and planted his corn so he could tend it both ways and it looks quite different to most of the corn around here.

Sam, you know how they put in corn and tended when you was here, they do that yet and the weeds are getting to be a perfect nuisance. Uriah has 13½ acres of corn he thinks will yield 60 bushels per acre and 4 acres that looks well but will not yield as much as it was planted late, our cane looks well, we will have our share of squashes again and some pumpkins, our watermellons are not so plenty as last year, was planted too late. Potatoes are not near so good a yield as last year as the bugs are so bad we will have more than we can make use of as we have quite a lot planted. Some vines are entirely striped; ours are not hurt much yet. We will feast on Fried Chicken & Sweet pototaoes after while as both chickens and sweet potatoes are doing well. I had a hugh mess of cabbage yesterday for dinner, will have plenty from now on. I have the best cabbage in the neighborhood. You bet I worked for it. We have had to do without cabbage every winter since we have been here and I was determined to have it this season if it could be raised. My tomatoes will soon be ripe, have a nice lot of them. The barley yielded 28½ bushels to the acre. Uriah wants to cut our wheat a Thursday. This may sound quite strange to you to cut wheat the middle of August. It is a very late wheat and was sowed late, have but 5 acres but it is good. The Robinsons' boys are going to cut it with their harvester.

Charlie, I wish you could spend next summer here and see

how they take care of their grain and see the machinery run. The headers are going to go ahead of everything here in very few years for lots of men say they will not pull any more bands after this year. When they cut grain with a header, when they are done cutting they are done stacking. I tell you it looks nice to see a header running. Combs headed our barley. I rode across with them in the header box and could have a good view. All the machinery goes before the horses. Uriah done his own stacking and stacked considerable for Combs. He says it is the easiest way to harvest he ever seen. The Headers put the grain in the stack for the same the Harvester puts it in the shock, 1.50 per acre they can cut any kind of grain and they have a machine here called the self binder. One man can cut and bind his own grain. I have not seen that work yet but the boys have. It is no uncommon occurance here for one man to have 100 acres of harvesting and some 160 acres.

Uriah is up at Giles today helping him put up his flax. Well I will stop writing about harvesting and crops or my letter will all be taken up for that. Oh yes, Giles will start with the thresher now soon. Sade will stay here most of the time, or she thinks to, and at Sam's part time. I have had lots of pie plant to use, had enough to make eight pies for threshers, have had eight Raspberries, one bush of them you sent us is growing, the blackberries all died.

Well the next is things in general. Net, you ask me some time ago what Giles had in their house. Well they are like ourselves and all the rest here, they have not got much furniture. They have a cook stove and as few cooking utensils as can do with, a small sink, two short benches, dishes enough to set a small table, 1 bed stead (Seal Morgans' bed stead), a Lounge, homemade, Giles' sheetiron trunk, a blue Chest that Sade brought, looking glass like ours only a little longer, two pictures, two chairs, the ones Giles brought from home, and a home made table. Sade has 25 yds of carpet that her Pa bought for her when she started out here but she dont want to put it down until they finish the house. Sade has a tolerable good bed. Sade did not bring as much from home as I thought she would, for the old man is in good circumstance but as tight as the bark on a beach tree in Feb. He knows how to keep his money, he give Sade 25 dollars when she left home, he bought Sade a meal sive and coffe mill while he was here and bought Sade Wheeler a set of knives & forks, and Sade's sister sent Sam's little girl three yards of calico. Was all the presents he brought so you may know they are all tight, or they would have sent more than that. All thoug I think Giles has a good woman, she will help him save for she is no spend thrift. They only get just what they have to have and she is very saving in anything she goes at. I think as much of her as any sister-in-law I have. She is willing to do any way and any thing to save expenses and she is very careful of everything she has. You may know she is not very proud when she has rode Giles saddle to church all summer and Giles rides on a horse blanket.

Now you need not think because they have nothing more that they are about to come on the county for we are all home-steaders here and are all on equality and all live about alike. If you think you could not enjoy yourselves here with us and our little dab of home made furniture and one room houses you know what you can do, but let me tell you, you would find as much sociability and I believe a little more than you will find in the east. Sam Ward is back on his place again, says Neb is one of the jolliest places he ever seen. Mrs. Ward has not seen hardly a well day since she left here. They have another boy or girl, I do not know. Uriah has that note yet he is going to see him the first day he gets time. Well I think Georges takes the rag off the bush.

Mother, what do you think by this time about George not having a big family? I think they are in as fare away for a big family as we are if Gussie was old when married. I think they are leaving us clear behind and if Giles does not hurry up Geo. will not give him any show at all.

Charlie, I was in hopes we would get your choice names but I guess George are going to beat us. Well Stell is our baby and will be for a long time. She likes her niny as well as ever but I have threatened to take it from her next month if it is cool and she keeps well, and I expect I will have a dreadful time of it for she is so bad after it. Ella is trying to feed her pup & we have another to raise but I expect will be like all the rest, when we get it raised we will loose it. She calls it Jo Turk. She says Jo is its given name. I named it Turk.

Oh yes, wish you could see my flowers. We have the prettiest Petunias here I ever seen grow, they are as big again as they grow in Ind. I have saved my honey suckel until it is in full bloom. I tell you I am proud of it. It is all the one I know. I have a prickle pear and Mrs Griffith brought me one of the prettiest cactis I ever seen from the Republican Valley. It resembles the pincushion cactis only much prettier. Have you got your Oleander yet? If you have I want you to send me a slip. You can send it in a paper. Cut off two or three slips, stick wax on the ends and they will only be on the road a few days and I believe they will grow. If you send Giles things this fall I want you to stick in a few bulbs of Tulips and Lillies if it is only one or two of each, just so we can get a start.

I would like so well to have a Peonia, have not seen any here.

Nett, we read your letter containing your pictures. I dont think you picture is nearly as good the one you sent me. Married life certainly cannot agree with you. You look nearly as old and peaked and lantern jawed as I do. What in the land ailed you anyhow, you look as though you was in deep distress. Was your dress pinching you or is that a kind of style you have got to putting on? It dont fit you if it is. I dont believe you are fattening up on *Peaches this fall.* Stright looks very much as I thought he would but I dont believe he is any better looking than my own man. I feel just like taking hold of the goatee and pulling him across the house. Well I guess there will be no danger of beauty killing either of our men nor will we quarrel over their good look, for as pretty is pretty does, but I shall look for Stright's picture soon. Be sure and send me a piece of your wedding dress this fall for my log cabin. I am working at it, and all the pieces of the worsted dresses you can get.

I think Aggie Norris has done well, better have some one to appologise for her. If my memory serves me right she was married the after part of Sept. or in Oct. I call it quick work. I suppose Sallie Mc will be next. Is there any talk of Sallie Homs marrying or does she have any beauxs? Does she look like she use too? I wish you could tell me just the half of what I want to know when you write.

Sam, I send you a Geneva paper. I got it soiled by laying it over pies, makes it look bad but you can read it any how.

Nett, if you find so much pleasure in writing to your new kinsfolks why dont Stright write to his new kinsfolks? I think him and Sade are both alike, they are slow at forming acquaintances. I think you will get a letter from Sade soon for she is a poor hand to write. She is with her pictures like Giles is with his, she thinks she does not make a good picture. Well neither of them is killed with beauty and how can they expect pretty pictures? The picture Giles had of Sade I thought was better looking than she is for Sade is not very handsome, for like the rest of us she has a big nose, but it is a pitty that two should get together and neither of them made a good picture. Nett, did you do like Giles & Will, get a democrat, so you have to keep still? I thought I would tell you how we had been getting along this summer. Wrote in this letter about being out of money that want you to send us money. That was not my object at all.

Mother, you said in your letter for us to keep a stiff upper lip, that would get some fruit this fall. Well that is no trouble for us any more for we have had to keep a stiff upper lip so much since we have been here that they have about grown stiff. Wish you could see the girls. Ella has been riding Stella in the grain scoop but she has upset her and Stella is mad as a wet hen. You better think they are wild, but there they go again. Sam Dave Robinson is married; he married one of the Brown girls and lives over south. I expect there are some big mistakes in this letter for the young ones have nearly teased the life out of me. Oh yes, we spent the Fourth in Fairmont. We had a splendid time. Well there is a poor sight for Uriah to write any in this letter. I did not suppose he would have time to write so I have not left any room for him. We are all well.

Write soon.

31. Shortcomings in Public Land Policy

N. C. McFarland, Land Commissioner, discovered that in North Dakota in the 1880s both the Homestead and Timber Culture Acts left much to be desired. Not only had vast areas of public lands served as a lodestone which drew people to the frontier, even to great stretches of arid lands west of the 98th meridian, but it also made rascals out of them. The proponents of the Timber Culture Act had hoped that it would help modify the climate and bring about some moisture preservation. In the opinion of Commissioner McFarland, "Frauds have been so extensively perpetrated under the timber culture act, that the practical operation of the act has been to prevent instead of promote the cultivation of trees. . . ."

In the Territory of Dakota, which cast 50,000 votes at the last election [1884], the number of agricultural entries to the present date exceeds 150,000, and such entries are now being made at the rate of more than 50,000 yearly. As a very considerable portion of the inhabitants are settled on railroad lands and school sections, it is manifest that the number of entries of public lands is far beyond the actual occupation of such lands, and far beyond the entries that could legally have been made. The governor of this Territory in his last annual message to the legislative assembly, makes the following statement:

N. C. McFarland, "Land Office Commissioner's Report," *Senate Document* 61, 47th Congress, Second Session (Washington: Government Printing Office, 1885), pp. 3, 4.

"The well-intended acts of Congress, allowing the entry of
160 acres of lands as a tree claim, have been so completely
nullified by the manipulations of land sharks that our broad
and fertile prairies are comparatively treeless."

The governor recommends that a certain number of acres
of land be exempted from Territorial and local taxation in order
to encourage the growth of trees and homesteads, for the reason expressly given, that frauds have been so extensively perpetrated under the timber-culture act, that the practical operation of that act has been to prevent instead of promote the
cultivation of trees. . . .

Complaints of frauds, and appeals for the protection of bona
fide settlers from the exactions and oppressions of those who
commit or cause these frauds to be committed, are constantly
coming up to this office. A flood-tide of illegal appropriations
seems to be sweeping over the new states and Territories,
threatening to engulf the entire public domain.

The time has arrived when, in my serious judgment, either
a complete radical change in public land laws and administration, or some adequate means for enforcing the penalties or
existing law, has become an alternative that can no longer be
disregarded.

32.   Administering the Public Lands

Further confusion over land policy was added onto an already impossible situation in a movement on the part of the Department of
Interior to let the matter of public land distribution calm down
until some arrangement could be made for better administration.
By this time, however, so much of the economy of Dakota Territory
was based on land titles that any change promised to bring disaster
to farmers, speculators, and bankers alike. Frontier farmers in
Dakota felt that they were being discriminated against by the cen-

From *The* [Bismark] *Daily Press and Dakotian,* April 28, 1885.

tral government, and Washington quickly learned that once a practice was begun it could not be changed without considerable emotional reaction at the grass-roots level of the American constituency.

Parties in the land and loan business in this city, have recently been presented with circulars from Washington, which contain an order from the general land office, under date of April 3rd, suspending final action upon all entries of public lands in Dakota, and other western territories and states. The order excepts from its provision all private cash entries and scrip entries. It applies, therefore directly to homestead, pre-emption and timber culture entries. In other words, persons are permitted to file upon lands, but are not permitted to prove up and secure title to their possessions. The suspension of final action is indefinite. It stands during the pleasure of the land commissioner and his superior office, the secretary of the interior. Filings, payments and proofs may proceed and if these preliminaries are found to be legally correct, applications will be approved for patent. Here the matter will rest until the circumstances connected with each claim are examined by government detective, after which the government will consider the propriety of granting title.

Thus the settler must wait indefinitely, while the speculator who puts up the cash or covers his acres with scrip secures his patent with no delay. That this course is not in the interest of settlement of the west is clearly apparent upon the fact of the order. It is significant that while the order includes all the western states and territories which contain government land, it does not apply to any of the southern states. Its effect upon this portion of the country can be well imagined. The poor but industrious settler upon the prairies of the east is peremptorily denied the privileges the law undertakes to guarantee, while the speculator is encouraged to secure and hold in their wild, undeveloped condition the lands which make up the public domain. The entire west is to suffer from a general suspicion of fraud and its progress must halt while slow investigation preceeds, but to the south there attaches no such suspicion and its public lands may become private property without delay or a danger that the settler, after having invested his all may finally be deprived of his rights.

The effect will be disastrous in Dakota. It will drive money from our midst. Foreign capital, upon which we so much depend for the development of our resources, will retire from the field, because the security behind its investment is swept away by this official order. Men cannot borrow upon an uncertain title—a title which depends upon future contingencies for confirmation. If the land department had made a studied effort to cut off all progress in the new west it could not have succeeded better than in this.

33. Circumventing the Land Laws

The conflict between the settler, corporate landholder, land grabber, and speculator was continuous. No doubt the basic intent of most of the important public land acts of Congress was to give the little homestead settler the advantage. One of the basic concepts of manifest destiny as an applied idea of westward expansion was that this would be true. It was hard, however, to draw the line as to who was a settler. There were hundreds, maybe even thousands of claimants. Once these people made a claim they could transfer it or otherwise dispose of it in a way that thwarted the intent of the law. The following three letters to N. C. McFarland, Public Land Commissioner, reflect this fact.

[From] *Mrs. L. L. Snowden, Granada, Bent County, Colorado,*
April 1, 1882

Why are the "land grabbers" allowed to hold their way here? If a poor man goes to deed up, the land officers and lawyers

N. C. McFarland, "Violations Relating to Public Lands," *Messages from the President of the United States, Chester A. Arthur, Senate Document* 61, 47th Congress, Second Session, vol. 3 (Washington: Government Printing Office, 1883), 8, 10, 32.

are bribed or are held on as it were, in the hollow of the "land grabber's" hands, so that a poor man does not get justice. If emigrants want to settle here they say there is no vacant land; because they have money and are cattle men of some note, they are allowed to fence in whole townships, buy their herders land rights, pick out the best land, and have them pretend to settle on it three or four months, and, in fact, do as they please, and are a great enemy of anyone who will not kneel to them, for they have all the say and influence, having for a justice of the peace an Englishman, who although he served in the Army of the late war, has not declared his intention of becoming a citizen. He jumped our claim, and they furnished him the means to law, and, of course, the office at Pueblo decided for them; my husband was told our lawyer [was] bought so another appealed the case, for nothing. I am still hopeful; I would like to know before we do any planting; should I have to wait until fall my planting will be of no avail, as these parties, through their claim, will hold their claim on my stock so you see my desire.

It is no uncommon thing to be asked, "What will you take for your homestead of pre-emption right?"

Enclosed are the notices of five that has sold or rather has agreed to let themselves be used for that purpose, for fifty dollars; am prepared to prove the Kuhler case. I would think, if there was a detective sent out on the 9th instant, he would find none of the parties at the clerk's office. I think it is time for these grabbers to be checked.

As we will have a new register, at Pueblo, Colo., he should be started in a justifiable way, and fulfill the law, and encourage the actual settler.

[From] *S. C. Crosby, Manchester, Iowa,*
December 10, 1882

I have just returned from an extensive trip to the Dakota Territory with a view of a "new house." I find the law of locating land is not complied with, or else the law as it is condensed in newspapers is very imperfect. Not one pre-emptor in ten has

made final proof as an occupant now or ever has for four weeks
prior to "notice of final proof;" same of "commuted homesteads."

I believe that it is as great a fraud upon the government as
the star route steal and "not half the trouble and expense to
prove it" and stop it. Not one tree claim in fifty is made by a
settler of the Territory, but are located and then put in the
hands of agents for speculation, the party being in Iowa or
Missouri, Wisconsin or Minnesota. Should not the tree claim
in justice be for the resident of the county? Cannot a few cases
in each county be made by the Government where it is easily
shown that they have done it to speculate.

I believe it would stop it, can you send me an authentic
copy of these laws as they are.

> [From] *D. L. Greene, Grangeville, Idaho,*
> *November 27, 1882*

I write to inform you of the great abuse of the homestead
pre-emption, and timber laws in this section. Land is being
taken up here under the above laws by parties who do not
comply with the laws in regard to residing upon the lands, etc,
and in fact do not comply with the law in scarcely one particular. Such is the case with old residents, some of whom have
from 320 to 500 acres and over, and still are taking up more
under the above laws, and keeping back newcomers who
would be actual settlers. And this is done openly, without any
attempt at secrecy. It (sic) because so many are doing it, and
they won't inform on each other.

I know of three parties, two of whom have taken pre-
emptions adjoining me, and not one has just proved on his,
and he has never done a thing on it but haul a couple of load
of rail on it.

The second has a small house on his; says he will fence
three or four acres in the spring and prove up, after which he
wants to sell house, fence etc.

The third party was around trying to sell his house on both
homestead and pre-emption immediately after proving up.

These parties generally get their witnesses from the loafers and irresponsible fellows that are lying around saloons, who are ready to swear to most anything for a few dollars. This land that is taken that way is mostly held for speculation. Some of them possibly intend to live on it themselves sometime or other when it will suit their convenience. I know of others taken in the way described, but it is not necessary to mention any more cases, as I just wished to give you an idea of how the government land is being gobbled up here. I have no doubt there are scores of claims here that ought to be canceled on account of fraud.

My motive in making this statement is that the land is kept from actual settlers. I would like to have the land settled by *bona fide* settlers in my neighborhood at this moment and not sham settlers. If you should send an agent here to enquire into this matter, I think he would be astonished at the amount of fraud practiced here in taking up land. In case you shall enquire into this matter, I will give further information if desired but do not wish to have my name used, as some of the perjurers might injure my property if they knew I informed on them.

V

The Indian Frontier

The westward movement created many new problems for the westering pioneer and for the nation, and none was more vexing than that of the Indian. The very fact of the Indian's presence was a problem: his presence blocked the free expansion of settler and speculator onto public lands.

And the white man's appropriation of more and more land was a continuing threat to the basics of Indian economy and existence. He not only took up the Indian's hunting and trapping and farming grounds, as well as his homeland, but his constant pressure often brought tribes into conflicts with each other. These tribal conflicts not only impressed the frontiersmen with their ferocity, but they also encouraged the maintenance of a substantial United States Army in the West; the army protected whites from atrocious Indian raids and it also lessened to some degree at least tribal frictions and warfare.

The white man never seemed to learn the whole truth about the Indian. For all the Indian's ferocity and understandable resistance, a romance attached to him and to his customs, and it is to be found reflected in the accounts of travelers who visited tribes beyond the lines of settlement.

For more than a century the government wrestled with the Indian problem. It held innumerable conferences with the tribes, made repeated treaties, removed thousands of Indians to special territories and reservations, used the Army against the more militant, and even allowed church groups to participate in Indian affairs. Responsibility for the Indian shifted from the Army to the Department of Interior, and finally Congress passed the Dawes Act as a step toward raising the Indian to the status of homesteader, "civilized man," and citizen.

34. Indian Favor and the British Traders

Conrad Weiser, Pennsylvania's official interpreter and chief advisor on Indian affairs in the mid-eighteenth century, established a handsome reputation for being able to deal with the red man in western Pennsylvania and along the Ohio. On one occasion he represented the president and council of Pennsylvania in an effort to explain to the Indians why, during a lull in the conflict between the British and French, the colony had been unable to deliver arms which had been promised the Indians. His account and speech is an interesting specimen of early Indian diplomacy compounded of two parts hot air and one part trader's goods.

17th [1748]. It rained very hard, but in the Afternoon it held up for about 3 hours; the Deputies of the several Nations met in Council & I delivered them what I had to say from the President & Council of Pennsylvania by Andrew Montour.

"Brethren, you that live on Ohio: I am sent to You by the President & Council of Pennsylvania, & I am now going to Speak to You on their behalf I desire You will take Notice & hear what I shall say."—Gave a String of Wampum.

"Brethren: Some of You have been in Philadelphia last Fall & acquainted us that You had taken up the English Hatchet, and that You had already made use of it against the French, & that the French had very hard heads, & your Country afforded nothing but Sticks & Hickerys which was not sufficient to break them. You desir'd your Brethren wou'd assist You with some Weapons sufficient to do it. Your Brethren the Presid^t. & Council promis'd you then to send something to You next Spring by Tharachiawagon [Weiser], but as some other Affairs prevented his Journey to Ohio, you receiv'd a

"Journal of Conrad Weiser, 1748–1765," Reuben Gold Thwaites, ed., *Early Western Travels, 1748–1846*, 4 vols. (Cleveland: Arthur H. Clark, 1904), vol. I, pp. 38–43.

Supply by George Croghan sent you by your said Brethren; but before George Croghan came back from Ohio News came from over the Great Lake that the King of Great Britain & the French King had agreed upon a Cessation of Arms for Six Months & that a Peace was very likely to follow. Your Brethren, the President & Council, were then in a manner at a loss what to do. It did not become them to act contrary to the command of the King, and it was out of their Power to encourage you in the War against the French; but as your Brethren never miss'd fulfilling their Promises, they have upon second Consideration thought proper to turn the intended Supply into a Civil & Brotherly Present, and have accordingly sent me with it, and here are the Goods before your Eyes, which I have, by your Brethren's Order, divided into 5 Shares & layd in 5 different heaps, one heap whereof your Brother Assaraquoa sent to You to remember his Friendship and Unity with You; & as you are all of the same Nations with whom we the English have been in League of Friendship, nothing need be said more than this, that the President & Council & Assaraquoa have sent You this Present to serve to strengthen the Chain of Friendship between us the English & the several Nations of Indians to which You belong. A French Peace is a very uncertain One, they keep it no longer than their Interest permits, then they break it without provocation given them. The French King's People have been almost starv'd in old France for want of Provision, which made them wish & seek for Peace; but our wise People are of opinion that after their Bellies are full they will quarrel again & raise a War. All nations in Europe know that their Friendship is mix'd with Poison, & many that trusted too much on their Friendship have been ruin'd.

"I now conclude & say, that we the English are your true Brethren at all Events, In token whereof receive this Present." The Goods being then uncover'd I proceeded. "Brethren: You have of late settled the River of Ohio for the sake of Hunting, & our Traders followed you for the sake of Hunting also. You have invited them yourselves. Your Brethren, the President & Council, desire You will look upon them as your Brethren & see that they have justice done. Some of your Young Men have robbed our Traders, but you will be so honest as to compel them to make Satisfaction. You are now become a People of Note, & are grown very numerous of late Years, & there is no doubt some wise Men among you, it therefore becomes you to Act the part of wise men, & for the future be more regular than You have Been for some Years past, when only a few Young Hunters lived here."— Gave a Belt.

"Brethren: You have of late made frequent Complaints against the Traders bringing so much Rum to your Towns, & desir'd it might be stop't; & your Brethren the President & Council made an Act accordingly & put a stop to it, & no Trader was to bring any Rum or strong Liquor to your Towns. I have the Act here with me & shall explain it to You before I leave you; But it seems it is out of your Brethren's Power to stop it entirely. You send down your own Skins by the Traders to buy Rum for you. You go yourselves & fetch Horse loads of strong Liquor. But the other Day an Indian came to this Town out of Maryland with 3 Horse loads of Liquor, so that it appears you love it so well that you cannot be without it. You know very well that the Country near the endless Mountain affords strong Liquor, & the moment the Traders buy it they are gone out of the Inhabitants & are travelling to this Place without being discover'd; besides this, you never agree about it—one will have it, the other won't (tho' very few), a third says we will have it cheaper; this last we believe is spoken from your Hearts (here they Laughed). Your Brethren, therefore, have order'd that every cask of Whiskey shall be sold to You for 5 Bucks in your Town, & if a Trader offers to sell Whiskey to You and will not let you have it at that Price, you may take it from him & drink it for nothing."—Gave a Belt.

"Brethren: Here is one of the Traders who you know to be a very sober & honest Man; he has been robbed of the

value of 300 Bucks, & you all know by whom; let, therefore, Satisfaction be made to the Trader."—Gave a String
of Wampum.

"Brethren, I have no more to say."

I delivered the Goods to them, having first divided them
into 5 Shares—a Share to the Senekas another to the Cajukas,
Oneidos, the Onontagers, & Mohawks, another to the Delawares, another to the Owendaets, Tisagechroanu, & Mohic-
kons, and the other to the Shawonese.

The Indians signified great Satisfaction & were well pleased
with the Cessation of Arms. The Rainy Weather hasted them
away with the Goods into the Houses.

18th. The Speech was delivered to the Delawares in their
own Language, & also to the Shawonese in their's, by Andrew
Montour, in the presence of the Gentlemen that accompanied
me. I acquainted the Indians I was determined to leave them
to-morrow & return homewards.

19th. Scaiohady, Tannghrishon, Oniadagarehra, with a few
more, came to my lodging & spoke as follows:

"Brother Onas, We desire you will hear what we are going to
say to You in behalf of all the Indians on Ohio; their Deputies
have sent us to You. We have heard what you have said to us,
& we return you many thanks for your kindness in informing
us of what pass'd between the King of Great Britain & the
French King, and in particular we return you many thanks
for the large Presents; the same we do to our Brother Assaraquoa, who joined our Brother Onas in making us a Present.
Our Brethren have indeed tied our Hearts to their's. We at
present can but return thanks with an empty hand till another
opportunity serves to do it sufficiently. We must call a great
Council & do every thing regular; in the mean time look upon
us as your true Brothers.

"Brother: You said the other Day in Council if any thing
befell us from the French we must let you know of it. We will
let you know if we hear any thing from the French, be it
against us or yourself. You will have Peace, but it's most cer-

tain that the Six Nations & their Allies are upon the point of
declaring War against the French. Let us keep up true Corris-
pondence & always hear of one another."—They gave a Belt.

35. Trader Diplomacy

That convivial Irishman, George Croghan, was one of the cleverest
of all Indian traders and a foremost negotiator with the western
tribes. In 1751 he was joined in an official diplomatic mission to
the Indians by Andrew Montour, an impudent, hard-drinking but
able half-breed interpreter and Indian diplomat. Like Weiser in
1748, Croghan and Montour endeavored passionately to woo away
from the French the Indian tribes and groups about the head of the
Ohio, in the western Ohio country, and in the Great Lakes region.
The trader-diplomats and the Indians vied with each other for the
loftiest and vaguest terms in which to express themselves; both
were masters in pretending great hurt and under the lubricating
effect of rum achieved lofty promises.

[August] 23ᵈ [1751]—Colᵒ Campbell & I had a Meeting with
the Twightwees, Wawiotanans, Pyankeshas, Kickapoos and
Musquattamies, when they produced the several Belts sent
them by Colᵒ Ntsfdytrry, in consequence of which Invitation
they came here.

   Then they spoake to the Six Nations Delawares & Shawanese
on several Belts & Pipes, beging in the most abject manner
that they would forgive them for the ill conduct of their Young
Men, to take Pity on their Women & Children & grant yᵐ peace.

   They then spoake to the Colᵒ & me on several Pipes & Belts
Expressing their great satisfaction at a firm and lasting Peace
settled between their Bretheren the English, & the several
Indian Nations in this Country, that they saw the heavy Clouds
that hung over their heads for some time past were now dis-

"Journal of George Croghan," Thwaites, ed., *Early Western Travels,* vol.
I, pp. 154–162.

persed, and that the Sun shone clear & bright & that as their Father the King of England had conquered the French in that [this] Country & taken into his Friendship all the Indian Nations, they hoped for the future they would be a happy people, & that they should always have reason to call the English their Fathers & beged we would take pity on their Women & Children, & make up the difference subsisting between them and the Shawanese, Delawares & Six Nations, and said as they were come here in consequence of Col° Bradstreet's Invitation, & that he had not met them they hoped their Fathers would pity their necessity & give them a little clothing, and a little rum to drink on the road, as they had come a great way to see their Fathers. Then the Wyondats spoake to the Shawanese, & all the Western Nations on severall Belts & strings, by which they exhorted the several Nations to behave themselves well to their Fathers the English, who had now taken them under their Protection, that if they did, they would be a happy People, that if they did not listen to the Councils of their Fathers, they must take the Consequences, having assured them that all Nations to the Sun rising had taken fast hold of their Fathers the English by the hand, & would follow their Advice, & do every thing they desired them, & never would let slip the Chain of Friendship now so happily renewed.

August 24th—We had another Meeting with the Several Nations, when the Wawiotanans, Twightwees, Pyankeshas, Kickapoos & Musquatamies made several speeches to Col° Campbell & me, in presence of all the other Nations, when they promised to become the Children of the King of Great Britain & farther acknowledged that they had at Ouiatonon before they came there [here] given up the Sovereignty of their Country to me for His Majesty, & promised to support his subjects in taking possession of all the Posts given up by the French their former Fathers, to the English, now their present Fathers, all which they confirmed with a Belt.

25th—We had another meeting with the same Indians, when Col° Campbell & I had made them several speeches in answer to theirs of the 23 & 24th then delivered them a Road Belt in the name of Sir William Johnson Baronet, to open a Road from the rising to the setting of the Sun which we charged them to keep open through their Country & cautioned them to stop their Ears against the Storys or idle reports of evil minded People & continue to promote the good Works of Peace, all which they promised to do in a most sincere manner.

26th—Colo Campbell & I made those Nations some presents, when after taking leave of us, they sett off for their own Country well satisfied.

27th—We had a Meeting with Pondiac & all the Ottawa Tribes, Chipwaes & Puttewatamies wth the Hurons of this Place & the chiefs of those settled at Sandusky & the Miamis River, when we made them the following Speeches.

CHILDREN PONDIAC & ALL OUR CHILDREN THE OTTAWAS, PUTTE-WATAMIES, CHIPWAYS & WYONDATTS: We are very glad to see so many of our Children here present at your Antient Council Fire, which has been neglected for some time past, since those high winds has arose & raised some heavy clouds over your Country, I now by this Belt dress up your Antient Fire & throw some dry wood upon it, that the blaze may ascend to the Clouds so that all Nations may see it, & know that you live in Peace & Tranquility with your Fathers the English.—A Belt.

By this Belt I disperse all the black clouds from over your heads, that the Sun may shine clear on your Women and Children, that those unborn may enjoy the blessings of this General Peace, now so happily settled between your Fathers the English & you & all your younger Brethren to the Sun setting.—A Belt.

Children: By this Belt I gather up all the Bones of your deceased friends, & bury them deep in the ground, that the herbs & sweet flowers of the earth may grow over them, that we may not see them any more.—A Belt.

Children: with this Belt I take the Hatchet out of your Hands & I pluck up a large tree & bury it deep, so that it may never be found any more, & I plant the tree of Peace, where all our children may sit under & smoak in Peace with their Fathers.—A Belt.

Children: We have made a Road from the Sun rising to the Sun setting, I desire that you will preserve that Road good and pleasant to Travel upon, that we may all share the blessings of this happy Union. I am sorry to see our Children dispersed thro' the Woods, I therefore desire you will return to your Antient Settlements & take care of your Council Fire which I have now dressed up, & promote the good work of Peace.—A Belt.

After which Wapicomica delivered his Messages from Sir William Johnson to Pondiac & the rest of the several Chiefs.

Aug. 28th—We had a Meeting with Pondiac & the several Nations when Pondiac made the following Speeches.

FATHER: We have all smoaked out of the Pipe of Peace its your Childrens Pipe & as the War is all over, & the Great Spirit and Giver of Light who has made the Earth & every thing therein, has brought us all together this day for our mutual good to promote the good Works of Peace, I declare to all Nations that I had settled my Peace with you before I came here, & now deliver my Pipe to be sent to Sir William Johnson that he may know I have made Peace, & taken the King of England for my Father, in presence of all the Nations now assembled, & whenever any of those Nations go to visit him, they may smoak out of it with him in Peace. Fathers we are oblidged to you for lighting up our old Council Fire for us, & desiring us to return to it, but we are now settled on the Miamis River, not far from hence, whenever you want us you will find us there ready to wait on you, the reason I choose to stay where we are now settled, is, that we love liquor, and did we live here as formerly, our People would be always drunk, which might occasion some quarrels between the Soldiers & them, this Father is all the reason I have for not returning to our old Settlements, & that we live so nigh this place, that when we want to drink, we can easily come for it.—Gave a large Pipe with a Belt of Wampum tied to it.

FATHER: Be strong and take pity on us your Children as our former Father did, 'tis just the Hunting Season of our children, our Fathers the French formerly used to credit his Children for powder & lead to hunt with, I request in behalf of all the Nations present that you will speak to the Traders now here to do the same, my Father, once more I request you will take pity on us & tell your Traders to give your Children credit for a little powder & lead, as the support of our Family's depend upon it, we have told you where we live, that whenever you want us & let us know it, we will come directly to you.—A Belt.

FATHER: You stopped up the Rum Barrel when we came here, 'till the Business of this Meeting was over, as it is now finished, we request you may open the barrel that your Children may drink & be merry.

August 29th—A Deputation of several Nations sett out from Detroit for the Illinois Country with several Messages from me & the Wyondats, Six Nations, Delawares, Shawanese & other Nations, in answer to theirs delivered me at Ouiatonon.

30th—The Chiefs of the several Nations who are settled on the Ouabache returned to Detroit from the River Roche, where they had been encamped, & informed Colo Campbell & me, they were now going off for their own Country, & that nothing gave them greater pleasure, than to see that all the Western Nations & Tribes had agreed to a general Peace, & that they should be glad [to know] how soon their Fathers the English, would take possession of the Posts in their Country, formerly possessed by their late Fathers the French, to open a Trade for them, & if this could not be done this Fall, they desired that some Traders might be sent to their Villages to supply them for the Winter, or else they would be oblidged to go to the Illinois and apply to their old Fathers the French for such necessarys as they might want.

They then spoke on a Belt & said Fathers, every thing is now settled, & we have agreed to your taking possession of the posts in our Country. we have been informed, that the English where ever they settle, make the Country their own, & you tell us that when you conquered the French they gave you this Country.—That no difference may happen hereafter, we tell you now the French never conquered us neither did they purchase a foot of our Country, nor have they a right to give it to you, we gave them liberty to settle for which they always rewarded us, & treated us with great Civility while they had it in their power, but as they are become now your people, if you expect to keep these Posts, we will expect to have proper returns from you.—A Belt.

Sept^br 2^d—The chiefs of the Wyondatts or Huron, came to me & said they had spoke last Summer to Sir Willm Johnson at Niagara about the lands, on which the French had settled near Detroit belonging to them, & desired I would mention again to him. they never had sold it to the French & expected their new Fathers the English would do them justice, as the French were become one People with us.—A Belt.

4th—Pondiac with several chiefs of the Ottawas, Chippawaes & Potowatamies likewise complained that the French had settled part of their country, which they never had sold to them, & hoped their Fathers the English would take it into Consideration, & see that a proper satisfacton was made to them. That their Country was very large, & they were willing to give up such part of it, as was necessary for their Fathers the English, to carry on Trade at, provided they were paid for it, & a sufficient part of the Country left them to hunt on.—A Belt.

6th—The *Sagina* Indians came here, & made a speech on a Belt of Wampum expressing their satisfaction on hearing that a general Peace was made with all the Western Nations & with Pondiac, they desired a little Powder, Lead & a few knives to enable them to hunt on their way home, & a little rum to drink their new Fathers health.—A Belt.

9th—*Altewaky* and *Chamindiway* Chiefs of a Band of Ottawas from Sandusky with 20 Men came here and informed me that their late conduct had been peaceable, that on hearing there was a great Meeting of all Nations at this place, they came to hear what would be done, & on their way here they had been informed that a General Peace was settled with all Nations to the Sun setting, & they now came to assure us of their attachment to the English Interest, & beged for some Powder, Lead, some Blankets and a little rum to help them to return to their town.—A String.

Septbr 11th—Col[o] Campbell & I gave the above parties some presents & a little rum & sent them away well satisfied.

12th—The Grand Sautois came with his band and spoke as follows.

FATHER: You sent me a Belt from the Miamis, & as soon as I received it, I set off to meet you here, on my way I heard what had past between you & the several Tribes that met you here, you have had pity on them, & I beg in behalf of myself & and the people of Chicago that you will have pity on us also. 'tis true we have been Fools, & have listened to evil reports, & the whistling of bad birds, we red people, are a very jealous and foolish people, & Father amongst you White People, there are bad people also, that tell us lyes & deceive us, which has been the occasion of what has past, I need not say much on this head, I am now convinced, that I have been wrong for some years past, but there are people who have behaved worse than I & my people, they were pardoned last year at this place, I hope we may meet with the same, that our Women & Children may enjoy the blessings of peace as the rest of our Bretheren the red people, & you shall be convinced by our future conduct that we will behave as well as any Tribe of Ind[s] in this Country.—A Belt.

He then said that the St. Joseph Indians would have come along with him, but the English Prisoner which their Fathers want from them, was some distance off a hunting, & as soon as they could get him in, they would deliver him up and desire forgiveness.

36.   The Indian Tragedy of 1774

The old upper Ohio frontier between 1740 and 1781 was a hotbed of conflict, confusion, and intrigue. The British, French, colonial,

Alexander Scott Withers, *Chronicles of Border Warfare, or a History of the Settlements by the Whites of Northwestern Virginia* . . . (Clarksburg: R. Israel, 1831), 111–120.

and Indian were involved in the troubles of the region. Pennsylvania and Virginia traders, land scouts, and soldiers came this way. British-French warring over the territory disturbed its peace for a decade; and then pressure from land speculator and prospective settler brought its own tensions. An outstanding Indian in 1774 was Chief John Logan. It was Logan and his family who became victims of the Greathouse tragedy, a preliminary incident to the outbreak of Dunmore's War. In his narrative, Alexander Scott Withers revealed the blameworthy actions of the colonial militiamen and emissaries of Lord Dunmore in provoking the short and abortive war which ended in the rendition of Chief Logan's famous oration and the making of the Treaty of Charlotte.

The outbreak of Dunmore's War was to disrupt the beginnings of Harrod's settlement in Kentucky. It, however, gave such frontiersmen as George Rogers Clark, Simon Kenton, Isaac Shelby, and Simon Girty a taste of border warfare.

If other evidence were wanting, to prove the fact that the war of 1774 had its origin in a determination of the Indians to repress the extension of white settlements, it could be found in the circumstance, that although it was terminated by the treaty with Lord Dunmore, yet it revived as soon as attempts were again made to occupy Kentucky, and was continued with increased ardour, 'till the victory obtained over them by General Wayne. For, notwithstanding that in the struggle for American liberty, those Indians became the allies of Great Britain, yet when independence was acknowledged, and the English forces withdrawn from the colonies, hostilities were still carried on by them; and, as was then well understood, because of the continued operation of those causes, which produced the war of 1775. That the Canadian traders and British emissaries, prompted the Indians to aggression, and extended to them every aid which they could, to render that aggression more effectually oppressive and overwhelming, is readily admitted. Yet this would not have led to a war, but for the encroachments which have been mentioned. French influence, united to the known jealousy of the Natives, would have been unavailingly exerted to array the Indians against Virginia, at the com-

mencement of Braddock's war, but for the proceedings of the
Ohio company, and the fact that the Pennsylvania traders
represented the object of that association to be purely territorial. And equally fruitless would have been their endeavor
to involve them in a contest with Virginians at a later period,
but for a like manifestation of an intention to encroach on their
domain.

In the latter end of April 1774, a party of land adventurers,
who had fled from the dangers which threatened them below,
came in collision with some Indians, near the mouth of Captina,
sixteen miles below Wheeling. A slight skirmish ensued, which
terminated in the discomfiture of the whites, notwithstanding
they had only one man wounded, and one or two of the enemy
were killed. About the same time, happened the affair opposite
the mouth of Yellow creek; a stream emptying into the Ohio
river from the northwest, nearly midway between Pittsburg
and Wheeling.

In consequence of advices received of the menacing conduct of the Indians, Joshua Baker (who lived at this place)
was preparing, together with his neighbors, to retire for
safety, into some of the nearer forts, or to go to the older
and more populous settlements, remote from danger. There
was at that time a large party of Indians, encamped on both
sides of Yellow creek, at its entrance into the river; and although in their intercourse at Baker's, they had not manifested
an intention of speedily commencing depredations, yet he
deemed his situation in the immediate contiguity of them, as
being far from secure, and was on the eve of abandoning it,
when a party of whites, who had just collected at his house,
fired upon and killed some Indians, who were likewise there.—
Among them were the brother and daughter of the celebrated
chief, Logan.

Apprized of impending danger, many of the inhabitants on
the frontiers of North Western Virginia, retired into the interior, before any depredations were committed, in the upper
country; some took refuge in forts which had been previously

built; while others, collecting together at particular houses, converted them into temporary fortresses, answering well the purposes of protection, to those who sought shelter in them. Fort Redstone, which had been erected after the successful expedition of General Forbes; and Fort Pitt, at the confluence of the Alleghany and Monongahela rivers, afforded an asylum to many. Several private forts were likewise established in various parts of the country; and every thing which individual exertion could effect, to ensure protection to the border inhabitants, was done. . . .

Early in June, the troops destined to make an incursion into the Indian country, assembled at Wheeling, and being placed under the command of Colonel Angus McDonald, descended the Ohio to the mouth of Captina. Debarking, at this place, from their boats and canoes, they took up their march to Wappatomica, an Indian town on the Muskingum. The country through which the army had to pass, was one unbroken forest, presenting many obstacles to its speedy advance, not the least of which was the difficulty of proceeding directly to the point proposed. To obviate this, however, they were accompanied by three persons in the capacity of guides; whose knowledge of the woods, and familiarity with those natural indices, which so unerringly mark the direction of the principal points, enabled them to pursue the direct course.—When they had approached within six miles of the town, the army encountered an opposition from a party of fifty or sixty Indians lying in ambush; and before these could be dislodged, two whites were killed, and eight or ten wounded;—one Indian was killed and several wounded. They then proceeded to Wappatomica without further molestation.

When the army arrived at the town, it was found to be entirely deserted. Supposing that it would cross the river, the Indians had retreated to the opposite bank, and concealing themselves behind trees and fallen timber, were awaiting that movement in joyful anticipation of a successful surprise.— Their own anxiety and the prudence of the commanding officer, however, frustrated that expectation. Several were discovered peeping from their covert, watching the motion of the army; and Colonel McDonald, suspecting their object, and apprehensive that they would recross the river and attack him in the rear, stationed videttes above and below, to detect any such purpose, and to apprise him of the first movement towards effecting it. Foiled by these prudent and precautionary measures and seeing their town in possession of the enemy, with no prospect of wresting it from them, 'till destruction would have done its work, the Indians sued for peace; and the commander of the expedition consenting to negotiate with them, if he could be assured of their sincerity, five chiefs were sent over as hostages, and the army then crossed the river, with them in front.

When a negotiation was begun, the Indians asked, that one of the hostages might be permitted to go and convoke the other chiefs, whose presence, it was alleged, would be necessary to the ratification of a peace. One was accordingly released; and not returning at the time specified, another was then sent, who in like manner failed to return. Colonel McDonald, suspecting some treachery, marched forward to the next town, above Wappatomica, where another slight engagement took place, in which one Indian was killed and one white man wounded. It was then ascertained, that the time which should have been spent in collecting the other chiefs, preparatory to negotiation, had been employed in removing their old men, their women and children, together with what property could be readily taken off, and for making preparations for a combined attack on the Virginia troops. To punish this duplicity and to render peace really desirable, Col. McDonald burned their towns and destroyed their crops; and being then in want of provisions, retraced his steps to Wheeling, taking with him the three remaining hostages, who were then sent on to Williamsburg. . . .

A council was next convoked to resolve on the fate of Robinson; and then arose in his breast, feelings of the most anxious inquietude. Logan assured him, that he should not be killed; but the council appeared determined that he should die, and he was tied to the stake. Logan then addressed them, and with much vehemence, insisted that Robinson too should be spared; and had the eloquence displayed on that occasion been less than Logan is believed to have possessed, it is by no means wonderful that he appeared to Robinson (as he afterwards said) the most powerful orator he ever heard. But commanding as his eloquence might have been, it seems not to have prevailed with the council; for Logan had to interpose otherwise than by argument or entreaty, to succeed in the attainment of his object. Enraged at the pertinacity with which the life of Robinson was sought to be taken, and reckless of the consequences, he drew the tomahawk from his belt, and severing the cords which bound the devoted victim to the stake, led him in triumph, to the cabin of an old squaw, by whom he was immediately adopted.

After this, so long as Logan remained in the town where Robinson was, he was kind and attentive to him; and when preparing to go again to war, got him to write the letter which was afterwards found on Holstein at the house of a Mr. Robertson, whose family were all murdered by the Indians. Robinson remained with his adopted mother, until he was redeemed under the treaty concluded at the close of the Dunmore campaign.

37. The Moravian Massacre

No single act in Indian-white relations prior to the Sand Creek Massacre in Colorado in 1864 provoked so much controversy as that related by Henry Howe in an early history of Ohio. The white man had often excused his own savage assaults on the Indian by characterizing the red man as a heathen unworthy of mercy, but the American conscience found it difficult to erase the slaughter of Indians in 1782 who had been converted to Christianity by the

Henry Howe, *Historical Collections of Ohio* (Cincinnati: Derby, Bradley, and Co., 1847), 38–43.

Moravians and who had placed their trust in both the white man and the white man's religion.

The first white inhabitants of Tuscarawas county, were the Moravian missionaries and their families. The Rev. Frederick Post and Rev. John Heckewelder had penetrated thus far into the wilderness previous to the commencement of the revolutionary war. Their first visits west of the Ohio date as early as the years 1761 and '62. Other missionary auxiliaries were sent out by that society, for the purpose of propagating the Christian religion among the Indians. Among these was the Rev. David Zeisberger, a man whose devotion to the cause was attested by the hardships he endured and the dangers he encountered.

Had the same pacific policy which governed the society of Friends in their first settlement of eastern Pennsylvania, been adopted by the white settlers of the west, the efforts of the Moravian missionaries in Ohio would have been more successful. But our western pioneers were not, either by profession or practice, friends of peace. They had an instinctive hatred to the aborigines, and were only deterred, by their inability, from exterminating the race. Perhaps the acts of cruelty practiced by certain Indian tribes on prisoners taken in previous contests with the whites, might have aided to produce this feeling on the part of the latter. Be that as it may, the effects of this deep-rooted prejudice greatly retarded the efforts of the missionaries.

They had three stations on the river Tuscarawas, or rather three Indian villages, viz.: Shoenbrun, Gnadenhutten and Salem. The site of the first is about two miles south of New Philadelphia; seven miles farther south was Gnadenhutten, in the immediate vicinity of the present village of that name; and about five miles below that was Salem, a short distance from the village of Port Washington. The first and last mentioned were on the west side of the Tuscarawas, now near the margin of the Ohio canal. Gnadenhutten is on the east side of the river. It was here that a massacre took place on the 8th of March, 1782, which, for cool barbarity, is perhaps unequalled in the history of the Indian war.

The Moravian villages on the Tuscarawas were situated about mid-way between the white settlements near the Ohio, and some warlike tribes of Wyandots and Delawares on the Sandusky. These latter were chiefly in the service of England, or at least opposed to the colonists, with whom she was then at war. There was a British station at Detroit, and an American one at Fort Pitt, (Pittsburgh,) which were regarded as the nucleus of western operations by each of the contending parties. The Moravian villages of friendly Indians on the Tuscarawas were situated, as the saying is, between two fires. As Christian converts and friends of peace, both policy and inclination led them to adopt neutral grounds. With much difficulty they sustained this position, partially unmolested, until the autumn of 1781. In the month of August, in that year, an English officer named Elliott, from Detroit, attended by two Delaware chiefs, Pimoacan and Pipe, with three hundred warriors, visited Gnadenhutten. They urged the necessity of the speedy removal of the Christian Indians further west, as a measure of safety. Seeing the latter were not inclined to take their advice, they resorted to threats, and in some instances to violence. They at last succeeded in their object. The Christian Indians were forced to leave their crops of corn, potatoes and garden vegetables, and remove, with their unwelcome visitors, to the country bordering on the Sandusky. The missionaries were taken prisoners to Detroit. After suffering severely from hunger and cold during the winter, a portion of the Indians were permitted to return to their settlements on the Tuscarawas, for the purpose of gathering in the corn left on the stalk the preceding fall.

About one hundred and fifty Moravian Indians, including women and children, arrived on the Tuscarawas in the latter part of February, and divided into three parties, so as to work at the three towns in the corn-fields. Satisfied that they had escaped from the thraldom of their less civilized brethren west, they little expected that a storm was gathering among the white settlers east, which was to burst over their peaceful habitations with such direful consequences.

Several depredations had been committed by hostile Indians, about this time, on the frontier inhabitants of western Pennsylvania and Virginia, who determined to retaliate. A company of one hundred men was raised and placed under the command of Col. Williamson, as a corps of volunteer militia. They set out for the Moravian towns on the Tuscarawas, and arrived within a mile of Gnadenhutten on the night of the 5th of March. On the morning of the 6th, finding the Indians were employed in their corn-field, on the west side of the river, sixteen of Williamson's men crossed, two at a time, over a large saptrough, or vessel used for retaining sugar-water, taking their rifles with them. The remainder went into the village, where they found a man and a woman, both of whom they killed. The sixteen on the west side, on approaching the Indians in the field, found them more numerous than they expected. They had their arms with them, which were usual on such occasions, both for purposes of protection and for killing game. The whites accosted them kindly, told them they had come to take them to a place where they would be in future protected, and advised them to quit work, and return with them to the neighborhood of Fort Pitt. Some of the Indians had been taken to that place in the preceding year, had been well treated by the American governor of the fort, and been dismissed with tokens of warm friendship. Under these circumstances, it is not surprising that the unsuspecting Moravian Indians readily surrendered their arms, and at once consented to be controlled by the advice of Colonel Williamson and his men. An Indian messenger was dispatched to Salem, to apprize the brethren there of the new arrangement, and both companies then returned to Gnadenhutten. On reaching the village, a number of mounted militia started for the Salem settlement, but e'er they reached it, found that the Moravian Indians at that place had already left their cornfields, by the advice of the messenger, and were on the road to join their brethren at Gnadenhutten. Measures had been adopted by the militia to secure the Indians whom they had at first decoyed into their power. They were bound, confined in two houses, and well guarded. On the arrival of the Indians from Salem, (their arms having been previously secured without suspicion of any hostile intention,) they were also fettered, and divided between the two prison-houses, the males in one, the females in the other. The number thus confined in both, including men, women and children, have been estimated from ninety to ninety-six.

A council was then held to determine how the Moravian Indians should be disposed of. This self-constituted military court embraced both officers and privates. The late Dr. Dodridge, in his published notes on Indian wars, &c., says: "Colonel Williamson put the question, whether the Moravian Indians should be taken prisoners to Fort Pitt, or *put to death?*" requesting those who were in favor of saving their lives to step out and form a second rank. Only eighteen out of the whole number stepped forth as advocates of mercy. In these, the feelings of humanity were not extinct. In the majority, which was large, no sympathy was manifested. They resolved to *murder* (for no other word can express the act) the whole of the Christian Indians in their custody. Among these were several who had contributed to aid the missionaries in the work of conversion and civilization—two of whom emigrated from New Jersey after the death of their spiritual pastor, the Rev. David Brainard. One woman, who could speak good English, knelt before the commander and begged his protection. Her supplication was unavailing. They were ordered to prepare for death. But the warning had been anticipated. Their firm belief in their new creed was shown forth in the sad hour of their tribulation, by religious exercises of preparation. The orisons of these devoted people were already ascending the throne of the Most High!—the sound of the Christian's hymn and the Christian's prayer found an echo in the surrounding woods, but no responsive feeling in the bosoms of their executioners. With gun, and spear, and tomahawk, and scalping-knife, the work of death progressed in these slaughterhouses, till not a sigh or moan was heard to proclaim the existence of human life within—all, save two—two Indian boys escaped, as if by a miracle, to be witnesses in after times of the savage cruelty of the white man towards their unfortunate race.

Thus were upwards of ninety human beings hurried to an untimely grave by those who should have been their legitimate protectors. After committing the barbarous act, Williamson and his men set fire to the houses containing the dead, and then marched off for Shoenbrun, the upper Indian town. But here the news of their atrocious deeds had preceded them. The inhabitants had all fled, and with them fled for a time the hopes of the missionaries to establish a settlement of Christian Indians on the Tuscarawas. The fruits of ten years' labor in the cause of civilization, was apparently lost.

38.   The Making of Frontier Indian Legend

This description of "Big Joe Logston" was written from memory by Felix Renick for John S. Williams and publication. It is the kind of material from which many of the frontier legends were created. For instance, there were the largely unsubstantiated descriptions of Daniel Boone's many hairbreadth exploits; of McColloch's famous leap near Wheeling, West Virginia; and of numerous other superhuman exploits. In later years, the dime novelists used stories such as this one of the Logstons to give full body to many of their breathless tales of personal prowess and heroism. Joe Logston had emigrated from Virginia to the early Ohio frontier by way of Kentucky.

The elder Logston, whose name was Joesph, and his wife, whose name, I think, was Mary, with an only son bearing his name, lived, when I first knew them, in Virginia, near the source of the north branch of the Potomac, in one of the most inhospitable regions of the Alleghany mountains, some twenty or thirty miles from any settlement. There never was, perhaps, a family better calculated to live in such a place. Old Joe (for they were soon known as Old Joe and Young Joe Logston) was a very large athletic man, with uncommon muscular strength. The old lady was not so much above the ordinary height of women, but like the Dutchman's horse, was built up from the ground; and it would have taken the strength of two or three common women to equal hers. The son was no discredit to either in the way of strength, size, or activity. In fact he soon outstripped his father. What little he lost in height was more than compensated in the thickness and muscle of the mother, so that when he came to his full size and strength, he went by the name of Big Joe Logston. I would not venture to say his physical powers were equal to those of the strong man of old, but such they were as to become proverbial. It was often said to stout looking, growing young men, "You will soon be as big as Big Joe Logston."

Joe sometimes descended from his mountain heights into the valleys, in order to exchange his skins for powder, lead, and other articles for the use of the family. While in society he entered, with great alacrity, into all the various athletic sports of the day. No Kentuckian could ever, with greater propriety than he, have said, "I can out-run, out-hop, out-jump, throw down, drag out, and whip any man in the country." And as to the use of the rifle, he was said to be one of the quickest and surest centre shots to be found. With all this, as is usual with men of real grit, Joe was good natured, and never sought a quarrel. No doubt many a bullying, bragging fellow would have been proud of the name of having whipped Big Joe Logston, but that, on taking a close survey of him, thought "prudence the better part of valor," and let him return to his mountain without raising his dander.

About the time Joe arrived at manhood, his father, and perhaps his mother, were called hence, leaving him single handed to contend, not only with the Spitzbergen winters of the mountains, but with the bears, panthers, wolves, rattle-snakes, and all the numerous tribes of dangerous animals, reptiles and insects, with which the mountain regions abound. Joe, however, maintained his ground for several years, until the settlements had begun to encroach on what he had been accustomed to consider his own premises. One man sat down six miles east of him, another about the same distance in another direction, and finally one, with a numerous family, had the temerity to come and pitch his cabin within two miles of him. This Joe could not stand, and he pulled up stakes and decamped to seek a neighborhood where he could hear the crack of no man's rifle but his own.

Of all the men I ever knew he was the best qualified to live on a frontier where there were savages, either animal or human, to contend with. His uncommon size and strength, and inclination to be entirely free from restraint, made him choose his residence a little outside of the bounds of law and civil liberty. I do not know the precise time he left the Alleghanies, but believe it was between the years of 1787 and '91. The next that we heard of Joe was, that he had settled in Kentucky, south of Green river, I think on Little Barren river, and of course, a little in advance of the settlements. The frontiers were frequently compelled to contend with the southern Indians. There was not a particle of fear in Joe's composition; that ingredient was left out of his nature. I never knew such a man in my life. There he would be. He soon had an introduction to a new acquaintance. So far he had been acquainted only with savage beasts, but now savage man came in his way, and as it "stirs the blood more to rouse the lion than to start a hare," Joe was in his delight. The Indians made a sudden attack, and all that escaped were driven into a rude fort for preservation, and, though reluctantly, Joe was one. This was a new life to him and did not at all suit his taste. He soon became very restless, and every day insisted on going out with others to hunt up the cattle. Knowing the danger better, or fearing it more, all persisted in their refusals to go with him.

To indulge his taste for the Woodman's life, he turned out alone, and rode till the after part of the day without finding any cattle. What the Indians had not killed were scared off. He concluded to return to the fort. Riding along a path which led in, he came to a fine vine of grapes. He laid his gun across the pommel of his saddle, set his hat on it, and filled it with grapes. He turned into the path and rode carelessly along, eating his grapes, and the first intimation he had of danger, was the crack of two rifles, one from each side of the road. One of the balls passed through the paps of his breast, which, for a male, were remarkably prominent, almost as much so as those of many nurses. The ball just grazed the skin between the paps, but did not injure the breast bone. The other ball struck his horse behind the saddle, and he sunk in his tracks. Thus was Joe eased off his horse in a manner more rare than welcome. Still he was on his feet in an instant, with his rifle in his hands and might have taken to his heels; and I will venture the opinion, that no Indian could have caught him. That, he said, was not his sort. He had never left a battle ground without leaving his mark, and he was resolved that that should not be the first. The moment the guns fired, one very athletic Indian discovered this, he jumped behind two pretty large saplings, some small distance apart, neither of which were large enough to cover his body, and to save himself as well as he could, he kept springing from one to the other.

Joe, knowing he had two enemies on the ground, kept a lookout for the other by a quick glance of the eye. He presently discovered him behind a tree loading his gun. The tree was not quite large enough to hide him. When in the act of pushing down his bullet, he exposed pretty fairly his hips. Joe, in the twinkling of an eye, wheeled and let him have his load in the part exposed. The big Indian then, with a mighty "Ugh!" rushed towards him with his raised tomahawk. Here were two warriors met, each determined to conquer or die,— each the Goliath of his nation. The Indian had rather the advantage in size of frame, but Joe in weight and muscular strength. The Indian made a halt at the distance of fifteen or twenty feet, and threw his tomahawk with all his force, but Joe had his eye on him and dodged it. It flew quite out of the reach of either of them. Joe then clubbed his gun and made at the Indian, thinking to knock him down. The Indian sprang into some brush, or saplings, to avoid his blows. The Indian depended entirely on dodging with the help of the saplings. At length Joe, thinking he had a pretty fair chance, made a side blow with such force, that missing the dodging Indian, the gun, now reduced to the naked barrel, was drawn quite out of his hands, and flew entirely out of reach. The Indian now gave another exulting "Ugh!" and sprang at him with all the savage fury he was master of. Neither of them had a weapon in his hands, and the Indian, seeing Logston bleeding freely, thought he could throw him down and dispatch him. In this he was mistaken. They seized each other and a desperate scuffle ensued. Joe could throw him down, but could not hold him there. The Indian being naked, with his hide oiled, had greatly the advantage in a ground scuffle, and would still slip out of Joe's grasp and rise. After throwing him five or six times, Joe found, that between loss of blood and violent exertions, his wind was leaving him, and that he must change the mode of warfare or lose his scalp, which he was not yet willing to spare. He threw the Indian again, and without attempting to hold him, jumped from him, and as he rose, aimed a fist blow at his head, which caused him to fall back, and as he would rise, Joe gave him several blows in succession, the Indian rising slower each time. He at last succeeded in giving him a pretty fair blow in the burr of the ear, with all his force, and he fell, as Joe thought, pretty near dead. Joe jumped on him, and thinking he could dispatch him by choaking, grasped his neck with his left hand, keeping his right one free for contingencies. Joe soon found the Indian was not so dead as he thought, and that he was making some use of his right arm which lay across his body, and on casting his eye down discovered the Indian was making an effort to unsheath a knife that was hanging at his belt.

The knife was short and so sunk in the sheath that it was necessary to force it up by pressing against the point. This the Indian was trying to effect, and with good success. Joe kept his eye on it, jerked it out of the sheath, and sunk it up to the handle into the Indian's breast, who gave a death groan and expired.

Joe now thought of the other Indian, and not knowing how far he had succeeded in killing or crippling him, sprang to his feet. He found the crippled Indian had crawled some distance towards them, and had propped his broken neck against a log and was trying to raise his gun to shoot him, but in attempting to do which he would fall forward and had to push against his gun to rise himself again. Joe seeing that he was safe, concluded he had fought long enough for healthy exercise that day, and not liking to be killed by a crippled Indian, he made for the fort. He got in about nightfall, and a hard looking case he was—blood and dirt from the crown of his head to the sole of his foot, no horse, no hat, no gun— with an account of the battle that some of his comrades could scarce believe to be much else than one of his big stories in which he would sometimes indulge. He told them they must go and judge for themselves.

39.   The Raisin Massacre

Few of the bloody incidents of the frontier left a deeper scar than the massacre that occurred on the River Raisin in the War of 1812. On January 21, 1813, British Colonel Henry Proctor, with a force half Indian in composition, overwhelmed an American militia force near present day Monroe, Michigan. Leaving the wounded prisoners behind in the village of Frenchtown, he marched the rest to Detroit. The wounded at first expected the mercy and protection of their

William Atherton, *Narrative of the Suffering and Defeat of the Northwestern Army, under General Winchester* (Frankfort, Ky: A. G. Hodges, 1842), 60–71.

British captors; but, as one of them, William Atherton, began to suspect the next day, Proctor's Indians had plans of their own. When the night of the twenty-second was through, "Remember the River Raisin" became a rallying cry for the Northwestern American Army.

After the departure of this Indian chief, (for I have but little doubt but what he was among the principal leaders of the Indian forces,) some conversation ensued among ourselves in reference to the designs of this crafty and intelligent chief.

There was, as well as I can recollect, but one opinion expressed on the subject; and I believe it was the opinion of all, that that would be the last night with most of us. We dreaded an attack during the night; for this Indian, just as he left, said "I am afraid some of the mischievious boys will do some mischief before morning." After remaining in this state of suspense for more than an hour, expecting every moment that the savages would come rushing upon us; but every thing becoming quiet, we laid down upon our blankets to rest: but rested very little during this dismal night. Dreadful as was the night, the morning was more fearful. Just as the sun had risen upon us, and our hopes began to rise; and just as we were about to eat the morsel of bread left us by our friends who had been marched off the day before, that we might be ready at a moments warning to leave, should the British send sleighs for us, we heard a noise in the passage, and before we had time to think, the door of our room was forced open by an Indian, who entered with tomahawk in hand, ready to commence his bloody work. He was quickly followed by others. Their first object was plunder. They had no sooner entered the door of our room, than they began, in the most cruel manner, to strip the blankets and clothes off the wounded as they lay upon the floor. Fortunately for me, I was at the opposite side of the room from the door at which the Indians entered, near a door leading into the front room of the house; and finding there was no time to lose, I immediately passed out into the front room, where I met one of the most savage looking

Indians I ever beheld. His very appearance was enough to terrify the stoutest heart. His face painted as black as charcoal could make it, plainly indicative of his deadly design; a bunch of long feathers fastened on his head, almost as large as a half bushel; a large tomahawk, the instrument of death, in his right hand; a scalping knife fastened to his belt. He instantly seized me by the collar, and led me out at the front door. At first I manifested some unwillingness to go with him. He then spoke very earnestly in his own language, and at the same time pulled me along forcibly, as if to remove me from the scene of death within. He led me through the front gate, and down the river about one hundred yards to the other houses, in which were Captains Hart, Hickman, and others. After leading me through the front gate, he left me. Just at this time, Captain Hart came out of his room, barefooted, with nothing on but shirt and drawers. In this condition he stood in the snow for some length of time pleading for his life. I here met with the chief who had been in our room in the evening. Captain Hart understanding the designs of Proctor and Elliott, and knowing that the only possible chance for life, under the circumstances, was to make some arrangement with the Indians. For this purpose he sought an interview with this one, as he seemed to be a leader, and very intelligent. They met in the front yard, near the gate, about the time I came in.

I stood by and heard the conversation. Captain Hart's first remark, if I mistake not, was, that he was an acquaintance of Colonel Elliott's, and that he (Elliott) had promised to send his own sleigh for him. The Indian replied, "Elliott has deceived you—he does not intend to fulfill his promise." Well, said Capt. Hart, "if you will agree to take me, I will give you a horse, or a hundred dollars. You shall have it on our arrival at Malden," The Indian said, "I cannot take you." "Why?" asked Captain Hart. "You are too badly wounded," said the Indian. Captain Hart then asked the Indian, what they intended to do with them? "Boys," said the Indian, raising himself up into an attitude and air of consequence and insult, "you are all to be killed." Though involved in the same calamity myself, I could but notice the calmness and composure with which the brave officer received the sentence of death. The only reply which I heard him make was in the language of prayer to Almighty God to sustain him in this hour of trial. Feeling that the awful sentence included myself as well as all the rest, my heart seemed to sink within me, expecting every moment to receive the fatal blow. Just at this moment an Indian dragged Captain Hickman out of the house by one arm, and threw him down near where I stood, with his face on the snow. He was tomahawked, but not yet dead. He lay strangling in his blood. From this scene I turned away, and walking around the end of the house, towards the back yard, met an Indian at the corner of the house, who took hold of me and searched my pockets for money, but finding none, passed on. I then passed on round the house, leaving the main building on my right, and walking slowly that I might not appear to have any design, and that I might not attract the attention of the enemy. I thought, possibly, I might reach a small log building which I discovered not far from the house. As there was but one small entrance into it, as it appeared dark within, it seemed to present the only possible refuge; and as there was no time to lose, and as life and death were depending, I determined to make the attempt to gain this place of retreat. But as I was within a few paces of my hiding place, an Indian coming from the opposite direction met me, and taking hold of me, asked me where I was wounded: I placed my hand upon my shoulder. He then felt of it, and finding that the wound was not bad, he took me back to the house where he had deposited his plunder; put a blanket around me, gave me a hat, then took me to the back door of the house in which the wounded lay, and gave me his gun and plunder in charge. In a moment every thing seemed to wear a different aspect. I now experienced one of those sudden transitions of mind impossible to be either conceived or expressed, except by those unhappy lot it has been, to be placed in like circumstances. Until now, despair had spread its gloomy mantle over me; but hope, that cheering companion, again visited my sinking heart and I again saw a faint prospect that my life might be spared. Thus situated, I had time to see what was passing around me. I had command of the way leading to Malden; and I saw but one road. I remained in this position about two hours, during which time I saw several pass—I suppose all who were able. Here I saw a striking example of the estimate a man places on life. I saw some of our own company—old acquaintances who were so badly wounded that they could scarcely be moved in their beds, understanding that those who could not travel on foot to Malden were all to be tomahawked, pass on their way to Malden, hobbling along on sticks. Poor fellows, they were soon overtaken by their merciless enemies and inhumanly butchered. A few moments after being placed here by the Indian who claimed me, another Indian set fire to the house. The fire was built in the passage near the back door where I stood. After the fire had taken considerable hold of the house, an Indian came running down stairs with a keg of powder in his hand, with the head out. Just as he got to the foot of the stairs his foot slipped, and he come very near falling into the fire with the powder. Had the powder caught, both he and I would have perished.

The general opinion, I believe is, in reference to Captain Hart, that an Indian engaged to take him to Malden; and that another Indian, unwilling that he should go, shot him on the road. This may be true, but has always appeared to me improbable. From the position I occupied, having command of the way to Malden, I believe I saw all who passed in that direction, but saw nothing of Captain Hart. Upon the whole, I am induced to think that Captain Hart met his fate in the front yard where I left him.

I remained here until the roof of the house set on fire had fallen in. I heard no cry within, from which I infered that the wounded were killed before the house was burnt.

My Indian finally returned, bringing with him one of the United States' pack horses: and placing his bundle of plunder on him, gave me the bridle, making signs to march on towards

Malden. I soon found the bodies of those poor hapless boys who had made the attempt, but were too badly wounded to travel, massacred, scalped, and stripped. When we reached the woods, we halted a short time by the fire. We then went on to Stony creek, where the British had encamped the night before the battle. Their wounded were still there, waiting to be conveyed to Malden.

Here the Indians made a large fire of rails, and gave the prisoners some bread. Our number was eight or ten. As we were eating, one of the Indians deliberately walked up to his prisoner, a fine looking young man, a son of Dr. Blythe of Lexington, and struck the tomahawk into his head. I was looking the young man in the face when he received the deadly blow; he closed his eyes, and sunk under the first stroke of the deadly weapon. After he had fallen, and received two or three strokes from the hand of the Indian, an old Frenchman took the weapon out of the hand of the savage and gave the dying man another stroke upon the head, which stilled him in death. This greatly alarmed us. There appeared to be nothing in his case, that we could see, that made it necessary for him to die and not the rest of us. We now expected every moment to share the same barbarity. One of our company, a young man by the name of Jones, was so terrified that he began to weep, and moved to the opposite side of the fire, thinking that those nearest the danger would be the first victims. We urged him to be still, and not to uncover such marks of fear, or that he would certainly be killed. The Indian who had taken me, and claimed me as his, was at this time a few steps from us, adjusting his pack; I stepped up to him, and asked him if they were going to kill us all. He answered "yes." I went back to the fire and tried to eat, as well as I could, without an appetite. It was now about two o'clock, P.M., and having eaten but little for three days past, and that day had taken nothing until we arrived at Stony creek; but this awful cold-blooded butchery took away all desire for food. I soon saw that he did not understand my question, and I was then somewhat relieved. It had been said, and perhaps with due regard to truth, that many of the Indians engaged in this dreadful havoc, were under the influence of rum. They were supplied with it by the British, and when under its influence were more savage than savages.

40. Shaping a Federal Indian Policy

Shaping an official United States Indian policy was an act that required long and patient consideration. There was also, mixed in with patience, a tremendous amount of expediency and willingness to move the problem on deeper into the West. Every president of the United States had to deal with the Indians, but President James Monroe was the first to enunciate the new policy of Indian removal.

First Annual Message to Congress

From several of the Indian tribes inhabiting the country bordering on Lake Erie purchases have been made of lands on conditions very favorable to the United States, and, as it is presumed, not less so to the tribes themselves.

By these purchases the Indian title, with moderate reservations, has been extinguished to the whole of the land within the limits of the State of Ohio, and to a part of that in the Michigan Territory and the State of Indiana. From the Cherokee tribe a tract has been purchased in the State of Georgia and an arrangement made by which, in exchange for lands beyond the Mississippi, a great part, if not the whole, of the land belonging to that tribe eastward of that river in the States of North Carolina, Georgia, and Tennessee, and in the Alabama Territory will soon be acquired. By these acquisitions, and others that may reasonably be expected soon to

James Monroe, "First Annual Message," March 4, 1817, J. D. Richardson, ed., *Compilation of the Messages and Papers of the Presidents, 1789–1897*, 10 volumes (Washington: Government Printing Office, 1907), vol. X. pp. 16, 17. "Eighth Annual Message," December 7, 1824, *ibid.*, p. 261.

follow, we shall be enabled to extend out settlements from the inhabited parts of the State of Ohio along Lake Erie into the Michigan Territory, and to connect our settlements by degrees through the State of Indiana and the Illinois Territory to that of Missouri. A similar and equally advantageous effect will soon be produced to the south, through the whole extent of the States and territory which border on the waters emptying into the Mississippi and the Mobile. In this progress, which the rights of nature demand and nothing can prevent, marking a growth rapid and gigantic, it is our duty to make new efforts for the preservation, improvement, and civilization of the native inhabitants. The hunter state can exist only in the vast uncultivated desert. It yields to the more dense and compact form and greater force of civilized population; and of right it ought to yield, for the earth was given to mankind to support the greatest number of which it is capable, and no tribe or people have a right to withhold from the wants of others more than is necessary for their own support and comfort. It is gratifying to know that the reservations of land made by the treaties with the tribes on Lake Erie were made with a view to individual ownership among them and to the cultivation of the soil by all, and that an annual stipend has been pledged to supply their other wants. It will merit the consideration of Congress whether other provision not stipulated by treaty ought to be made for these tribes and for the advancement of the liberal and humane policy of the United States toward all the tribes within our limits, and more particularly for their improvement in the arts of civilized life.

Among the advantages incident to these purchases, and to those which have preceded, the security which may thereby be afforded to our inland frontiers is peculiarly important. With a strong barrier, consisting of our own people, thus planted on the Lakes, the Mississippi, and the Mobile, with the protection to be derived from the regular force, Indian hostilities, if they do not altogether cease, will henceforth lose their terror. Fortifications in those quarters to any extent will not be necessary, and the expense attending them may be saved.

A people accustomed to the use of firearms only, as the Indian tribes are, will shun even a moderate works which are defended by cannon. Great fortifications will therefore be requisite only in future along the coast and at some points in the interior connected with it. On these will the safety of our towns and the commerce of our great rivers, from the Bay of Fundy to the Mississippi, depend. On these, therefore, should the utmost attention, skill, and labor be bestowed.

A considerable and rapid augmentation in the value of all the public lands, proceeding from these and other obvious causes, may henceforward be expected. The difficulties attending early emigrations will be dissipated even in the most remote parts. Several new States have been admitted into our Union to the west and south, and Territorial governments, happily organized, established over every other portion in which there is vacant land for sale. In terminating Indian hostilities, as must soon be done, in a formidable shape at least, the emigration, which has heretofore been great, will probably increase, and the demand for land and the augmentation in its value be in like proportion. The great increase of our population throughout the Union will alone produce an important effect, and in no quarter will it be so sensibly felt as in those in contemplation. The public lands are a public stock, which ought to be disposed of to the best advantage for the nation. The nation should therefore derive the profit proceeding from the continual rise in their value. Every encouragement should be given to the emigrants consistent with a fair competition between them, but that competition should operate in the first sale to the advantage of the nation rather than of individuals. Great capitalists will derive all the benefit incident to their superior wealth under any mode of sale which may be adopted. But if, looking forward to the rise in the value of the public lands, they should have the opportunity of amassing at a low price vast bodies in their hands, the profit will accrue to them and not to the public. They would also have the power in that degree to control the emigration and settlement in such a manner as their opinion of their respective interests might dictate. I submit this subject to the consideration of Congress, that such further provision may be made in the sale of the public lands, with a view to the public interest, should any be deemed expedient, as in their judgment may be best adapted to the object.

Eighth Annual Message to Congress

The condition of the aborigines within our limits, and especially those who are within the limits of the States, merits likewise particular attention. Experience has shown that unless the tribes be civilized they can never be incorporated into our system in any form whatever. It has likewise shown that in the regular augmentation of our population with the extension of our settlements their situation will become deplorable, if their extinction is not menaced. Some well-digested plan which will rescue them from such calamities is due to their rights, to the rights of humanity, and to the honor of the nation. Their civilization is indispensable to the safety, and this can be accomplished only by degrees. The process must commence with the infant state, through whom some effect may be wrought on the parental. Difficulties of the most serious character present themselves to the attainment of this very desirable result on the territory on which they now reside. To remove them from it by force, even with a view to their own security and happiness, would be revolting to humanity and utterly unjustifiable. Between the limits of our present States and Territories and the Rocky Mountains and Mexico there is a vast territory to which they might be invited with inducements which might be successful. It is thought if that territory should be divided into districts by previous agreement with the tribes now residing there and civil governments be established in each, with schools for every branch of instruction in literature and the arts of civilized life, that all the tribes now within our limits might gradually be drawn there. The execution of this plan would necessarily be attended with expense, and that not inconsiderable, but it is doubted whether any other can be devised which would be less liable to that objection or more likely to succeed.

41. Indian Removal, an Official Rationale

In his second annual message to Congress in 1833, Andrew Jackson came to grips at last with the long impending problem of Indian relations. In this message he set in motion the official actions which resulted in the removal of the Choctaws, Chickasaws, Cherokees, Greeks, and Seminole Indians from North Carolina, Tennessee, Georgia, Florida, Alabama, and Mississippi to territory set aside for their exclusive use west of the Mississippi. In his message Jackson not only called upon Congress to take immediate action to see that this removal was carried out, but he also expressed one of the basic concepts that large numbers of Americans had about both the West and the Indian.

It gives me pleasure to announce to Congress that the benevolent policy of the Government, steadily pursued for nearly thirty years, in relation to the removal of the Indians beyond the white settlements is approaching to a happy consummation. Two important tribes have accepted the provision made for their removal at the last session of Congress, and it is believed that their example will induce the remaining tribes also to seek the same obvious advantages.

The consequences of a speedy removal will be important to the United States, to individual States, and to the Indians themselves. The pecuniary advantages which it promises to the Government are the least of its recommendations. It puts an end to all possible danger of collision between the authorities of the General and State Governments on account of the Indians. It will place a dense and civilized population in large

Andrew Jackson, "Messages to Congress, Dec. 6, 1833," James D. Richardson, ed., *Messages and Papers* (Washington: Bureau of National Literature and Arts, X vols., 1908), vol. II, pp. 519–523.

tracts of country now occupied by a few savage hunters. By opening the whole territory between Tennessee on the north and Louisiana on the south to the settlement of the whites it will incalculably strengthen the southwestern frontier and render the adjacent States strong enough to repel future invasions without remote aid. It will relieve the whole State of Mississippi and the western part of Alabama of Indian occupancy, and enable those States to advance rapidly in population, wealth, and power. It will separate the Indians from immediate contact with settlements of whites; free them from the power of the States; enable them to pursue happiness in their own way and under their own rude institutions; will retard the progress of decay, which is lessening their numbers, and perhaps cause them gradually, under the protection of the Government and through the influence of good counsels, to cast off their savage habits and become an interesting, civilized, and Christian community. These consequences, some of them so certain and the rest so probable, make the complete execution of the plan sanctioned by Congress at their last session an object of much solicitude.

Toward the aborigines of the country no one can indulge a more friendly feeling than myself, or would go further in attempting to reclaim them from their wandering habits and make them a happy, prosperous people. I have endeavored to impress upon them my own solemn convictions of the duties and powers of the General Government in relation to the State authorities. For the justice of the laws passed by the States within the scope of their reserved powers they are not responsible to this Government. As individuals we may entertain and express our opinions of their acts, but as a Government we have as little right to control them as we have to prescribe laws for other nations.

With a full understanding of the subject, the Choctaw and the Chickasaw tribes have with great unanimity determined to avail themselves of the liberal offers presented by the act of Congress, and have agreed to remove beyond the Mississippi River. Treaties have been made with them, which in due season will be submitted for consideration. In negotiating these treaties they were made to understand their true condition, and they have preferred maintaining their independence in the Western forests to submitting to the laws of the States in which they now reside. These treaties, being probably the last which will ever be made with them, are characterized by great liberality on the part of the Government. They give the Indians a liberal sum in consideration of their removal, and comfortable subsistence on their new homes. If it be their interest to maintain a separate existence, they will there be at liberty to do so without the inconveniences and vexations to which they would unavoidably have been subject in Alabama and Mississippi.

Humanity has often wept over the fate of the aborigines of this country, and Philanthropy has been long busily employed in devising means to avert it, but its progress has never for a moment been arrested, and one by one have many powerful tribes disappeared from the earth. To follow to the tomb the last of his race and to tread on the graves of extinct nations excite melancholy reflections. But true philanthropy reconciles the mind to these vicissitudes as it does to the extinction of one generation to make room for another. In the monuments and fortresses of an unknown people, spread over the extensive regions of the West, we behold the memorials of a once powerful race, which was exterminated or has disappeared to make room for the existing savage tribes. Nor is there anything in this which, upon a comprehensive view of the general interests of the human race, is to be regretted. Philanthropy could not wish to see this continent restored to the condition in which it was found by our forefathers. What good man would prefer a country covered with forests and ranged by a few thousand savages to our extensive Republic, studded with cities, towns, and prosperous farms, embellished with all the improvements which art can devise or industry execute, occupied by more than 12,000,000 happy people, and filled with all the blessings of liberty, civilization and religion?

The present policy of the Government is but a continuation of the same progressive change by a milder process. The tribes which occupied the countries now constituting the Eastern States were annihilated or have melted away to make room for the whites. The waves of population and civilization are rolling to the westward, and we now propose to acquire the countries occupied by the red men of the South and West by a fair exchange, and, at the expense of the United States, to send them to a land where their existence may be prolonged and perhaps made perpetual. Doubtless it will be painful to leave the graves of their fathers; but what do they more than our ancestors did or than our children are now doing? To better their condition in an unknown land our forefathers left all that was dear in earthly objects. Our children by thousands yearly leave the land of their birth to seek new homes in distant regions. Does Humanity weep at these painful separations from everything, animate and inanimate, with which the young heart has become entwined? Far from it. It is rather a source of joy that our country affords scope where our young population may range unconstrained in body or in mind, developing the power and faculties of man in their highest perfection. These remove hundreds and almost thousands of miles at their own expense, purchase the lands they occupy, and support themselves at their new homes from the moment of their arrival. Can it be cruel in this Government when, by events which it can not control, the Indian is made discontented in his ancient home to purchase his lands, to give him a new and extensive territory, to pay the expense of his removal, and support him a year in his new abode? How many thousands of our own people would gladly embrace the opportunity of removing to the West on such conditions! If the offers made to the Indians were extended to them, they would be hailed with gratitude and joy.

And is it supposed that the wandering savage has a stronger attachment to his home than the settled, civilized Christian? Is it more afflicting to him to leave the graves of his fathers than it is to our brothers and children? Rightly considered, the policy of the General Government toward the red man is not only liberal, but generous. He is unwilling to submit to the laws of the States and mingle with their population. To save him from this alternative, or perhaps utter annihilation, the General Government kindly offers him a new home, and proposes to pay the whole expense of his removal and settlement.

In the consummation of a policy originating at an early period, and steadily pursued by every Administration within the present century—so just to the States and so generous to the Indians—the Executive feels it has a right to expect the cooperation of Congress and of all good and disinterested men. The States, moreover, have a right to demand it. It was substantially a part of the compact which made them members of our Confederacy. With Georgia there is an express contract; with the new States an implied one of equal obligation. Why, in authorizing Ohio, Indiana, Illinois, Missouri, Mississippi, and Alabama to form constitutions and become separate States, did Congress include within their limits extensive tracts of Indian lands, and, in some instances, powerful Indian tribes? Was it not understood by both parties that the power of the States was to be coextensive with their limits, and that with all convenient dispatch the General Government should extinguish the Indian title and remove every obstruction to the complete jurisdiction of the State governments over the soil? Probably not one of those States would have accepted a separate existence—certainly it would never have been granted by Congress—had it been understood that they were to be confined forever to those small portions of their nominal territory the Indian title to which had at the time been extinguished.

It is, therefore, a duty which this Government owes to the new States to extinguish as soon as possible the Indian title to all lands which Congress themselves have included within their limits. When this is done the duties of the General Government in relation to the States and the Indians within their limits are at an end. The Indians may leave the State or not, as they choose. The purchase of their lands does not alter in the least their personal relations with the State government. No act of the General Government has ever been deemed necessary to give the States jurisdiction over the persons of the Indians. That they possess by virtue of their sovereign power within their own limits in as full a manner before as after the purchase of the Indian lands; nor can this Government add to or diminish it.

May we not hope, therefore, that all good citizens, and none more zealously than those who think the Indians oppressed by subjection to the laws of the States, will unite in attempting to open the eyes of those children of the forest to their true condition, and by a speedy removal to relieve them from all the evils, real or imaginary, present or prospective, with which they may be supposed to be threatened.

42.   Departing the Home Land

The shrewd French observer Alexis de Tocqueville has left one of the most graphic descriptions of the Indian removal. Standing on the banks of the Mississippi at Memphis he saw Indians of the Choctaw tribe cross in raw weather to the west bank to begin life anew in a strange land. Even the Choctaws' dogs appeared as tragic figures in their loyal pursuit of their masters. Tocqueville sensed the fact that removal after all was not the answer to the Indian-white conflict in the rivalry for land. Within a short time white hordes would overtake the Indians in Oklahoma and again snatch their lands away from them with baubles, too little money, and faithless promises.

Bold adventurers soon penetrate into the country the Indians have deserted, and when they have advanced about fifteen or twenty leagues from the extreme frontiers of the Whites, they began to build habitations for civilized beings in the

Alexis de Tocqueville, *Democracy in America* (New York: George Dearborn, 1838), 320–322.

midst of the wilderness. This is done without difficulty, as the territory of a hunting-nation is ill defined; it is the common property of the tribe, and belongs to no one in particular, so that individual interests are not concerned in the protection of any part of it.

A few European families settled in different situations at a considerable distance from each other, soon drive away the wild animals which remain between their places of abode. The Indians, who had previously lived in a sort of abundance, then find it difficult to subsist, and still more difficult to procure the articles of barter which they stand in need of.

To drive away their game is to deprive them of the means of existence, as effectually as if the fields of our agriculturists were stricken with barrenness; and they are reduced, like famished wolves, to prowl through the forsaken woods in quest of prey. Their instinctive love of their country attaches them to the soil which gave them birth, even after it has ceased to yield anything but misery and death. At length they are compelled to acquiesce, and to depart: they follow the traces of the elk, the buffalo, and the beaver, and are guided by these wild animals in the choice of their future country. Properly speaking, therefore, it is not the Europeans who drive away the native inhabitants of America; it is famine which compels them to recede; a happy distinction which had escaped the casuists of former times, and for which we are indebted to modern discovery!

It is impossible to conceive the extent of the sufferings which attend these forced emigrations. They are undertaken by a people already exhausted and reduced; and the countries to which the new comers betake themselves are inhabited by other tribes which receive them with jealous hostility. Hunger is in the rear, war awaits them, and misery besets them on all sides. In the hope of escaping from such a host of enemies, they separate, and each individual endeavors to procure the means of supporting his existence in solitude and secrecy, living in the immensity of the desert like an outcast in civilized society. The social tie, which distress had long since weakened, is then dissolved: they have lost their country, and their people soon deserts them; their very families are obliterated; the names they bore in common are forgotten, their language perishes, and all traces of their origin disappear. Their nation has ceased to exist, except in the recollection of the antiquaries of America and a few of the learned of Europe.

I should be sorry to have my reader suppose that I am coloring the picture too highly: I saw with my own eyes several of the cases of misery which I have been describing; and I was the witness of sufferings which I have not the power to portray.

At the end of the year 1831, whilst I was on the left bank of the Mississippi at a place named by Europeans Memphis, there arrived a numerous band of Choctaws (or Chactas, as they are called by the French in Louisiana.) These savages had left their country, and were endeavoring to gain the right bank of the Mississippi, where they hoped to find an asylum which had been promised them by the American Government. It was then the middle of winter, and the cold was unusually severe; the snow had frozen hard upon the ground, and the river was drifting huge masses of ice. The Indians had their families with them; and they brought in their train the wounded and the sick, with children newly born, and old men upon the verge of death. They possessed neither tents nor wagons, but only their arms and some provisions. I saw them embark to pass the mighty river, and never will that solemn spectacle fade from my remembrance. No cry, no sob was heard amongst the assembled crowd: all were silent. Their calamities were of ancient date, and they knew them to be irremediable. The Indians had all stepped into the bark which was to carry them across, but their dogs remained upon the bank. As soon as these animals perceived that their masters were finally leaving the shore, they set up a dismal howl, and, plunging all together into the icy waters of the Mississippi, they swam after the boat.

The ejectment of the Indians very often takes place at the present day, in a regular, and, as it were, a legal manner.

When the European population begins to approach the limit of the desert inhabited by a savage tribe, the Government of the United States usually dispatches envoys to them who assemble the Indians in a large plain, and having first eaten and drunk with them, accost them in the following manner: "What have you to do in the land of your fathers? Before long you must dig up their bones in order to live. In what respect is the country you inhabit better than another? Are there no woods, marshes, or prairies, except where you dwell? And can you live nowhere but under your own sun? Beyond those mountains which you see at the horizon, beyond the lake which bounds your territory on the West, there lie vast countries where beasts of chase are found in great abundance; sell your lands to us, and go to live happily in those solitudes." After holding this language, they spread before the eyes of the Indians fire-arms, woollen garments, kegs of brandy, glass necklaces, bracelets of tinsel, ear-rings, and looking-glasses. If when they have beheld all these riches, they still hesitate, it is insinuated that they have not the means of refusing their required consent, and that the Government itself will not long have the power of protecting them in their rights. What are they to do? Half convinced, and half compelled, they go to inhabit new deserts, where the importunate Whites will not let them remain ten years in tranquility. In this manner do the Americans obtain at a very low price whole provinces, which the richest sovereigns of Europe could not purchase.

43. The Stain of the Sand Creek Massacre

Atrocities were not always committed by the red man. On November 29, 1864, a militia colonel and former Methodist minister named John Milton Chivington, leading Colorado volunteers, fell

Helen Hunt Jackson, *A Century of Dishonor* (Boston: Roberts Brothers, 1885), 343–350.

upon the encampment of some five hundred Cheyennes under Chief Black Kettle who thought he was under the protection of Fort Lyon. Obeying the governor's order to report to the fort to declare himself friendly, Black Kettle was said to be flying both an American and a white flag. However, Chivington and his men swept over the Sand Creek village in an orgy of slaughter. And the "Chivington massacre" has been a matter of controversy with writers on western America ever since. Helen Hunt Jackson vented her wrath in the *New York Tribune* in 1879; her letter drew a reply from William N. Byars of the *Rocky Mountain News*. Both letters became part of her book, *A Century of Dishonor*.

In June, 1864, Governor Evans, of Colorado, sent out a circular to the Indians of the Plains, inviting all friendly Indians to come into the neighborhood of the forts, and be protected by the United States Troops. Hostilities and depredations had been committed by some bands of Indians, and the Government was about to make war upon them. This circular says:

> In some instances they (the Indians) have attacked and killed soldiers, and murdered peaceable citizens. For this the Great Father is angry, and will certainly hunt them out and punish them; but he does not want to injure those who remain friendly to the whites. He desires to protect and take care of them. For this purpose I direct that all friendly Indians keep away from those who are at war, and go to places of safety. Friendly Arapahoes and Cheyennes belonging to the Arkansas River will go to Major Colby, United States Agent at Fort Lyon, who will give them provisions and show them a place of safety.

In consequence of this proclamation of the governor, a band of Cheyennes, several hundred in number, came in and settled down near Fort Lyon. After a time they were requested to move to Sand Creek, about forty miles from Fort Lyon, where they were still guaranteed "perfect safety" and the protection of the Government. Rations of food were issued to them from time to time. On the 27th of November, Colonel J. M. Chivington, a member of the Methodist Episcopal Church in Denver, and Colonel of the First Colorado Cavalry, led his regiment by forced march to Fort Lyon, induced some of the United States troops to join him, and fell upon this camp of friendly Indians at daybreak. The chief, White Antelope, always known as friendly to the whites, came running toward the soldiers holding up his hands and crying, "Stop! Stop!" in English. When he saw that there was no mistake, that it was a deliberate attack, he folded his arms and waited till he was shot down. The United States flag was floating over the lodge of Black Kettle, the head chief of the tribe; below it was tied also a small white flag as additional security– a precaution Black Kettle had been advised by United States officers to take if he met troops on the Plains. In Major Wynkoop's testimony, given before the committee appointed by Congress to investigate this massacre, is the following passage:

> Women and children were killed and scalped, children shot at and children were killed and scalped, children shot at their mothers' breasts, and all the bodies mutilated in the most horrible manner. . . . The dead bodies of females profaned in such a manner that the recital is sickening, Colonel J. M. Chivington all the time inciting his troops to their diabolical outrages.

Another man testified as to what he saw on the 30th of November, three days after the battle, as follows:

> I saw a man dismount from his horse and cut the ear from the body of an Indian, and the scalp from the head of another. I saw a number of children killed; they had bullet-holes in them; one child had been cut with some sharp instrument across its side. I saw another that both ears had been cut off. . . . I saw several of the Third Regiment cut off fingers to get rings off them. I saw Major Sayre scalp a dead Indian. The scalp had a long tail of silver hanging to it.

Robert Bent testified:

> I saw one squaw lying on the bank, whose leg had been broken. A soldier came up to her with a drawn saber. She raised her arm to protect herself; he struck, breaking her arm. She rolled over, and raised her other arm; he struck, breaking that, and

then left her without killing her. I saw one squaw cut open, with an unborn child lying by her side.

Major Anthony testified:

There was one little child, probably three years old, just big enough to walk through the sand. The Indians had gone ahead, and this little child was behind, following after them. The little fellow was perfectly naked, travelling in the sand. I saw one man get off his horse at a distance of about seventy-five yards and draw up his rifle and fire. He missed the child. Another man came up and said, "Let me try the son of a b——. I can hit him." He got down off his horse, kneeled down, and fired at the little child, but he missed him. A third man came up, and made a similar remark, and fired, and the little fellow dropped.

The Indians were not able to make much resistance, as only a part of them were armed, the United States officers having required them to give up their guns. Luckily they had kept a few.

When this Colorado regiment of demons returned to Denver they were greeted with an ovation. *The Denver News* said: "All acquitted themselves well. Colorado soldiers have again covered themselves with glory;" and at a theatrical performance given in the city, the scalps taken from Indians were held up and exhibited to the audience, which applauded rapturously.

After listening, day after day, to such testimonies as these I have quoted, and others so much worse that I may not write and *The Tribune* could not print the words needful to tell them, the committee reported: "It is difficult to believe that beings in the form of men, and disgracing the uniform of the United States soldiers and officers, could commit or countenance the commission of such acts of cruelty and barbarity;" and of Colonel Chivington: "He deliberately planned and executed a foul and dastardly massacre, which would have disgraced the veriest savage among those who were victims of his cruelty."

This was just fifteen years ago, no more. Shall we apply the same rule of judgment to the white men of Colorado that the Government is now applying to the Utes? There are 130,000 inhabitants of Colorado; hundreds of them had a hand in this massacre, and thousands in cool blood applauded it when it was done. There are 4000 Utes in Colorado. Twelve of them, desperate, guilty men, have committed murder and rape, and three or four hundred of them did, in the convenient phrase of our diplomcy, "go to war against the Government." I.E., they attempted, by force of arms, to restrain the entrance upon their own lands– lands bought, owned and paid for– of soldiers that the Government had sent them, to be ready to make war upon them, in case the agent thought it best to do so! This is the plain English of it. This is the plain, naked truth of it.

And now the Secretary of the Interior has stopped the issue of rations to 1000 of these helpless creatures; rations, be it understood, which are not, and never were, a charity, but are the Utes rightful dues, on account of lands by them sold; dues which the Government promised to pay "annually forever." Will the American people justify this? There is such a thing as the conscience of a nation– as a nation's sense of justice. Can it not be roused to speak now? Shall we sit still, warm and well fed, in our homes, while five hundred women and little children are being slowly starved in the bleak, barren wilderness of Colorado? Starved, not because storm or blight, or drouth has visited their country and cut off their crops; not because pestilence has laid its hand on them and slain the hunters who brought the meat, but because it lies within the promise of one man, by one word, to deprive them of one-half of their necessary food for as long a term of years as he may please; and "the Secretary of the Interior cannot consistently feed a tribe that has gone to war against the Government."

We read in the statutes of the United States that certain things may be done by "executive order" of the President. Is it not time for the President to interfere when hundreds

of women and children are being starved in his Republic by
the order of one man? Colonel J. M. Chivington's method
was less human by far. To be shot dead is a mercy, and a
grace for which we will all sue, if to be starved to death were
our only other alternative.

New York, January 31st, 1880.   H. H.

LETTER II

To the Editor of the Tribune:

Sir,– In your edition of yesterday appears an article, under
the above caption, which arraigns the people of Colorado as
a community of barbarous murderers, and finally elevates
them above the present Secretary of the Interior, thereby
placing the latter gentlemen in a most unenviable light if
the charges averred be true. "The Sand Creek Massacre" of
1864 is made the text and burden of the article; its application is to the present condition of the White River band of
Utes in Colorado. Quotations are given from the testimony
gathered, and the report made thereon by a committee of
Congress charged with a so-called investigation of the Sand
Creek affair. That investigation was made for a certain selfish
purpose. It was to break down and ruin certain men. Evidence was taken upon one side only. It was largely false,
and infamously partial. There was no answer for the defence.

The Cheyenne and Arapahoe Indians assembled at Sand
Creek were not under the protection of a United States fort.
A few of them had been encamped about Fort Lyon and
drawing supplies therefrom, but they gradually disappeared
and joined the main camp on Dry Sandy, forty miles from
the fort, separated from it by a waterless desert, and entirely
beyond the limit of its control or observation. While some
of the occupants were still, no doubt, occasional visitors at
the fort, and applicants for supplies and ammunition, most of
the warriors were engaged in raiding the great Platte River
Road, seventy-five miles farther north, robbing and burning
trains, stealing cattle and horses, robbing and destroying the

the United States mails, and killing white people. During the summer and fall they had murdered over fifty of the citizens of Colorado. They had stolen and destroyed provisions and merchandise, and driven away stock worth hundreds of thousands of dollars. They had interupted the mails, and for thirty-two consecutive days none were allowed to pass their lines. When satiated with murder and arson, and loaded with plunder, they would retire to their sacred refuge on Sand Creek to rest and refresh themselves, recruit their wasted supplies of ammunition from Fort Lyon– begged under the garb of gentle, peaceful savages– and return to the road to relieve their tired comrades, and riot again in carnage and robbery. These are facts; and when the "robbers' roost" was cleaned out, on that sad but glorious 27th day of November, 1864, they were sufficiently proven. Scalps of white men not yet dried; letters and photographs stolen from the mails; bills of lading and invoices of goods; bales and bolts of goods themselves, addressed to merchants in Denver; half-worn clothing of white women and children, and many other articles of like character, were found in that poetical Indian camp, and recovered by the Colorado soldiers. They were brought to Denver, and those were the scalps exhibited in the theatre of that city. There was also an Indian saddle blanket entirely fringed around the edges with white women's scalps, with the long, fair hair attached. There was an Indian saddle over the pommel of which was stretched skin stripped from the body of a white woman. Is it any wonder that soldiers flushed with victory, after one of the hardest campaigns ever endured by men, should indulge– some of them– in unwarranted atrocities after finding evidence of barbarism, and while more than forty of their comrades were weltering in their own blood upon the field?

If "H. H." had been in Denver in the early part of that summer, when the bloated, festering bodies of the Hungate family– father, mother, and two babes– were drawn through the streets naked in an ox wagon, cut, mutilated, and scalped– the work of those same red fiends who were so justly punished at Sand Creek; if later, "H. H." had seen an upright and most estimable business man go crazy over the news of his son's being tortured to death a hundred miles down the Platte, as I did; if "H. H." had seen one-half the Colorado homes made desolate that fateful season, and a tithe of the tears that were caused to flow, I think there would have been one little word of excuse for the people of Colorado– more than a doubtful comparison with an inefficient and culpable Indian policy. Bear in mind that Colorado had no railroads then. Her supplies reached her by only one road– along the Platte– in wagons drawn by oxen, mules, or horses. That line was in full possession of the enemy. Starvation stared us in the face. Hardly a party went or came without some persons being killed. Sand Creek saved Colorado, and taught the Indians the most salutary lesson they had ever learned. And now, after fifteen years, and here in the shadow of the Nation's Capital, with the spectre of "H. H.'s" condemnation staring me in the face, I am neither afraid nor ashamed to repeat the language then used by *The Denver News*: "All acquitted themselves well. Colorado soldiers have again covered themselves with glory."

Thus much of the history is gone over by "H. H." to present in true dramatic form the deplorable condition of the White River Utes, 1000 in number, who are now suffering the pangs of hunger and the discomfort of cold in the wilds of Western Colorado, without any kind agent to issue rations, provide blankets, or build fires for them. It is really too bad. A painful dispensation of Providence has deprived them of their best friend, and they are desolate and bereaved. He placed his life and its best efforts, his unbounded enthusiams for their good, his great Christian heart– all at their service. But an accident befell him, and he is no more. The coroner's jury that sat upon his remains found that his dead body had a barrel stave driven in to his mouth, a log-chain around his neck, by which it had been dragged about like a dead hog, and sundry bullet-holes through his body. The presumption was that from the effect of some one of these accidents he died; and, alas! he is no longer to serve out weekly rations to his flock of gentle Utes. There is no sorrow over his death or desolation wrought, but there is pity, oceans of pity, for the Indians who are hungry and cold. True, at the time he died they took the flour, the pork, and salt, and coffee, and sugar, and tobacco, and blankets, and all supplies that he would have issued to them through this long winter had he lived. With his care these would have lasted until spring, and been sufficient for their wants; but, without it, "H. H." is suspicious that they are all gone, and yet it is but just past the middle of winter. Can "H. H." tell why this is thus? It is also true that they drove away the large herd of cattle from the increase of which that same unfortunate agent and his predecessors had supplied them with beef for eleven years past, and yet the consumption did not keep pace with the natural increase. They took them all, and are presumed to have them now. True, again, they had at the beginning of winter, or at the period of the melancholy loss of their best friend, about 4000 horses that were rolling fat, and three acres of dogs– not bad food in an emergency, or for an Indian thanksgiving feast– some of which should still remain.

But "H. H." intimates that there is an alleged excuse for withholding rations from these poor, persecuted red angels. "Twelve" of them have been bad, and the tyrant at the head of the Interior Department is systematically starving all of the 1000 who constitute the band, and their 4000 horses, and 1800 cattle, and three acres of dogs, and six months' supplies, because those twelve bad Indians cannot conscientiously pick themselves out and be offered up as a burnt-offering and a sacrifice to appease the wrath of an outraged and partly civilized nation. This is the present indictment, and the Secretary and the President are commanded to stand up and plead "guilty or not guilty, but you know you are guilty, d–n you." Now I challenge and defy "H. H.," or any other person living, to pick out or name twelve White River male Utes, over sixteen years of age, who were *not* guilty, directly or indirectly, as principals or accomplices before the fact, in the

Thornburgh attack or in the Agency massacre. I know these Indians well enough to know that these attacks were perfectly understood and deliberately planned. I cannot be made to believe that a single one of them, of common-sense and intelligence, was ignorant of what was to take place, and that knowledge extended far beyond the White River band. There were plenty of recruits from both the Los Pinos and the Uintah bands. In withholding supplies from the White River Utes the Secretary of the Interior is simply obeying the law. He cannot, except upon his own personal responsibility, issue supplies to a hostile Indian tribe, and the country will hold him accountable for a departure from his line of duty. Inferentially the Indians are justified by "H. H." in their attack upon Thornburgh's command. Their object was to defend "their own lands– lands bought, owned, and paid for." Bought of whom pray? Paid for by whom? To whom was payment made? The soldiers were making no attack; they contemplated none. The agent had no authority to order an attack. He could proclaim war. He could have no control whatever over the troops. But his life was in danger. The honor of his family was at stake. He asked for protection. "H. H." says he had no right to it. His life and the honor of his aged wife and of his virgin daughter are gone, and "H. H." is the champion of the fiends who wrought the ruin.

Washington, D.C., February 6th, 1880.   Wm. N. Byars

44. The Lingering Problems of the Red Man

By 1881 the historian could write that the United States government had largely failed in its many efforts to solve the Indian

Chester A. Arthur, "First Annual Message to Congress, December 6, 1881," Richardson, ed., *Compilation of the Messages* . . . , vol. VIII, pp. 54–57.

problem. The old frontier treaties had failed because they were idealistic in concept, unrealistic in long-range application, and many times insincere. The Indian removal plan of the 1830s had only delayed and aggravated the Indian decision, and President Ulysses S. Grant's attempt to use the churches to bring peace in the West was hopelessly impractical. On the other hand, the use of the army was not an answer to the lingering troubles. Somehow the Congress had to come to grips with this matter in such a way that a stable solution could be found. In 1881 the public was becoming aroused by the questions of inhumanity and unfairness. General Philip Sheridan's philosophy of "killing off the problem" was not in keeping with the rising humanitarianism of the time. President Chester A. Arthur, like many of his predecessors, responded with a statement of the position of the federal government.

Prominent among the matters which challenge the attention of Congress at its present session is the management of our Indian affairs. While this question has been a cause of trouble and embarrassment from the infancy of the Government, it is but recently that any effort has been made for its solution at once serious, determined, consistent, and promising success.

It has been easier to resort to convenient makeshifts for tiding over temporary difficulties ·than to grapple with the great permanent problem, and accordingly the easier course has almost invariably been pursued.

It was natural, at a time when the national territory seemed almost illimitable and contained many millions of acres far outside the bounds of civilized settlements, that a policy should have been initiated which more than aught else has been the fruitful source of our Indian complications.

I refer, of course, to the policy of dealing with the various Indian tribes as separate nationalities, of relegating them by treaty stipulations to the occupancy of immense reservations in the West, and of encouraging them to live a savage life, undisturbed by any earnest and well-directed efforts to bring them under the influences of civilization.

The unsatisfactory results which have sprung from this policy are becoming apparent to all.

As the white settlements have crowded the borders of the reservations, the Indians, sometimes contentedly and sometimes against their will, have been transferred to other hunting grounds, from which they have again been dislodged whenever their newfound homes have been desired by the adventurous settlers.

These removals and the frontier collisions by which they have often been preceded have led to frequent and disastrous conflicts between the races.

It is profitless to discuss here which of them has been chiefly responsible for the disturbances whose recital occupies so large a space upon the pages of history. We have to deal with the appalling fact that though thousands of lives have been sacrificed and hundreds of millions of dollars expended in an attempt to solve the Indian problem, it has until within the past few years seemed scarcely nearer a solution than it was a century ago. But the Government has of late been cautiously but steadily feeling its way to the adoption of a policy which has already produced gratifying results, and which, in my judgment, is likely, if Congress and the Executive accord in its support, to relieve us ere long from the difficulties which have hitherto beset us.

For the success of the efforts now making to introduce among the Indians the customs and pursuits of civilized life and gradually to absorb them into the mass of our citizens, sharing their rights and holden to their responsibilities, there is imperative need for legislative action.

My suggestions in that regard will be chiefly as have been already called to the attention of Congress and have received to some extent its consideration.

First, I recommend the passage of an act making the laws of the various states and territories applicable to the Indian reservations within their borders and extending the laws of the State of Arkansas to the portion of the Indian Territory not occupied by the Five Civilized Tribes.

The Indian should receive the protection of the law. He should be allowed to maintain in court his rights of person and property. He has repeatedly begged for this privilege. Its exercise would be very valuable to him in his progress toward civilization.

Second, Of even greater importance is a measure which has been frequently recommended by my predecessors in office, and in furtherance of which several bills have been from time to time introduced in both Houses of Congress. The enactment of a general law permitting the allotment in severalty, to such Indians, at least, as desire it, of a reasonable quantity of land secured to them by patent, and for their own protection made inalienable for twenty or twenty-five years, is demanded for their present welfare and their permanent advancement.

In return for such considerate action on the part of the Government, there is reason to believe that the Indians in large numbers would be persuaded to sever their tribal relations and to engage at once in agricultural pursuits. Many of them realize the fact that their hunting days are over and that it is now for their best interests to conform their manner of life to the new order of things. By no greater inducement than the assurance of permanent title to the soil can they be led to engage in the occupation of tilling it.

The well-attested reports of their increasing interest in husbandry justify the hope and belief that the enactment of such a statute as I recommend would be at once attended with gratifying results. A resort to the allotment system would have a direct and powerful influence in dissolving the tribal bond, which is so prominent a feature of savage life, and which tends so strongly to perpetuate it.

Third, I advise a liberal appropriation for the support of Indian schools, because of my confident belief that such a course is consistent with the wisest economy.

VI

The Magic of the Rivers

The great river channels cut into all parts of the frontier. The Mississippi and Missouri with their branches reached into the whole upper expanse of the continent. Beyond the headwaters of the Missouri, streams that flowed westward opened still newer paths west. Flatboatmen succeeded those who paddled canoes on the Ohio and Mississippi, and hardier keelboatmen knew what it meant to tug against the currents of the rivers in traveling both directions. Millions of tons of farm produce floated southward to market, and hundreds of thousands of settlers followed along the western streams to new homes.

After 1811, the steamboat appeared on the western waters. By 1820 this vessel had become so significant in frontier river traffic that it brought about the rise of some towns and the decline of others. It speeded up the penetration of much of the Mississippi Valley portion of the continent and brought the entire country into closer communication. A restlessness appeared to infect the people. All along the rivers they were on the move, some traveling to new homes, some in search of adventure, some seeking amusement, and some were scoundrels looking for easy victims. Whatever the purpose of the traveler, the river society, from shanty boater and flatboatman to the most refined traveler, constituted a highly virile segment of frontier society. Economically, the river traffic was a commercial lifeline.

45. The Flatboat

Produce from all the Mississippi Valley was drifted southward to market. In time, four or five types of river craft were in use. The keelboat was pulled, shoved, and dragged up stream by the expenditure of an enormous amount of human energy. Its blood sister, the flatboat, was too cumbersome to be towed upstream, but it was a monstrous carrier of heavy goods. Not only did the flatboat float down the annual harvests from the ever expanding fields of the valley, it also helped to condition a peculiar breed of men to the life of the river and to produce a new folklore of the frontier. A more expansive orator might have viewed the scene described by Timothy Flint and proclaimed that it was a prologue to the opening of a much greater American empire.

The Keel boat is of a long, slender and elegant form, and generally carries from fifteen to thirty tons. Its advantage is its small draft of water, and the lightness of its construction. It is still much used on the Ohio and upper Mississippi in low stages of water, and on all the boatable streams, where steam boats do not yet run. Its propelling power is by oars, sails, setting poles, cordelle, and when the waters are high, and the boat runs on the margin of the bushes, 'bush-whacking,' or pulling up by the bushes. Before the invention of steam boats, these boats were used in the proportion of six to one at the present time.

The ferry flat is a scow-boat, and when used as a boat of descent for families, has a roof, or covering. These are sometimes, in the vernacular phrase, called 'sleds.' The Alleghany or Mackinaw skiff is a covered skiff, carrying from six to ten tons; and is much used on the Alleghany, the Illinois, and the rivers of the upper Mississippi and Missouri. Periogues are sometimes hollowed from one very large tree, or from the trunks of two trees united, and fitted with a plank rim. They carry from one to three tons. There are common skiffs, canoes and 'dug-outs,' for the convenience of crossing the rivers; and a select company of a few travellers often descend in them to New Orleans. Hunters and Indians, and sometimes passengers, make long journeys of ascent of the rivers in them. Besides these, there are anomalous water crafts, that can hardly be reduced to any class, used as boats of passage or descent. We have seen flat boats, worked by a wheel, which was driven by the cattle, that were conveying to the New Orleans market. There are horse boats of various constructions, used for the most part as ferry boats; but sometimes as boats of ascent. Two keel boats are connected by a platform. A circular pen holds the horses, which by different movements propel wheels. We saw United States' troops ascending the Missouri by boats, propelled by tread wheels; and we have, more than once, seen a boat moved rapidly up stream by wheels, after the steam boat construction, propelled by a man, turning a crank.

But the boats of passage and conveyance, that remain after the invention of steam boats, and are still important to those objects, are keel boats and flats. The flat boats are called, in the vernacular phrase, 'Kentucky flats,' or 'broad horns.' They are simply an oblong ark, with a roof of circular slope, to shed rain. They are generally about fifteen feet wide, and from fifty to eighty, and sometimes an hundred feet in length. The timbers of the bottom are massive beams; and they are intended to be of great strength; and to carry a burthen of from two to four hundred barrels. Great numbers of cattle, hogs and horses are conveyed to market in them. We have seen family boats of this description, fitted up for the descent of families to the lower country, with a stove, comfortable apartments, beds, and arrangements for commodious habitancy. We see in them ladies, servants, cattle, horses, sheep, dogs and poultry, all floating on the same bottom; and on the roof the looms, ploughs, spinning wheels and domestic implements of the family.

Nine tenths of the produce of the upper country, even after the invention of steam boats, continues to descend to New Orleans in Kentucky flats. They generally carry three hands; and perhaps a supernumerary fourth hand, a kind of supercargo. This boat, in the form of a parallelogram, lying flat and dead in the water, and with square timbers below its bottom planks, and carrying such a great weight, runs on to a sandbar with a strong headway, and ploughs its timbers into the sand; and it is, of course, a work of extreme labor to get the boat afloat again. Its form and its weight render it difficult to give it a direction with any power of oars. Hence, in the shallow waters, it often gets aground. When it has at length cleared the shallow waters, and gained the heavy current of the Mississippi, the landing such an unwieldy water craft, in such a current, is a matter of no little difficulty and danger.

All the toil, and danger, and exposure, and moving accidents of this long and perilous voyage, are hidden, however, from the inhabitants, who contemplate the boats floating by their dwellings on beautiful spring mornings, when the verdant forest, the mild and delicious temperature of the air, the delightful azures of the sky of this country, the fine bottom on the one hand, and the romantic bluff on the other, the broad and smooth stream rolling calmly down the forest, and floating the boat gently forward, present delightful images and associations to the beholders. At this time there is no visible danger, or call for labor. The boat takes care of itself, and little do the beholders imagine, how different a scene may be presented in half an hour. Meantime one of the hands scrapes a violin, and the others dance. Greetings, or rude defiances, or trials of wit, or proffers of love to the girls on the shore, or saucy messages, are scattered between them and the spectators along the banks. The boat glides on, until it disappears behind the point of wood. At this moment, perhaps, the bugle, with which all the boats are provided, strikes up its note in the distance over the water. These

scenes, and these notes, echoing from the bluffs of the beautiful Ohio, have a charm for the imagination, which, although
we have heard them a thousand times repeated, at all hours
and in all positions, even to us present the image of a tempting and charming youthful existence, that almost inspires a
wish, that we were boatmen. . . .

The bayou at New Madrid has an extensive and fine eddy,
into which boats float, almost without exertion, and land in
a remarkably fine harbor. It may be fairly considered the
central point, or the chief meridian of boats, in the Mississippi valley. This bayou generally brings up the descending
and ascending boats; and this is an excellent point of observation, from which to contemplate their aspect, the character
of boating, and the descriptions and the amount of produce
from the upper country. You can here take an imaginary
voyage to the falls of St. Anthony, or Missouri; to the lead
mines of Rock river, or Chicago or lake Michigan; to Tip-
pecanoe or the Wabash, Oleanne point of the Alleghany,
Brownsville of the Monongahela, the Saline of the Kenahwa,
or the mountains, round whose bases winds the Tennessee;
or, if you choose, you may take the cheap and rapid journey
of thought along the courses of an hundred others; and in
the lapse of a few days' residence in the spring, at this point,
you may see boats, which have arrived here from all these
imagined places. One hundred boats have landed here in a
day.—The boisterous gaiety of the hands, the congratulations
of acquaintances, who have met here from immense distances,
the moving picture of life on board the boats, in the numerous
animals, large and small, which they carry, their different
ladings, the evidence of the increasing agriculture above, and,
more than all, the immense distances, which they have already
traversed, afford a copious fund of meditation. In one place
there are boats loaded with pine plank, from the pine forests
of the southwest of New York. In another quarter are landed
together the boats of 'old Kentucky,' with their whiskey, hemp,
tobacco, bagging and bale rope; with all the other articles of

the produce of their soil. From Tennessee there are the same articles, together with boats loaded with bales of cotton. From Illinois and Missouri, cattle, horses, and the general produce of the western country, together with peltry and lead from Missouri. Some boats are loaded with corn in bulk, and in the ear. Others are loaded with pork in bulk. Others with barrels of apples and potatoes, and great quantities of dried apples and peaches. Others have loads of cider, and what is called 'cider royal,' or cider, that has been strengthened by boiling, or freezing. Other boats are loaded with furniture, tools, domestic and agricultural implements; in short, the numerous products of the ingenuity, speculation, manufacture and agriculture of the whole upper country of the West. They have come from regions, thousands of miles apart. They have floated to a common point of union.—The surfaces of the boats cover some acres. Dunghill fowls are fluttering over the roofs, as invariable appendages. The piercing note of the chanticleer is heard.— The cattle low. The horses trample, as in their stables. The swine utter the cries of fighting with each other. The turkeys gobble. The dogs of an hundred regions become acquainted. The boatmen travel about from boat to boat, make enquiries and acquaintances, agree to 'lash boats,' as it is called, and form alliances to yield mutual assistance to each other on the way to New Orleans. After an hour or two passed in this way, they spring on shore, to 'raise the wind' in the village. If they tarry all night, as is generally the case, it is well for the people of the town, if they do not become riotous in the course of the evening; in which case, strong measures are adopted, and the proceedings on both sides are summary and decisive. With the first dawn all is bustle and motion; and amidst shouts, and trampling of cattle, and barking of dogs, and crowding of the dunghill fowls, the fleet is in a half an hour all under way; and when the sun rises, nothing is seen, but the broad stream rolling on, as before. These boats unite once more at Natchez and New Orleans; and although they live on the same river, it is improbable, that they will ever meet again on the earth.

46. Rivermen, Kentucky Style

The Kentucky flatboatmen oftentimes represented a segment of the Westerner's faith in himself by his raucous boasts that he could outrun, outfight, knock-down-and-drag-out all creation. This boast was not so much a belief that he could actually do these things, as an expression of a sense of expansionism which could be felt at every turn on the frontier. Both the issuance of such brag and the calling of a bluff were parts of western confidence.

We are not content to wait. We are dissatisfied, if, upon the first experiment, we do not exceed all other people; and not only so, but boast in anticipation of success. If defeat ensue, which not unfrequently occurs, mortification follows, our self-love is reproved, and we render ourselves liable to the just criticism and ridicule of the world.

This national foible was, in early days, exhibited at a landing on the Mississippi, frequented by flat boats, in the person of a fearless young Kentuckian, who, so soon as the boat, on which he had floated down the river, was made fast, jumped ashore, and, giving three or four caracoles in the air with the necessary whoops, declared that he had the fastest horse, the truest rifle and the prettiest sister, on the western waters—threatening summary chastisement to any who would maintain the contrary. A crowd soon gathered, and the bravado was listened to, for some time, without any reply—some being intimidated and others not disposed to provoke a row. At length a quiet, slow-moving sort of a body walked up, and, addressing the fiery Kentuckian, asked him if he had his horse with him. The reply was, that he was aboard the boat. The quiet man remarked,

J. D. B. DeBow, "National Vanity," *DeBow's Review of the Southern and Western States* (New Orleans: DeBow's Review, 1850), vol. IX, pp. 140, 141.

that he was willing to try his speed with a sorry pony that he had brought down with him. A small wager was made, the two horses were brought out, the riders mounted and the race run. The flash Kentuckian was shamefully beaten and made the laughing stock of the assembly. After the race, a long-shanked Tennesseean, with buckskin leggings and hunting shirt, stepped up, and, addressing the braggart, said: "Stranger, I haven't seed your rifle, but here is an old flint-lock that I will try agin your'n, at one hundred paces, for a treat to the company." The banter was accepted, the distance measured, and the Kentuckian again defeated, to the renewed merriment of the crowd. The drink was taken, and some disposition shown for ending all dispute; but, at the moment, a well-set, stout young boatman walked up, with one handkerchief round his head and another tightly tied about the loins, with his shirt sleeves rolled up to the shoulder, and told our hero, that he should like to see him *"walk out his sister."* The Kentuckian replied, that she was not aboard, but he was willing to fight on his brag. Rules for fair play were established, a manly stand up made, and the Kentuckian served with a pair of black eyes, and compelled to acknowledge that there was one "gal" in the West as pretty as his sister. Now, this Kentuckian represented Brother Jonathan as he, at this day, stands—enterprising, brave, good natured and strong, but not sufficiently modest and prudent.

47. River Country

In 1806 the flatboat *Non Pareil* left Marietta, Ohio, for New Orleans. The boat was built in Marietta and carried a crew of five men; two of them were Frenchmen and three were Irishmen. An account of one of her voyages was written by the early Ohio Valley historian Samuel P. Hildreth. The section of the river he described

Samuel P. Hildreth, "History of a Voyage from Marietta to New Orleans in 1805," *The American Pioneer*, 2 vols. (Cincinnati: Logan Historical Society, 1842), vol. 1, pp. 132–134.

as a link of the voyage, reached from Cape Giradeau, Missouri, to Baton Rouge, Louisiana. The boat made rather fast time going from Cincinnati to New Orleans in twenty-one days. The country spreading back from this stretch of the river was wild and exotic.

Shortly after leaving Fort Pickering a striking change was noticed in the vegetable productions of the country. The dark brown foliage of the cypress, with its thickly clustering branches, had been seen for the last few days along the swampy borders of the river, but now the "Spanish moss," (*tillandsia usneoides,*) appeared hanging in festoons from its trunk and limbs. This parasitic plant is peculiar to the lower Mississippi and the country bordering the gulf of Mexico; imparting a funereal and melancholy expression to the forests, reminding one of mourning weeds and sepulchral drapery, as the wind sighs and moans through its thread-like texture. It however, has its uses; affording food to the wild deer and cattle, when they can find no better, and a valuable article for stuffing beds and mattresses. The palmetto, (*chemcrops latanier,*) with its evergreen foliage, also reminds the voyager from the upper waters that he is approaching the warmer regions of the South.

In addition to these new tenants of the land, the ill favored and unsightly form of the alligator is seen; lying on a stationary pile of drift wood, or stretched on a sandbar, enjoying his "siesta" in the warm rays of the sun. Barker, who had navigated this river before, was familiar with their appearance, but to Charles and Graham the sight was novel and exciting. They soon made up their minds to pick a quarrel with them the first good opportunity, and requested the captain, who was always at the helm and keeping a look out, to give them notice of the next one he saw asleep. It was not long before one was seen lying on a drift just above the mouth of the Arkansas river. They immediately sprang into the little skiff that was towing along at the stern of the schooner, armed with their pistols, intending to give him a shot or two before he awakened. With great caution they dropped the skiff slowly along to within a few feet of the sleeping monster, and Graham was just raising his pistol for a shot, when, with a sudden flirt, he rolled into the water so near them as nearly to upset their little boat. Their first thought was that he would attack them in the river, being his favorite residence, when Charles, putting all his strength to the oars, pulled directly for the schooner, pleased to escape from the contest with no further harm than a good fright.

In three days after leaving Fort Pickering they reached the "Walnut hills," where was a small village of log huts inhabited chiefly by hunters. It is now the site of Vicksburgh, a large flourishing town and a port from which is shipped a great portion of the cotton grown in the state of Mississippi. Since leaving the mouth of the Ohio they had passed but few flat boats, it being rather late in the season; and besides only a small number descended at this early day, the produce of the country on that river being mostly wanted for the support of the new settlers which were daily pouring in like a flood. Tennessee and Kentucky having been longer settled, had commenced sending considerable quantities of tobacco and flour to New Orleans, even while it was under the Spanish regime. Robert Williamson, a native of Tennessee, informed me that he had sent flour down the Cumberland river as early as the year 1787, which sold at New Orleans for twenty-two dollars a barrel; and again in 1793, when it brought only twelve dollars. There was then a duty on it of two dollars per barrel. A considerable number of barges had began to ascend the Mississippi, with groceries, and every few days they were greeted with the sight of one of these boats toiling upward with oar and line against the powerful current of the "father of rivers." On these occasions the lively songs and rude jokes of the boatmen served to enliven the way, and afford a theme for remark for several hours after. The amount of merchandise sent up the river in barges in 1805 could not have been great, as in 1810 it amounted only to three hundred tons. In 1813, the business had increased to three thousand tons, and more and larger boats were employed; while the price of freight had fallen to ninety dollars a ton to the falls of the Ohio. In the year 1812, the first steam-boat run on the river between New Orleans and

Natchez, performing the upward voyage in *seven* days, and the downward in *two* days. The price of a cabin passage up was twenty-five dollars, and down it was eighteen dollars. In the year 1815, the first steam-boat voyage was accomplished between New Orleans and Pittsburgh, by Captain Shreve, in the *Enterprise*. The trip upward was performed in fifty-four days, twenty of which it was said were spent in stoppages at intermediate ports. Such improvements have since taken place as to shorten the period to about one fourth of that time.

From the "Walnut hills" to Natchez, a distance of one hundred and twenty miles, nothing worthy of notice occurred. The country was more settled than above, and the openings and log cabins of the cotton planters were occasionally seen. The cultivation of this plant, now so important an article in the exports of the country, was begun by the Spaniards as early as the year 1772, in the vicinity of Natchez; but was greatly lessened in value from the difficulty of clearing it from the seeds, which tedious operation was performed by hand until the invention of the "cotton gin" by the ingenious Whitney. Natchez was at this time a town of considerable size, and next in importance to New Orleans. The *Nonpariel* had been twenty-one days in performing the voyage from Cincinnati.

48.   Southward Flowing Commerce

The western flatboat was a wilful, clumsy vehicle of travel, but as certain as rivers flowed southward and the currents kept up, they reached their destination. These crude vessels hauled millions of tons of western produce to market. In fact it was the flatboat that helped open frontier commerce and trade. Without them farmers would have had no market for the products of their freshly cleared fields, and downriver shipowners would have had no cargoes for their seagoing and coastal vessels. There was, however, the whim-

"John Smith," "Western Flatboatmen," Samuel Cumings, *The Western Pilot* (Cincinnati: G. Conclin, 1849), pp. 128–142.

sical side to flatboating on the western waters. A man, Samuel Cumings, called "John Smith," described the effects that boating had on men. Manning the oars and undergoing difficulties caused by low currents, whirlpools, treacherous snags, and river pirates kept a man on edge. Time hung heavy on the hands of crews as they drifted with the current, so it was only natural that they would get into meanness of one sort or another. Collectively these western boatmen formed one of the most rugged social groups in American history.

It was a beautiful Sabbath morning in the latter part of June that John Skalian let go the rope from the stake at the Cincinnati Landing, whilst the rest of the crew were hauling in planks, ropes, &c., and in a few minutes our noble broadhorn was headed for the middle of the stream. "Give her scissors," said our Captain, as his hoarse boatswain-voice lit down on us from the *quarter*—no—the steering-oar—and away glided our noble bark, with all the majesty of a mule. Then "Kentuck" struck up his favorite,

> Farewell to Ohio, Kentucky,

Also, likewise,

> To the gal that's neither constant nor true,
> Whilst now in a broadhorn to New Orleans I'll steer,
> Where many pretty girls on the banks shall appear.

And it was farewell, for the meanders of the river soon hid the smoke and the city from our view. "Ease oars, and let her float," said the Captain. That was always wholesome news. A cup of blue-ruin was passed around, as we drank to the friends we left behind, and the better acquaintance of ourselves on board. We were all strangers to each other, and we sat down to chat. Before the Captain called us to the oars again, we knew each other, where we were from, where we were going, what for, and all about it. Our Broadhorn was of the largest size, and well-built. She did honor to her Captain, and her Captain did honor to her. In resemblance they were not unlike; both very awk-ward-looking animals, having great respect for each other, as the Captain drank the whisky and ate the tobacco, and the Broadhorn carried it for him. This was our principal cargo, on which our captain said he intended to clear two thousand dol-lars—*sure.* The crew consisted in six of us—four besides the cook and captain: John Skalian, a good-natured Irishman, whom, of course, we *aliased* Paddy, Simon Roberts, a jolly Englishman, *alias* John Bull; Wm. Thompson, a full-blooded, wild, clever Kentuckian, *alias* Kentuck; and your humble ser-vant, John Smith. They did not choose to *alias* me, for Kentuck said I was but a Jimmy about the house, to carry wood and water, and have no share in the crop. We soon became ac-quainted with His Honor, the cook, his kettle that boiled the pork and beans, and his white cakes, with letters on them. Burnt rye was the substitute for coffee, and the first time we sat down, or, *stood up,* we ascertained the truth of the old saying, that "fingers were made before forks;" and, after a lecture from John Bull on etiquette, that he had learned in England from some relation of his, called Chesterfield, I be-lieve, we all were convinced that we were too well raised to go hungry, in this land of liberty and pork and beans. "Oars," cried the captain, and we all sprang to our feet as quick as if we were about to mount a snag, and swung around the sweeps in an instant. "Hold on," said our commander, "you need not row; I was only practicing you. I must get you in tune, that I can rely on you in case of necessity." I swung back my oar and took a squint at the captain's phiz, which resulted in my con-viction that he was "a little by the head," and addressed him thus: "Capt. Finney (that was his name), now, as I am, a tolerable sort of a boatman, and as we are past Big Bone Bar, I will stay up and watch the boat, if you will go to bunk." "Agreed," said he, "keep her off of the shores and sawyers, and I will lay down close by the tapp'd whisky-barrel, so that them fellows will not get drunk; at the same time, if the boat wants pumping the water will awake me, as I will lay on the floor: so,

good night; look out for snags;" and the captain made his exit
to the cabin. Reader, maybe you think there is no cabin on a
flatboat, if you do think so, and will take the trouble to go on
board one of these broadhorns, walk back on deck to the stern,
and you will perceive a hole, climb down that hole, and you
will find every thing in apple-pie order—the fireplace in the
middle, the captain's bunk on one side and the 'tater barrels
on the other. This is the cabin, and you may not like it; for so
it is, people that have not traveled much don't know much,
and, of course, don't appreciate such refinements. But, to my
tale. Scarcely had His Majesty left us, till down sat his motley
crew at spinning yarns, singing songs—with but little care for
the captain or his beast of a broadhorn—quite immaterial with
us whether she went side-way or end-way, head up or down
the river, so she kept off from the shores and snags. "Paddy,
give us a song." "I will," said Paddy, and he struck up,

"Oh, Charley McKeever, you have ruined me"

This is one of the old Irish rebel sons, and John Bull did not
relish it; but Kentuck insisted on the song, and the song was
sung, and stories were told till one after another fell asleep,
until Morpheus had us all wrapt under cover. The sun rose
next morning and found the nose of our broadhorn up stream,
and her watchful crew sound asleep on their backs. "Halloo,"
said a fellow from the shore, "are you bound up or down."
"Shut your mouth, you big Hoosier," replied Kentuck. The
Broadhorn had evidently turned around with Kentuck, as he
imagined the man hailing from the Hoosier (Indiana) shore.

The dialogue between Kentuck and the man on shore aroused
us all, and brought His Honor, the Captain, on deck. "John,"
said he to me, "where are we." "Here," said I. "Well, but where
abouts in the river are we." "About in the middle of it," said I.
"What town is that we are coming to," said Captain Finney.
"I don't know," said I, "but I think I can tell when we get close
to it." "Get close to it, you fool, we are going from it; we have
passed that town. I thought there was no such town on the

Kentuck shore. Turn the ship's head down stream. Kentuck, blow the horn. Ah, that horn brings to my memory again Major Wm. O. Butler and his poem. . . ."

Yes, reader, flatboating has its charms, and Kentuck blew his horn a blast, the vibrating sounds of which caused the mountains of Hanover to echo. "Cook, bring up a tin-cupful of anti-fog emetic. Boys, wash, bitter, and prepare for breakfast." At Jeffersonville, our captain sent me on shore in the canoe, for old Bowman, who piloted us over the Falls. The crooked channel over these rapids, the breaker-waves and counter-currents, the awful, sublime swiftness of a passage through the narrow channel over these Falls, gave rise to many remarks amongst the crew, and John Bull's pen ran glib and fast: he was writing down all he saw or heard in his "Diary on a Broadhorn." "Mr. Roberts," said Kentuck, "if you could get the character, the manners and customs of these wild Hoosiers, all written down and printed in a book, it would be a great curiosity in the old country, and would sell well. Now, these Hoosiers are a queer people, and if you write about them, you should know them well." "How am I to know them," said John Bull. "You must catch them," replied Kentuck, "and there are two ways of catching them. If you want to catch a she one, get a pack of hounds and run her down. The he ones are easier caught, as follows: take a basket of hoosier-bait, that is, ginger-cakes, go into the woods any where in Indiana, blow your horn; they will soon flock around you; drop the bait and as they pick it up throw the rope around them, and you have them." "Write that down," said Kentuck, to himself, as he twisted his quid of tobacco over to the other side of his mouth, and giving me a sly wink. Ere long, we were in view of Mt. Vernon, seven miles below. Mt. Vernon is in Posey county Indiana. "By-the-by, John Bull," said Kentuck, "did you ever hear of this Posey county, and of its extensive soap-mines." "Soap-mines?" ejaculated Johnny, "no, I have not: what about them." "Well, I will tell you. There is a Hoosier back of Mt. Vernon there about fifteen miles, in Posey, who once on a time got it in his head that he could find salt on his farm. So he dug and dug about a month, until he had got about four hundred feet deep, through gravel and solid rocks, when at last, as he was about giving it up as a bad job, he struck upon a vein of soft soap—yes, sir, on my honor, he did—but not being satisfied, he plug'd the vein and dug a little further and found the hard soap. He stopped there, as he could make as much money as he wanted without digging any further for the real Castile; and he has made his everlasting fortune. Why, sir, this Hoosier and his soap-mine has ruined every soap-boiler in the west." "And you may write that down too," said Kentuck, aside.

The sports and merriments of life on a broadhorn are various, and many the deer-chase in the river, the bear-hunt and wild turkey shooting on days we are compelled to lay by for head-wind, which lend to the enrichment of its charms. Then the herds of wild geese and ducks, the brants, the numerous flocks of large swan, the clouds of pelican, and sand-hill crane, when on the wing, infest the air with their deafening yell, give life and motion to the most torpid man. We are now approaching the great father of waters. The mouth of the Ohio is in sight. Johnny Bull, his pen and book in hand, writes down his conclusion that the Ohio is a nice river for a new country, and at this junction of the two rivers at some distant day, say five hundred years, there may be a settlement—may be a village— asks Kentuck's opinion of his written prediction. "Never will be a settlement there," replied Kentuck, "for the simple reason that the musketoes and gallinippers are so bad they can't build. Why, sir, the general government has been trying to erect a fort here for ten years. The object of the fort is to protect the flat-boatmen from the wild and desperate cane-biters of Arkansas; but it is given up—it cannot be accomplished. The fact is, Mr. Roberts, the government has sent about five hundren broadhorns, loaded with brick to build the fort with, but as fast as they were landed, these infernal gallinippers and musketoes carried them off under their wings to whet their bills with." And such, I suppose, is published in his work in England.

49. Heyday of the Steamboat

By 1850 the steamboat was an institution in the West. Operating a boat, however, was as big a speculation as conducting a fur company, dealing in western lands, or banking. It was a profitable venture if the owner had good luck and a disastrous one if he lost his luck. Nevertheless, the coming of the steamboat opened one of the fabulous chapters in western expansion. The Reverend Robert Baird quoted an English traveler.

The first steam-boat built in the Valley of the Mississippi was the *New Orleans,* which was launched at Pittsburgh in the year 1811. Consequently, twenty-two years have elapsed since the greatest improvements in river navigation which the world has ever seen, was introduced into this western region. Few steam-boats however were built before the year 1817. Since that period the number has annually and rapidly increased, until it has become astonishingly great. From documents in my possession, and which I believe are very accurate, I learn that, at the commencement of the year 1831, the number of *three hundred and forty-eight* had been running on these waters, and all, excepting a very few which were brought round from the East, were built, or were building, this year. So that there have been not less, probably, than 500 steam-boats built in the West, about one half of which are now in existence.

It is a fact, that the steam-boats in the West are far less durable than those in the East. One reason of this may be, that the wood of which they are made seems to be of more rapid growth, and consequently of a less solid and firm fibre. Another reason is, that they are hastily put together, and of materials little seasoned. And perhaps a greater is, that they suffer much hard usage, from the powerful application of steam, and more than all, from being so often run against rocks, sand-bars

Robert Baird, *View of the Valley of the Mississippi*, pp. 332, 333, 342.

and logs. Whatever may be the causes, they seldom are worth much after running five or six years. Some have run seven or eight; but this number is small. A few which were built of *live oak* have lasted nearly ten years.

It has been asserted that the cost of a steamboat in the West is about $100 per ton. This estimate as a general one, is, I am persuaded, too high. The relative cost of steam-boats in the West, as everywhere else, is inversely proportional to their size. A steam-boat of fifty tons costs more proportionately, than one of a hundred tons, or five hundred tons. At present a boat from seventy-five to one hundred tons may be completely finished and prepared, in every respect, for running, for about *eighty* dollars per ton; or at the highest, when most expensively finished, for *one hundred* dollars per ton; whilst a plain boat of five hundred tons, cost about $29,500; and the *Henry Clay*, a splendid boat of five hundred tons, cost near $43,000. Some idea of the large amount of capital invested in steam-boats in the West, may be obtained, from the above statement. The eighty steam-boats which were built last year, some of them being of the largest class, cost on an average from $12,000 to $15,000, each, in all from $960,000, to $1,200,000.

It has been said, that steam-boats in the West usually clear their prime cost during the first year's running, and after that, the proceeds—deducting of course the repairs and other expenses—are nett profit to the owners. I am confident that this is not true as a general fact. Whilst some boats which run very well, and are managed by capable and careful owners, and numerous agents in the various ports from Pittsburgh to New Orleans, do quite, and sometimes more than, pay their original cost during the first year, and afterwards for three or four years are a source of great profit to their owners, many do not clear their first cost in two or three years, and some never. It is considered well if they do so in two or three years. Even then, they prove in the end, very valuable stock. . . .

One of the large boats, filled with passengers, is almost a *world* in miniature. In the cabin you will find ladies and gentlemen of various claims to merit; on the forward part of the boat are the sailors, deck hands, and those *sons of Vulcan*—the firemen—possessing striking traits of character, and full of noise, and song, and too often of *whiskey;* while above, in the deck cabin, there is every thing that may be called *human*—all sorts of men and women, of all trades, from all parts of the world, of all possible manners and habits. There is the half-horse and half-alligator Kentucky boatmen, swaggering, and boasting his prowess, his rifle, his horse, and his wife. One is sawing away on a wretched old fiddle all day long; another is grinding a knife or a razor; here is a party *playing cards*; and in yonder corner is a dance to the sound of a Jew's harp; whilst few are trying to demean themselves soberly, by sitting in silence or reading a book. But it is almost impossible—the wondrous tale and horrible are telling; the bottle and the jug are freely circulating; and the boisterous and deafening laugh is incessantly raised, sufficient to banish every vestige of seriousness, and thought, and sense. A friend of mine, some time ago, went down from Cincinnati to New Orleans on board the steam-boat—which carried fifty cabin passengers, one or two hundred deck passengers; one negro-driver with his gang of negroes; a part of a company of soldiers; a menagerie of wild beasts; a whole circus; and a company of play actors!

50. Steamboat Travel on the Upper Mississippi

Many observers of the western scene described their steamboat experiences between New Orleans and St. Louis, but few of them got into the upper river. This narrator, John Regan, was an Ayrshire school teacher who decided to immigrate to North America. He gave almost no attention to his passage northward from New Orleans, but he described in highly graphic terms the hazards of river travel

John Regan, *The Emigrant's Guide to the Western States of America; or, Backwoods and Prairies* . . . (Edinburgh: Oliver & Bond, Tweedsdale Court, 1842), 28–38.

above St. Louis where the passenger spent about as much time walking on shore as he did aboard the boat on which he had paid his fare. Navigation was uncertain, and the levels of water in the river fluctuated with seasonal conditions.

Our passage money from New Orleans to St. Louis, 1100 miles, was four dollars, exclusive of provisions. When we got to the latter place several persons came aboard from the town making enquiries for workmen. . . . At this place we had to take a small steamer for the upper Mississippi. We embarked, accordingly, on board the *Indian Queen,* and on Saturday evening stopped for the night at the small village of Keokuk, on the Iowa side of the river, and at the foot of the Desmoins rapids. Here the greater part of the vessel's lading, including our more heavy chests, had to be removed into keelboats, to allow the steamer to pass up the rapids, as the water in the principal channel was not over four feet deep, though the river here, at 1500 miles up, is as wide as at its mouth. The rapids are caused by the river flowing at the rate of eight or nine miles an hour over a continuous bed of limestone rock, extending twelve miles to Montrose. On Sunday morning, all things being ready, before we got breakfast, the captain requested the men passengers, of whom there were about fifty, to take a short walk around the bend along the river side, as the river being at a low stage, his vessel would be much lightened. . . . Arrived at Montrose, which might contain about 200 inhabitants, we loitered about the place for two hours, but still no appearance of the steamer. Here we were informed that it was quite likely she had got fast on the rocks, and might have to remain there for a day or two. This was rather unlooked-for information, and we at once set off down the river, to ascertain her position. About a mile below Nashville, there she was, hard and fast upon the rocks, sure enough, toward the Illinois side of the river. We immediately hired a skiff and got on board. She had got fast by the head, and the men had out beams on each side in front, standing perpendicularly on the rock; to the upper end tackles were made fast, and these connected with strong timbers on deck. Sometimes the men hauled upon the ropes, and sometimes a turn was taken round the engine shaft. Two anchors were out about fifty yards ahead, to hold against the stream, if the beams should succeed in lifting her off. The "deck hands," as they were called, seemed to take the business very coolly—never at any time making a very desperate struggle—whether from incapacity or laziness, I will not say; but they kept humbugging at it till Wednesday. On the morning of that day we saw a steamer coming down with lead from Galena. Her own speed, and that of the current united, brought her down at a fearful rate. She appeared to be bearing right down upon us. The channel where we were was doubtless narrow, and her velocity, if she swerved to the shallow water, would have fixed her immoveably on the rocks till next spring freshets. Down came the vast moving structure, menacing destruction to the helpless *Indian Queen*. Every soul held his breath in intense suspense. No word arose from either vessel. Down! Down! escape was inevitable! The blow was struck! Our starboard keelboat, about 100 feet long, and strongly made received the full force of the collision! It was the work of a moment. A tremendous crash and the huge mass swept past apparently unscathed.

The keelboat, fortunately, was about level with the "guard" of the *Queen*, and being driven under it the force of the stroke was somewhat broken. The violence, however, with which the steamer herself was shaken showed that this had not entirely obviated the crushing effects of the stroke. In gushed waters by numerous breaches, and the entire boat had a fair prospect of soon going down. I had three heavy chests in it, and I determined they should not go down without a struggle. John Adams was at my side in a moment. While everyone was scrambling for his own, in an incredibly short space of time we succeeded in getting two of them upon the guard. We wrought with desperation. I then set John to dragging those two on the inner deck, while I should get the third, which was the smallest, up to the gunwale of the keelboat. I had just got it up, and was holding it by the ear rope to balance it upon the gunwale, when in the horrible confusion, a passenger leaped upon it from the steamboat, and immediately both passenger and chest were in the Mississippi. The fall sunk the man sufficiently to carry him clear beneath the paddle-wheel. He rose, however, immediately after, and, being a swimmer, struck out boldly upon the stream. No living man could make way against the desperate current. The small boat, which was made fast at the stern, was immediately manned, and went off in pursuit. The poor fellow, by wisely swimming with the stream had managed to support himself till he was picked up. He had received no injuries by the accident, but seemed to suffer considerably from fright and exhaustion. My chest got entangled in the paddle wheel, and, after some exertion, was rescued. By the aid of a few blankets and three or four pounds of tallow candles the leaks were stopped, and willing hands soon baled out the water which had got in.

As the concussion had removed the steamer somewhat off her former bed, and all were impatient to get away, ten or twelve tons of salt in bags were taken out of the hold that evening, and put into the keelboat. Our luggage was again put in, and the boat and all the passengers towed over to the Illinois bank, distant fifty yards. The steamer was then at dusk got once more into the channel, and ready for starting in the morning. We got our chests ashore, and encamped for the night on the banks. Reader, do you wish to know *how* we did it? Well, then: I had a large chest and two smaller ones: these two I placed side by side, with their ends abutting against the side of the large one. This formed a sleeping platform. A few bundles of grass served to smooth the descent from the big chest to its smaller neighbors: the mattress then was laid on. But still we were in the open air—we must have some protection from the dews. A piece of driftwood, five feet long, was now set at the centre of the bed head, and another at the foot. A large bed quilt was stretched over all, and at the gable ends other softer wares were exhibited. Thus defended on all sides, our bed was comfortable enough. But after we had got fairly in, we were unable to sleep, from the noise of our fellow passengers. The women objected to lie on the ground, for fear of snakes—for they had not all three chests at their disposal. At last, as sleep became more urgent, they sunk minor differences, and bye and bye we were all peace. During the night a few cows and a drove of hogs paid us a visit, which caused some little commotion, from the dangerous exposure of the provision baskets, &c. This new annoyance was tided over also; and in the morning– the dew having fallen heavily during the night, our sheltering quilt was saturated with moisture. "Well, well," thought we, "there are fortunes in wayfaring as well as in war, and they who can not manifest a little fortitude in the midst of the evil should not set out."

By sunup we were again on board the steamer, and, without anything peculiar happening, landed at Burlington, Desmoins County, on the Iowa shore, twenty-two miles above the rapids. . . . The Eastern and Middle states from which the population of Iowa chiefly came, have never produced a race of young men that will be poor and miserable in a country presenting every incitement to sobriety and industry, and to enterprise, and which affords a much larger reward to the cultivator of the soil than any of the older states and Canada.

Notwithstanding all of this I had made up my mind not to settle west of the Mississippi.

Those who have read Dickens' "American Notes," will doubtless remember what that great sketcher, whose genius appears to have stayed at home at Cockaigne, when he set out on his travels, has said of the Mississippi. The passage is short, but characteristic of a certain class of travellers.

> But what words shall describe the Mississippi, great father of rivers, who (praise be to Heaven) has no young children like him. An enormous ditch, sometimes two or three miles wide, running liquid mud, six miles an hour: its strong and frothing current choked and obstructed everywhere by huge logs and whole forest trees; now twining themselves together in great rafts, from the interstices of which a sedgy lazy foam works up to float upon the water's top; now rolling past like monstrous bodies, their entangled roots showing like matted hair; now

glancing singly by like giant leeches; and now writhing round and round in the vortex of some small whirlpool, like wounded snakes. The banks low, the trees dwarfish, the marshes swarming with frogs, the wretched cabins few and far between, their inmates hollow cheeked, and pale, the weather very hot, mosquitos penetrating into every crack and crevice of the boat, mud and slime everywhere, and on everything; nothing pleasant in its aspect but the harmless lightning which flickers every night upon the dark horizon.

For two days we toiled up this foul stream, striking constantly against the floating timber, or stopping to avoid those more dangerous obstacles the snags or sawyers, which are the hidden trunks of trees that have their roots below the tide. When the nights are very dark, the look-out stationed in the head of the boat knows by the ripple of the water if any great impediment is near at hand, and rings a bell beside him, which is the signal for the engine to be stopped; but always in the night this bell has work to do, and after every ring there comes a blow which renders it no easy matter to remain in bed.

We drank the muddy water of this river while we were upon it. It is considered wholesome by the natives, and is something more opaque than gruel. I have seen water like it at filter shops, but nowhere else.

VII

The Herder's Frontier

American frontier history in its more dramatic aspect is made up of the adventures of groups of people following specialized interests. The cowboys and sheepherders were to create rich chapters in the history of westward expansion. In human terms they were heroic in deeds and in romance. Riding long, almost endless trails, the western cowboy early became a folk hero. His job was no less arduous and sweaty than that of his counterpart on the old frontier who moved from one grazing ground to the next just ahead of the advancing settlement line. There was, however, a marked difference. The more modern cattle drover became America's man on horseback. Mixing American and Spanish customs and practices, the trailherders presented dashing figures with their colorful clothing, pointed shoes, revolvers, lariats, and highly ornamented saddles.

Driving a herd of cattle across the vast western ranges was risky business. Weather, aridity, animal predators, Indians, and physical exhaustion all figured prominently in the history of the drives. Perhaps no American frontiersman suffered more from isolation and loneliness than did the cowboy on the long drives. He was a victim both of boredom and nervous tension all the way. There was nothing intriguing about a plodding herd of cattle, and nothing more frightening than thundering stampedes, treacherous river crossings, and storms on the plains. It is little wonder that the horse became so prominent in this chapter of the frontier saga. It offered possible escape both from the dangers and the dullness of the drives; it even offered pleasing companionship.

Extension of the railroads to railhead cattle towns brought a gaudy if not godless kind of anti-social life, along with cattle buyers and railroad men. Girls, gamblers, saloon keepers, and camp followers of all sorts marked these places as the outskirts of settled and sedate society. The cowtown was as fleeting both in its life span and the nature of its society as were the railheads themselves. They were overrun by farmers, bankers, ministers of the gospel, schools, and churches. Within remarkably short time they passed into memory as rowdy places where law and order became distinguished only by its absence.

Where the cowboy, and all the trappings of transient frontier society associated with the long drives up from the plains of Texas, caught American imagination, the sheepherder was also an active figure on parts of the raw frontier. Lonely herders, driving from winter and summer grasslands and to market centers, produced an altogether different sort of pastoral story of the frontier. While no strong claims can be made for these lonely shepherds as trailbreakers, they certainly helped to broaden and mark the trails in the Northwest and Southwest.

Both cowboys and sheepherders figured prominently in the soberer field of expanding American economics and changing mores of food merchandising, banking, farming, railroad building, and the rise of big, commercial urbanization. In another field this moment in frontier history was to rival Indian wars and heroics in the literature of the westward movement as an ever appealing theme for writer, teller of folk tales, and the producers of movies and television programs.

51. The Great American Desert

Stephen H. Long's report not only added materially to the American's knowledge of the western territories, it also conditioned his mind for thinking about this vast region. It would be impossible to determine how many official decisions were made in Washington relating to the western plains on the basis of information contained in Long's report. And it would be most difficult to determine how much of American Indian policy after 1820 was formulated upon it. Perhaps the most important concept of the report presented was that of the "Great American Desert."

Stephen H. Long, "Account of an Expedition from Pittsburgh to the Rocky Mountains," Thwaites, ed., *Early Western Travels*, XVII, pp. 143–148.

The country of the Canadian above that last considered, or that portion of it west of the assumed meridian, appears to be possessed of a soil somewhat richer than the more northerly parts of the section, but exhibits no indications of extraordinary fecundity in any part of it. Proceeding westward, a very gradual change is observable in the apparent fertility of the soil, the surface becoming more sandy and sterile, and the vegetation less vigorous and luxuriant. The bottoms appear to be composed, in many places, almost exclusively of loose sand, exhibiting but few signs of vegetation. Knobs and drifts of sand, driven from the bed of the river by the violence of the wind, are piled in profusion along the margin of the river throughout the greater part of its length. It is remarkable, that these drifts are in many instances covered with grape vines of a scrubby appearance, bearing fruit in the greatest abundance and perfection. The vines grow to various heights, from eighteen inches to four feet, unaccompanied, in some instances, by any other vegetable, and bear a grape of a dark purple or black colour, of a delicious flavour, and of the size of a large pea or common gooseberry.

The waters of this section, almost in every part of it, appear to hold in solution a greater or less proportion of common salt and sulphate of magnesia, which, in many instances, render them too brackish or bitter for use. Saline and nitrous efflorescences frequently occur upon the surface, in various parts of the country, and incrustations of salt, of considerable thickness, are to be found in some few places south of the Arkansa river. As to the existence of rock salt in a mineral state some doubts are to be entertained, if the decision is to rest upon the character of the specimens exhibited as proofs of the fact. The several examples of this formation that we have witnessed, are evidently crystalline salt deposited by a regular process of evaporation and crystallization, and formed into concrete masses or crusts upon the surface of the ground.

Indications of coal are occasionally to be seen, but this mineral does not probably occur in large quantities. The geological character of this section is not such as to encourage the search for valuable minerals. A deep crust of secondary sandstone, occasionally alternating with breccia, with here and there a superstratum of rocks of a primitive type, are the principal formation that present themselves.

Of the animals of this region, the buffaloe or bison ranks first in importance, inasmuch as it supplies multitudes of savages not only with the principal part of their necessary food, but also contributes to furnish them with warm clothing. The flesh of this animal is equal, if not superior, to beef, and affords not only a savoury but a wholesome diet. A large proportion of this section, commencing at the assumed meridian, and extending westward to within one hundred miles of the Rocky Mountains, constitutes a part only of their pasture ground, over which they roam in numbers to an incredible amount. Their range extends northwardly and southwardly of the section, as far as we have any particular account of the country. The animal next in importance is the wild horse, a descendant, no doubt, of the Spanish breed of horses, to which its size, form and variety of colours, show that it is nearly allied. In regard to their contour, symmetry, &c. they afford all the varieties common to that breed of horses. They are considerably numerous in some parts of the country, but not abundant. They are generally collected in gangs, but are sometimes solitary.

Grizzly or white bears are frequently to be seen in the vicinity of the mountains. They are much larger than the common bear, endowed with great strength, and are said to be exceedingly ferocious. The black or common bears are numerous in some parts of the country, but none of these animals are found remote from woodlands, upon the products of which they in a great measure depend for their subsistence.

The common deer are to be met with in every part of this section, but are most numerous in the vicinity of woodlands. The black-tailed or mule deer is found only in the neighbourhood of the mountains; hilly and broken lands seem to afford them their favourite pasture ground. The elk is also an inhabitant of this section, but is not to be found remote from woodlands. The cabric wild goat, or, as it is more frequently called, the antelope, is common. They are numerous, and with the buffaloe are the common occupants of the plains, from which they retire only in quest of water.

Wolves are exceedingly numerous, particularly within the immediate range of the buffaloe. Of these there are many varieties, distinguishable by their shape, size and colour.

The marmot, commonly called the prairie dog, is more abundant throughout this section than any other quadruped. They live in villages scattered in every direction, and thickly inhabited; a single village in some instances occupying a tract of ground three or four miles in extent. Their habitations are burrows three or four inches in diameter, situated at the distance of fifteen or twenty paces asunder. Their habits and manners in other respects are peculiarly interesting. They subsist on vegetables; their flesh is similar to that of the ground hog, and their hair equally as coarse.

The beaver, otter, mink, and muskrat, are numerous upon the rivers, creeks, and rivulets issuing from the mountains, and generally upon those whose valleys are supplied with woodland.

Badgers, raccoons, hares, polecats, porcupines, many varieties of squirrels, panthers, wild cats, lynxes and foxes of several species, are also inhabitants of this section. Besides these, the country affords a great variety and abundance of reptiles and insects, both venomous and harmless.

Of the feathered tribes, no very considerable variety is observable. The turtle-dove, the jay, the barn swallow, the quail (partridge of the Middle States), the owl, whip-poor-will, and lark, which seen more widely distributed over the territory of the United States than any other birds, are found here. Several varieties of the hawk, containing some new species, the bald and gray eagle, the buzzard, raven, crow, jackdaw, magpie, turkey, two or three varieties of the grouse, pheasant, pigeon, many varieties of the sparrow and fly-catcher, the whooping or sandhill crane, curlew, sandpiper, together with a variety of other land and water fowls, are more or less numerous in this region. It is remarkable that birds of various kinds common to the sea-coast, and seldom found far in the interior, pervade the valley of the Mississippi to a great distance from the gulf of Mexico, and frequent the regions adjacent to the Rocky Mountains.

In regard to this extensive section of country, I do not hesitate in giving the opinion, that it is almost wholly unfit for cultivation, and of course uninhabitable by a people depending upon agriculture for their subsistence. Although tracts of fertile land considerably extensive are occasionally to be met with, yet the scarcity of wood and water, almost uniformly prevalent, will prove an insuperable obstacle in the way of settling the country.

52. The Noble Beast

The horse was brought to North America by the European. It adapted itself to the land and survived and multiplied without man's assistance. When the horse went wild and roamed at will, it became a heroic animal. No Greek legend glorified the horse more than did stories out of the West about wild herds led by magnificent stallions. George Catlin, an eastern lawyer turned painter, spent eight years among the Indians with his palette and brush and saw the wild horse in all its glory on the western plains.

The tract of country over which we passed, between the False Washita and this place, is stocked, not only with buffaloes, but with numerous bands of wild horses, many of which we saw every day. There is no other animal on the prairies so wild and so sagacious as the horse; and none other so difficult to come up with. So remarkably keen is their eye, that they will generally run "at the sight," when they are a mile distant; being, no doubt, able to distinguish the character of the enemy that

George Catlin, *Letters and Notes on the Manners, Customs, and Condition of the North American Indians*, 2 vols. (London: Tosswill and Myers, 1841), II, pp. 57, 58.

is approaching when at that distance; and when in motion, will seldom stop short of three or four miles. I made many attempts to approach them by stealth, when they were grazing and playing their gambols, without ever having been more than once able to succeed. In this instance, I left my horse, and with my friend Chadwick, skulked through a ravine for a couple of miles; until we were at length brought within gunshot of a fine herd of them, when I used my pencil for some time, while we were under cover of a little hedge of bushes which effectually screened us from their view. In this herd we saw all the colours, nearly, that can be seen in a kennel of English hounds. Some were milk white, some jet black—others were sorrel, and bay, and cream colour—many were of an iron grey; and others were pied, containing a variety of colours on the same animal. Their manes were very profuse, and hanging in the wildest confusion over their necks and faces—and their long tails swept the ground.

After we had satisfied our curiosity in looking at these proud and playful animals, we agreed that we would try the experiment of "creasing" one, as it is termed in this country; which is done by shooting them through the gristle on the top of the neck, which stuns them so that they fall, and are secured with the hobbles on the feet; after which they rise again without fatal injury. This is a practice often resorted to by expert hunters, with good rifles, who are not able to take them in any other way. My friend Joe and I were armed on this occasion, each with a light fowling-piece, which have not quite the preciseness in throwing a bullet that a rifle has; and having both levelled our pieces at the withers of a noble, fine-looking iron grey, we pulled trigger, and the poor creature fell, and the rest of the herd were out of sight in a moment. We advanced speedily to him, and had the most inexpressible mortification of finding, that we never had thought of hobbles or halters, to secure him—and in a few moments more, had the still greater mortification, and even anguish, to find that one of our shots had broken the poor creature's neck, and that he was quite dead.

The laments of poor Chadwick for the wicked folly of destroying this noble animal, were such as I never shall forget; and so guilty did we feel that we agreed that when we joined the regiment, we should boast of all the rest of our hunting feats, but never make mention of this.

53. Cowboys and Homesteaders

A. P. (Ott) Black was a master cowhand. He saw the trail driving industry grow from its clumsy start in Southwest Texas until it became big business. "Ott" Black had experiences everywhere in the West where men ran cattle. In good cowboy fashion his recollections are brief and pungent. They give a keen insight into the ordeals of cattle driving. Life had a sequence: "A few years of serenity—then barbed wire and nesters, next homesteaders and plowing."

Grass, long years in growing, billions of acres of it had been unmolested for centuries. Then sod was turned to sky; seed was planted to grow and thrive for pitifully few years on that deadened buried grass; and now, hot dry winds swirling along over the parched blackened earth, picking up the powdery clay and sweeping it to every corner of the country— nature and real beauty tampered with, angry and showering down it's wrath on a heedless world—a warning to selfish man in a world where pitifully little that is beautiful can hope to survive. . . .

In 1871 he [Black's father] stripped fifteen thousand acres of land in Parker County and decided to go into the cattle business. The land cost him fifteen cents an acre, but he always claimed that it was too much money. He picked up about two thousand head of "yellow-hammer" stuff over in the "piney woods" and drove them back to the ranch. That was when my brother, Sam Houston Black, named in honor of the Texas

A. P. [Ott] Black, _The End of the Long Horn Trail_ (Selfridge, N.D.: Selfridge Journal, n.d.), 1, 6, 7, 17–19.

president, got the hoof marks on his head. The cattle stampeded one day and knocked Sam off his horse right in front of the stampeding herd. My youngest brother rode in and dragged Sam behind a tree, using a bull whip to split the herd to either side. Nobody thought Sam would ever live, but we got him to a hammer-and-saw doctor who patched him up and gave him a new lease on life. He always carried those hoof marks on his head. I haven't heard of him in ten years, so I guess he must be dead by this time.

That was the beginning of the big cattle days in Texas. That year saw the start of the trail herds and the markings of the Chisholm trails– the east trail crossing at Red River Station and the west one at Doan's store. They were the days of big money and real men to spend it. Board sidewalks, high false fronted buildings, gambling houses with the click of poker chips, roulette wheels and dice, prostitution and everything that went with it. Livery barns at the ends of streets and dust covered, sweat stained riders with jingling spurs and wide brimmed hats. Dodge City and Honeywell, the end of the trails and the meccas of pleasure and entertainment. Thousands of dollars changing hands every hour. The Western wilderness was coming to life. Cattle grazing on grass untouched for centuries. Cattle pouring into railheads to entrain for Chicago and the East– jamming stockyards and bawling in the direction of distant ranges. Drunkedness, curses, laughter, anger and death. It only happened once; it'll never happen again. . . .

The first herds to come North were small and didn't amount to much in comparison to the big drives of a few years later. I met Bill LaForce, the man who drove the first herd of yearling steers from the Millet ranch in the early part of April, 1882. I'd been working with the rest of the hands, driving the cattle in from the winter range and throwing them back to the summer range as we did every year. On that particular spring just after we'd finished and were riding into headquarters with Bob Green, we ran into LaForce camped along the trail. The foreman introduced him to me. He was a tall, slender and some-

what dark complexioned man who showed his French blood.
He told Green that he'd been appointed to take the first herd
out and would like to get started by about the fifteenth of the
month. He said his trail horses, wagon and everything was
ready to go then. So we went to the ranch, got in a bunch of
cornfed cutting horses and started out to make up his herd.
We turned over twenty five hundred of the prettiest yearling
steers a man would ever want to see to LaForce up on the
Wichita River, the north end of the range.

We had to go along with his outfit until he got across the
Wichita to keep the old cows from trailing their calves. Did
you know they could trail like bloodhounds? We went on a
little further and helped cross the Red River into the Indian
territory. It took twenty-two riders to break them into the trail.
LaForce's cowpunchers were nothing but a bunch of cotton
pickers who didn't know the Jews killed Christ. It took a little
while to make a cowpuncher, but that crew didn't know a
damn thing. I don't think they ever saw a trail herd before in
their lives. The regular range crew had to hold the cattle from
dusk till midnight and the regular trail crew took over till daylight. One night we had to tie fifty head of yearlings to keep
them from running back to their mothers and their old trail
grounds.

The trail crew and equipment consisted of eight riders, a
horse wrangler and boss and cook. An ordinary wagon had a
mess box built into the back end with a wagon rod running
through the middle of it, and stood about four feet high. The
lid of the box was hinged and when the lid was folded over
a leg dropped out and supported it to make a table for the
cook. A pot rack was built under the mess box next to the
coupling pole, and a beef hide stretched between the four
wheels underneath the wagon was used to carry fuel. This fuel
was good at one time and no good at another. If it rained, the
sap got up in it and cooking was impossible. It was the original
prairie coal– cow chips– or I believe they call it cow dung or
some such thing in the best society. It could be found anywhere cattle ranged. Lots of Western farmers still use it. I've

found ponderous big piles of it in late years, stacked up as high as a house.

The cow punchers bed rolls piled up the rest of the wagon, and about all the space left for the cook was his spring seat. He slept under the wagon and hung a lantern in the top of the wagon so the cattle, if they stampeded on a dark night, would not run over him. The cowpunchers rolled out their beds wherever they liked.

The cattle, after they got out on the trail a few days, were pretty well broke in and knew exactly what was expected of them. The wagon usually went on ahead a little ways after the sun went down and the day's drive stopped. The cattle grazed along until they came up to the wagon, then they stopped and bedded down. They just seemed to know that that was as far as they were to go. If there happened to be a dew in the morning the cattle would just walk on up the trail until the sun dried off the grass. Those old range cattle would never eat if there was dew on the grass; they were different from dairy cows.

The shortest drive ever made from Texas to Montana was ninety days, but a hundred days was considered average. Each cowpuncher had to stand guard two and a half hours every night; two cowpunchers worked each shift from sundown to daybreak. I look back now and wonder how a man could stand sixteen hours work every day and have his rest disturbed at night, and live on sour dough biscuits and beef from one end of the year to the other.

54.   End of the Lonely Cattle Trail

The end of the long Texas cattle trail in the 1870s was the beginning of a second journey to the slaughterhouse for the cattle, and

Joseph G. McCoy, *Historic Sketches of the Cattle Trade* (Washington: The Rare Book Shop, 1932), pp. 138–142.

the long ride home for the cattlemen. Before he left for home the cowboy usually savored the pleasures of the railhead town. He got drunk, was fleeced by crooked gamblers, took a bath if water was available, got a haircut, and, sometimes, got run out of town. The dance floors with their free and easy girls held a well-nigh fatal attraction for men who had ridden the range many hundred, dusty miles. Women, virtuous or not, symbolized a taste of what at least passed for civilization. Joseph G. McCoy, a central figure in the early cattle trade and an early historian of the drives, has left one of the most dependable contemporary views of this part of the frontier activity.

When the herd is sold and delivered to the purchaser, a day of rejoicing to the cow-boy has come, for then he can go free and have a jolly time; and it is a jolly time they have. Straightway after settling with their employers the barber shop is visited, and three to six months' growth of hair is shorn off, their long-grown, sunburnt beard "set" in due shape, and properly blacked; next a clothing store of the Israelitish style is "gone through," and the cow-boy emerges a new man, in outward appearance, everything being new, not excepting the hat and boots, with star decorations about the tops, also a new ———, well, in short everything new. Then for fun and frolic. The barroom, the theatre, the gambling-room, the bawdy house, the dance house, each and all come in for their full share of attention. In any of these places an affront, or a slight, real or imaginary, is cause sufficient for him to unlimber one or more "mountain howitzers," invariably found strapped to his person, and proceed to deal out death in unbroken doses to such as may be in range of his pistols, whether real friends or enemies, no matter, his anger and bad whisky urge him on to deeds of blood and death.

At frontier towns where are centered many cattle and, as a natural result, considerable business is transacted, and many strangers congregate, there are always to be found a number of bad characters, both male and female; of the very worst class in the universe, such as have fallen below the level of the lowest type of the brute creation. Men who live a soulless, aimless life, dependent upon the turn of a card for the means of living. They wear out a purposeless life, ever looking blear-eyed and dissipated; to whom life, from various causes, has long since become worse than a total blank; beings in the form of men whose outward appearance would betoken gentlemen, but whose heartstrings are but a wisp of base sounding chords, upon which the touch of the higher and purer life have long since ceased to be felt. Beings without whom the world would be better, richer and more desirable. And with them are always found their counterparts in the opposite sex; those who have fallen low, alas! how low! They, too, are found in the frontier cattle town; and that institution known in the west as a dance house, is there found also. When the darkness of the night is come to shroud their orgies from public gaze, these miserable beings gather into the halls of the dance house, and "trip the fantastic toe" to wretched music, ground out by dilapidated instruments, by beings fully as degraded as the most vile. In this vortex of dissipation the average cow-boy plunges with great delight. Few more wild, reckless scenes of abandoned debauchery can be seen on the civilized earth, than a dance house in full blast in one of the many frontier towns. To say they dance wildly or in an abandoned manner is putting it mild. Their manner of practising the terpsichorean art would put the French "Can-Can" to shame.

The cow-boy enters the dance with a peculiar zest, not stopping to divest himself of his sombrero, spurs, or pistols, but just as he dismounts off of his cow-pony, so he goes into the dance. A more odd, not to say comical sight, is not often seen than the dancing cow-boy; with the front of his sombrero lifted at an angle of fully forty-five degrees; his huge spurs jingling at every step or motion; his revolvers flapping up and down like a retreating sheep's tail; his eyes lit up with excitement, liquor and lust; he plunges in and "hoes it down" at a terrible rate, in the most approved yet awkward country style; often swinging "his partner" clear off of the floor for an entire circle, then "balance all" with an occasional demoniacal yell, near akin to the war whoop of the savage Indian. All this he does, en-

tirely oblivious to the whole world "and the balance of mankind." After dancing furiously, the entire "set" is called to
"waltz to the bar," where the boy is required to treat his partner, and, of course, himself also, which he does not hesitate to
do time and again, although it cost him fifty cents each time.
Yet if it cost ten times that amount he would not hesitate, but
the more he dances and drink, the less common sense he will
have, and the more completely his animal passions will control
him. Such is the manner in which the cow-boy spends his hard
earned dollars. And such is the entertainment that many young
men—from the North and the South, of superior parentage
and youthful advantages in life—give themselves up to, and
often more, their lives are made to pay the forfeit of their sin-
ful foolishness.

After a few days of frolic and debauchery, the cow-boy is
ready, in company with his comrades, to start back to Texas,
often not having one dollar left of his summer's wages. To this
rather hard drawn picture of the cow-boy, there are many
creditable exceptions,—young men who respect themselves
and save their money, and are worthy young gentlemen,—but
it is idle to deny the fact that the wild, reckless conduct of the
cow-boys while drunk, in connection with that of the worth-
less northern renegades, have brought the *personnel* of the
Texas cattle trade into great disrepute, and filled many graves
with victims, bad men and good men, at Abilene, Newton,
Wichita, and Ellsworth. But by far the larger portion of those
killed are of that class that can be spared without detriment
to the good morals and respectability of humanity.

It often occurs when the cow-boys fail to get into a melee
and kill each other by the half dozen, that the keepers of those
"hell's half acres" find some pretext arising from "business
jealousies" or other causes, to suddenly become belligerent,
and stop not to declare war, but begin hostilities at once. It is
generally effective work they do with their revolvers and shot
guns, for they are the most desperate men on earth. Either
some of the principals or their subordinates are generally "done
for" in a thorough manner, or wounded so as to be miserable

cripples for life. On such occasions there are few tears shed, or even inquiries made, by the respectable people, but an expression of sorrow is common that, active hostilities did not continue until every rough was stone dead.

55. Hazards of Cattle Grazing

Cattle grazing on the western plains passed through many stages. Many an old timer lived through the burly years of the long drives, the development of markets, range laws, and cattlemen's associations, and other challenges. Disease, blizzards, drouths, and overgrazing all exacted tolls. Maverick steers caused equally as much anxiety. Sometimes these cattle of no markings and unestablished ownership meant the difference between profit and loss for the plainsman. Many a cattleman's assembly was disrupted by too vigorous discussion of this subject, as John Clay here relates.

The Wyoming Stock Growers' Association . . . was a mighty engine in its day and with the Cattle Growers' Association of Texas, it blazed the path for many important changes in our western cattle business. The first meeting I attended was in April, 1884. The range cattle business was then in full bloom and there was a big attendance. Judge Carey was in the Chair, and Mr. Thomas Sturgis was secretary, assisted by Mr. Harry Bush. The meeting was held in the Opera House of those days. It was a sort of free for all. We did not in those days have prepared papers over which the author had labored for days. The favorite theme of the railroads, the packers, public stockyards, the leasing of the public domain and many other ills real and imaginary were not thought of. Every cowman rode on a pass quite on an equality with the politicians, and the railroad manager or his assistants were very popular. The packers had not developed into the devils they are now painted and in the

John Clay, *My Life on the Range* (Chicago: Privately Printed, 1924), 114–117.

eyes of the average cowman a stockyard was looked on as a blessing, and in fact at this very meeting the South Omaha scheme was bursting into bloom and receiving enthusiastic support from the range owners.

The discussions at this meeting arose principally from the reports of various committees and these were mainly directed towards the preservation of property on the range. The maverick was one of the subjects of wordy warfare and many suggestions. He was a pariah in a way, and yet he was property. He had no mark or brand and yet he came from somewhere. He was a will o' the wisp, homeless, innocent, a wanderer, revolving round his birthplace and claimed by the owner who had a shadowy right over a certain amount of range. Cap Haskell told me that when he first worked the country north of the Sweetwater over on Poison and Muskrat Creeks, westward towards the Wind River and as far north as Bad Water, he branded on one round-up a hundred and fifty mavericks, some of them four-year-old steers and cows with calves at foot that had not a mark or an ear slit on them. This was the hour when an adventurous man could start a herd of cattle if he was able to register a brand as his mark and property. Many of them did and not a few respectable citizens of today made a beginning, adding on to it by other devious methods not necessary to explain. The maverick was clearly the property of the cattle owners, but the legal right was not definable. By courtesy, when the animal was found on what by common consent was admitted to be a certain owner's range, he was allowed by his neighbors to put his brand on the foundling, and there the matter remained, but the covetous owner or the enterprising cowboy began work on his own account before the round-up and means had to be devised to stop this semi-illegal proceeding. So a law was passed making the maverick practically the property of the state. At the round-ups in the different districts the captain sold them at the close of the day's work to the highest bidder, who put his brand on them, and the proceeds went to the state for the benefit of the cattlemen.

The real object of the meeting, namely the arrangement of the round-ups in the different districts, was all done by committees and the final results communicated to the meeting on big sheets of paper, which fixed the date and place of meeting and laid the plan of working the country out in a methodical way. It was very interesting to look over the diagram and see how completely the country was covered. The arrangements made here and published broadcast let every owner know just what he had to do, when and where the work would commence on his particular range, and in this way he could mobilize his force and perfect his plans. The fall or beef round-up generally followed the lines of the spring one, although they were not always identically the same. Carey, as chairman of those meetings, was fluent, fair, patient and in every way an ideal presiding officer. You could not stampede him and he held his audience well in hand. Sturgis was cool, concise and when he spoke he was logical, with a fine grasp of his subject. Hec Reel, the treasurer, was a good deal of a kicker, but generally speaking this meeting and others that followed were harmonious. Dr. Hopkins, the state veterinarian, was a windy chap, but he had a lot of knowledge and knew his business exceedingly well. His judgment was only fair and his methods out in the field were not very tactful, but he was earnest and indefatigable in his work. We had had several disease scares in the East and consequently the Doctor had a fertile field to work in. Not only at the meetings of the association did the Doctor keep driving his ideas home, but all round the state he hammered away at the stockmen, showing up the grave possibilities of disease working havoc on the plains. The seed bore fruit, as we shall see hereafter.

The social side of the meeting was a revelation to the outsider. The company was made up of all kinds of men. The owner and the cowpuncher were most in evidence, but there was an endless procession of railroad men, mostly from the traffic department, a strong contingent of Chicago commission men, managers of feed stations and a great miscellaneous

crowd, some of them hunting for locations or jobs, others looking on from curiosity or the simple love of adventure. During
the day Luke Murrin's saloon had great patronage. This was
the gentleman who sized up the book count business in epi-
gram. One stormy day when a blizzard was sweeping across
Wyoming and howling through the streets of Cheyenne, the
boys who liked their noon dram leaned up against Luke's bar.
Their faces very long and disconsolate, backed up by low
mutterings of loss on the range and visions of unpaid notes in
the fall, the witty but rather disreputable saloon keeper said:
"Cheer up boys, whatever happens the books won't freeze."
At night the Club had the call. In a way it was a brilliant
scene, for there were men from all points of the compass. The
wanderers from foreign shores were back to work. They had
their story to tell, and in return the stay-at-home imparted his
view of the winter, the state of the range and the different
trades that had gone through. Wine flowed freely, tongues got
limber, the different cliques broke away from one another. It
was a sort of love feast; no apple of discord appeared and no
cloud hung on the horizon.

56.   Man *versus* Arid Land

John Wesley Powell stirred much controversy over his sound observations relating to the arid plains area where the rainfall was twenty
inches or less annually. His demarcation, although not stated in a
sharp line, began roughly at the 98th meridian and extended in
more or less intensity westward to the Pacific. In his opinion agriculture without irrigation was impractical where rainfall was less
than twenty inches. There were many frontiersmen and railway
promoters and operators who took sharp exception to Powell's observations, but subsequent agricultural failure and dust storms supported his contentions.

John Wesley Powell, *Report of the Lands of the Arid Region of the
United States* (Washington: Government Printing Office, 1879), 1–4.

The eastern portion of the United States is supplied with abundant rainfall for agricultural purposes, receiving the necessary amount from the evaporation of the Atlantic Ocean and the Gulf of Mexico; but westward the amount of aqueous precipitation diminishes in a general way until at last a region is reached where the climate is so arid that agriculture is not successful without irrigation. This Arid Region begins about midway in the Great Plains and extends across the Rocky Mountains to the Pacific Ocean. But on the northwest coast there is a region of greater precipitation, embracing western Washington and Oregon and the northwest corner of California. The winds impinging on this region are freighted with moisture derived from the great Pacific currents; and where this waterladen atmosphere strikes the western coast in full force, the precipitation is excessive, reaching a maximum north of the Columbia River of 80 inches annually. But the rainfall rapidly decreases from the Pacific Ocean eastward to the summit of the Cascade Mountains. It will be convenient to designate this humid area as the Lower Columbia Region. Rain gauge records have not been made to such an extent as to enable us to define its eastern and southern boundaries, but as they are chiefly along high mountains, definite boundary lines are unimportant in the consideration of agricultural resources and the questions relating thereto. In like manner on the east the rain gauge records, though more full, do not give all the facts necessary to a thorough discussion of the subject; yet the records are such as to indicate approximately the boundary between the Arid Region, where irrigation is necessary to agriculture, and the Humid Region, where the lands receive enough moisture from the clouds for the maturing of crops. Experience teaches that it is not wise to depend upon rainfall where the amount is less than 20 inches annually, if this amount is somewhat evenly distributed throughout the year; but if the rainfall is unevenly distributed, so that "rainy seasons" are produced, the question whether agriculture is possible without irrigation depends upon the time of the "rainy season" and the amount of its rainfall. Any unequal distribution of rain through the year, though the inequality be so slight as not to produce "rainy seasons", affects agriculture either favorably or unfavorably. If the spring and summer precipitation exceeds that of the fall and winter, a smaller amount of annual rain may be sufficient; but if the rainfall during the season of growing crops is less than the average of the same length of time during the remainder of the year, a greater amount of annual precipitation is necessary. In some localities in the western portion of the United States this unequal distribution of rainfall through the seasons affects agriculture favorably, and this is true immediately west of the northern portion of the line of 20 inches of rainfall, which extends along the plains from our northern to our southern boundary.

The isohyetal or mean annual rainfall line of 20 inches, as indicated on the rain chart accompanying this report, begins on the southern boundary of the United States, about 60 miles west of Brownsville, on the Rio Grande del Norte, and intersects the northern boundary about 50 miles east of Pembina. Between these two points the line is very irregular, but in middle latitudes makes a general curve to the westward. On the southern portion of the line the rainfall is somewhat evenly distributed through the seasons, but along the northern portion the rainfall of spring and summer is greater than that of fall and winter, and hence the boundary of what has been called the Arid Region runs farther to the west. Again, there is another modifying condition, namely, that of temperature. Where the temperature is greater, more rainfall is needed; where the temperature is less, agriculture is successful with a smaller amount of precipitation. But geographically this temperature is dependent upon two conditions—altitude and latitude. Along the northern portion of the line latitude is an important factor, and the line of possible agriculture without irrigation is carried still farther westward. This conclusion, based upon the consideration of rainfall and latitude, accords with the experience of the farmers of the region, for it is a well-known fact that agriculture without irrigation is successfully carried on in the valley of the Red River of the North, and also in the southeastern portion of Dakota Territory. A much more extended series of rain-gauge records than we now have is necessary before this line constituting the eastern boundary of the Arid Region can be well defined. It is doubtless more or less meandering in its course throughout its whole extent from south to north, being affected by local conditions of rainfall, as well as by the general conditions above mentioned; but in a general way it may be represented by the one hundredth meridian, in some places passing to the east, in others to the west, but in the main to the east.

The limit of successful agriculture without irrigation has been set at 20 inches, that the extent of the Arid Region should by no means be exaggerated; but at 20 inches agriculture will not be uniformly successful from season to season. Many droughts will occur; many seasons in a long series will be fruitless; and it may be doubted whether, on the whole, agriculture will prove remunerative. On this point it is impossible to speak with certainty. A larger experience than the history of agriculture in the western portion of the United States affords is necessary to a final determination of the question.

In fact, a broad belt separates the Arid Region of the west from the Humid Region of the east. Extending from the one hundredth meridian eastward to about the isohyetal line of 28 inches, the district of country thus embraced will be subject more or less to disastrous droughts, the frequency of which will diminish from west to east. For convenience let this be called the Sub-humid Region. Its western boundary is the line already defined as running irregularly along the one hundredth meridian. Its eastern boundary passes west of the isohyetal line of 28 inches of rainfall in Minnesota, running approximately parallel to the western boundary line above described. Nearly one-tenth of the whole area of the United States, exclusive of Alaska, is embraced in this Sub-humid Region. In the western portion disastrous droughts will be frequent; in the eastern portion infrequent. In the western

portion agriculturists will early resort to irrigation to secure
immunity from such disasters, and this event will be hastened
because irrigation when properly conducted is a perennial
source of fertilization, and is even remunerative for this purpose alone; and for the same reason the inhabitants of the
eastern part will gradually develop irrigating methods. It may
be confidently expected that at a time not far distant irrigation will be practiced to a greater or less extent throughout
this Sub-humid Region. Its settlement presents problems differing materially from those pertaining to the region to the westward. Irrigation is not immediately necessary, and hence
agriculture does not immediately depend upon capital. The
region may be settled and its agricultural capacities more or
less developed, and the question of the construction of irrigating canals may be a matter of time and convenience. For
many reasons, much of the sub-humid belt is attractive to
settlers: it is almost destitute of forests, and for this reason
is more readily subdued, as the land is ready for the plow.
But because of the lack of forests the country is more dependent upon railroads for the transportation of building and
fencing materials and for fuel. To a large extent it is a region
where timber may be successfully cultivated. As the rainfall
is on a general average nearly sufficient for continuous successful agriculture, the amount of water to be supplied by irrigating canals will be comparatively small, so that its streams
can serve proportionally larger areas than the streams of the
Arid Region. In its first settlement the people will be favored
by having lands easily subdued, but they will have to contend
against a lack of timber. Eventually this will be a region of
great agricultural wealth, as in general the soils are good.
From our northern to our southern boundary no swamp lands
are found, except to some slight extent in the northeastern
portion, and it has no excessively hilly or mountainous districts. It is a beautiful prairie country throughout, lacking
somewhat in rainfall; but this want can be easily supplied by
utilizing the living streams; and, further, these streams will
afford fertilizing materials of great value.

VIII

The Fur Traders' Frontier

Back on the old Appalachian frontier hunters traded for furs and skins and broke trails across the mountains to the Ohio Valley. Men like George Croghan, Henry Skaggs, James Stewart, and Timothe Demunbreum carried on an extensive trade with the Indians. These long hunters were forerunners of settled civilization itself. By the outbreak of the American Revolution the long hunters and land scouts had gained more than a general knowledge of the western country.

In the first quarter of the nineteenth century the successors to the old frontier scouts and traders were opening trails into the far, Rocky Mountain West. Emanuel Lisa, the four Sublette brothers, Jedediah Smith, Thomas Fitzpatrick, James Ohio Pattie, and James Beckwourth were the long hunters of the newer frontier. The Sublette brothers were grandsons of the old Indian fighter William Whitley, who fell in 1813 in the battle of the Thames. All of these trappers and traders had sprung from the earlier settlements east of the Ohio.

The Rocky Mountain adventurers took American interests into one of the most dramatic geographical areas of the continent. Buried within the great mountainous folds were the holes and valleys where beaver thrived, and Indian tribes were concentrated. In this era of the mountain man, traders and trappers teetered on the line of demarcation between civilization and abject surrender to nature. It was an area where men were driven on by stern economic motives, yet entranced by the romance of splendid isolation. Long tramps over unmarked country, winter entrapments, and the excesses of the annual rendezvous all gave the mountain ventures romantic aura. No other frontier experience had been exactly like it. Furs, Indians, trading rivalries, and even skirmishes with resistant tribes all appealed to the men of the mountains.

With a background of Rocky Mountain spaciousness and fearful grandeur, the long hunters seem much sturdier men in comparison with the old Appalachian wanderers whose story had already appeared in folk literature. The mountain man on this new frontier made permanent contributions to American history, not so much as fur trader but as trailbreaker. Before the fur trading closed, settlers' wagons were lumbering across the Rockies to the Northwest and the Pacific Coast. Along the way the emigrants met the bull boats of the American Fur Company and the independent traders swirling down the shallow Platte and to market in St. Louis; they passed such landmarks as Fort Kearny, Chimney Rock, Scott's Bluff, Independence Rock, South Pass, and wandered up the Green River, and around the Great Basin Rim. Even the Santa Fe traders followed on the heels of the mountain men to that far away Southwest outpost. One frontier movement marched on the heels of another.

57.   Green River Country and Beyond

It was the mountain man who was almost the storybook pioneer. His wanderings took him into vast areas of unbroken country. He lived and trapped for long periods of time alone, suffering privations and hardships. Loneliness was his constant companion, so much so that many trappers became inveterate readers of the Bible, Shakespeare, and even of dry New England clerical commentaries. He was set out for the world to see by a number of writers, among them Washington Irving. Irving saw the mountain man when he traveled with the party of Captain B. L. E. Bonneville. Bonneville obtained a leave of absence from the army to engage in trading in 1831. He outfitted at Independence and traded as far west as Idaho. As a commercial venture his trip was a failure, and it added nothing to knowledge of the West, but it was highly productive of literary grist, for Irving wrote impressively of his trip with Bonneville and the sights he saw.

Washington Irving, *Adventures of Captain Bonneville, or Scenes Beyond the Rocky Mountains of the Far West*, 3 vols. (London: Richard Bentley, 1837), vol. II, pp. 109–135.

Leaving Captain Bonneville and his band ensconced within their fortified camp in the Green river valley, we shall step back and accompany a party of the Rocky Mountain Fur Company in its progress, with supplies from St. Louis, to the annual rendezvous at Pierre's Hole. This party consisted of sixty men, well mounted, and conducting a line of pack-horses. They were commanded by Captain William Sublette, a partner in the company, and one of the most active, intrepid, and renowned leaders in this half military kind of service. He was accompanied by his associate in business, and tried companion in danger, Mr. Robert Campbell, one of the pioneers of the trade beyond the mountains, who had commanded trapping parties there in times of the greatest peril.

As these worthy compeers were on their route to the frontier, they fell in with another expedition, likewise on its way to the mountains. This was a party of regular "down-easters," that is to say, people of New England, who, with the all penetrating, and all pervading spirit of their race, were now pushing their way into a new field of enterprise, with which they were totally unacquainted.

The party had been fitted out, and was maintained and commanded by Captain Nathaniel J. Wyeth, of Boston. This gentleman had conceived an idea, that a profitable fishery for salmon might be established on the Columbia River, and connected with the fur trade. He had, accordingly, invested capital in goods, calculated, as he supposed, for the Indian trade, and had enlisted a number of eastern men in his employ, who had never been in the far west, nor knew any thing of the wilderness. With these he was bravely steering his way across the continent, undismayed by danger, difficulty, or distance, in the same way that a New England coaster and his neighbours will cooly launch forth on a voyage to the Black sea, or a whaling cruise to the Pacific.

With all their national aptitude at expedient and resource, Captain Wyeth and his men felt themselves completely at a loss when they reached the frontier, and found that the wilder-

ness required experience and habitudes, of which they were
totally deficient. Not one of the party, except the leader, had
ever seen an Indian or handled a rifle; they were without guide
or interpreter, and totally unacquainted with "wood craft,"
and the modes of making their way among savage hordes,
and subsisting themselves, during long marches over wild
mountains and barren plains.

In this predicament, Captain Sublette found them, in a
manner becalmed, or rather run aground, at the little frontier town of Independence, in Missouri, and kindly took them
in tow. The two parties travelled amicably together; the frontier men of Sublette's party gave their Yankee comrades some
lessons in hunting, and some insight into the art and mystery
of dealing with the Indians, and they all arrived without accident at the upper branches of the Nebraska or Platte river.

In the course of their march, Mr. Fitzpatrick, the partner
of the company who was resident at that time beyond the
mountains, came down from the rendezvous at Pierre's Hole
to meet them, and hurry them forward. He travelled in company with them until they reached the Sweet Water; then
taking a couple of horses, one for the saddle, and the other
as a packhorse, he started off express for Pierre's Hole, to make
arrangements against their arrival, that he might commence
his hunting campaign before the rival company.

Fitzpatrick was a hardy and experienced mountaineer, and
knew all the passes and defiles. As he was pursuing his lonely
course up the Green river valley, he descried several horsemen
at a distance, and came to a halt to reconnoitre. He supposed
them to be some detachment from the rendezvous, or a party
of friendly Indians. They perceived him, and setting up the
war-whoop, dashed forward at full speed: he saw at once his
mistake and his peril—they were Blackfeet.

Springing upon his fleetest horse, and abandoning the other
to the enemy, he made for the mountains, and succeeded in
escaping up one of the most dangerous defiles. Here he concealed himself for a time, until he thought the Indians had
gone off, when he returned into the valley. He was again pur-

sued, lost his remaining horse, and only escaped by scrambling up among the cliffs. For several days he remained lurking among rocks and precipices, and almost famished, having but one remaining charge in his rifle, which he kept for self-defense.

In the meantime, Sublette and Campbell, with their fellow-traveller, Captain Wyeth, had pursued their march unmolested, and arrived in the Green river valley, totally unconscious that there was any lurking enemy at hand. They had encamped one night on the banks of a small stream, which came down from the Wind river mountains, when, about midnight, a band of Indians burst upon their camp, with horrible yells and whoops, and a discharge of guns and arrows. Happily no other harm was done than wounding one mule, and causing several horses to break loose from their pickets. The camp was instantly in arms; but the Indians retreated with yells of exultation, carrying off several of the horses, under covert of the night.

This was somewhat of a disagreeable foretaste of mountain life to some of Captain Wyeth's band, accustomed only to the regular and peaceful life of New England; nor was it altogether to the taste of Captain Sublette's men, who were chiefly creoles and townsmen from St. Louis. They continued their march the next morning, keeping scouts ahead and upon their flanks, and arrived without further molestation at Pierre's Hole.

The first inquiry of Captain Sublette, on reaching the rendezvous, was for Fitzpatrick. To his great concern he found he had not arrived, nor had any intelligence been received concerning him. Great uneasiness was now entertained, lest that gentleman should have fallen into the hands of the Blackfeet, who had made the midnight attack upon the camp. It was a matter of general joy, therefore, when he made his appearance, conducted by two half-breed Iroquois hunters. He had lurked for several days among the mountains, until almost starved; at length he escaped the vigilance of his enemies in the night, and was so fortunate as to meet the two Iroquois hunters, who, being on horseback, conveyed him without further difficulty to the rendezvous. He arrived there so emaciated, that he could scarcely be recognised.

The valley called Pierre's Hole, is about thirty miles in length, and fifteen in width, bounded to the west and south by low and broken ridges, and overlooked to the east by three lofty mountains, called the three Tetons, which domineer as landmarks over a vast extent of country.

A fine stream, fed by rivulets and mountain springs, pours through the valley towards the north, dividing it into nearly equal parts. The meadows on its borders are broad and extensive, covered with willow and cotton-wood trees, so closely interlocked and matted together, as to be nearly impassable.

In this valley was congregated the motley populace connected with the fur trade. Here the two rival companies had their encampments, with their retainers of all kinds: traders, trappers, hunters, and half-breeds, assembled from all quarters, awaiting their yearly supplies, and their orders to start off in new directions. Here, also, the savage tribes connected with the trade, the Nez Perces or Chopunnish Indians, and Flatheads, had pitched their lodges beside the streams, and with their squaws, awaited the distribution of goods and finery. There was, moreover, a band of fifteen free trappers, commanded by a gallant leader from Arkansas, named Sinclair, who held their encampment a little apart from the rest.

Such was the wild and heterogeneous assemblage, amounting to several hundred men, civilized and savage, distributed in tents and lodges in the several camps.

The arrival of Captain Sublette with supplies, put the Rocky Mountain Fur Company in full activity. The wares and merchandise were quickly opened, and as quickly disposed of to trappers and Indians; the usual excitement and revelry took place, after which, all hands began to disperse to their several destinations.

On the 17th of July, a small brigade of fourteen trappers, led by Milton Sublette, brother of the captain, set out with the intention of proceeding to the south-west. They were accompanied by Sinclair and his fifteen free trappers; Captain

Wyeth, also, and his New England band of beaver hunters
and salmon fishers, now dwindling down to eleven, took this
opportunity to prosecute their cruise in the wilderness, in company with such experienced pilots.

On the first day, they proceeded about eight miles to the
south-east, and encamped for the night, still in the valley of
Pierre's Hole. On the following morning, just as they were
raising their camp, they observed a long line of people pouring down a defile of the mountains. They at first supposed
them to be Fontenelle and his party, whose arrival had been
daily expected. Captain Wyeth, however, reconnoitred them
with a spyglass, and soon perceived they were Indians. They
were divided into two parties, forming, in the whole, about
one hundred and fifty persons, men, women, and children.
Some were on horseback, fantastically painted and arrayed,
with scarlet blankets fluttering in the wind. The greater part,
however, were on foot. They had perceived the trappers before
they were themselves discovered, and came down yelling
whooping into the plain. On nearer approach, they were
ascertained to be Blackfeet.

One of the trappers of Sublette's brigade, a half-breed,
named Antoine Godin, now mounted his horse, and rode forth
as if to hold a conference. He was the son of an Iroquois
hunter, who had been cruelly murdered by the Blackfeet, at
a small stream below the mountains, which still bears his
name. In company with Antoine rode forth a Flathead Indian,
whose once powerful tribe had been completely broken down
in their wars with the Blackfeet. Both of them, therefore,
cherished the most vengeful hostility against these marauders
of the mountains. The Blackfeet came to a halt. One of the
chiefs advanced singly and unarmed, bearing the pipe of
peace. This overture was certainly pacific; but Antoine and
the Flathead were predisposed to hostility, and pretended to
consider it a treacherous movement.

"Is your piece charged?" said Antoine to his red companion.
"It is."

"Then cock it, and follow me."

They met the Blackfoot chief half way, who extended his hand in friendship. Antoine grasped it.

"Fire!" cried he.

The Flathead levelled his piece, and brought the Blackfoot to the ground. Antoine snatched off his scarlet blanket, which was richly ornamented, and galloped off with it as a trophy to the camp, the bullets of the enemy whistling after him.

The Indians immediately threw themselves into the edge of a swamp, among willows and cotton-wood trees, interwoven with vines. Here they began to fortify themselves; the women digging a trench, and throwing up a breastwork of logs and branches, deep hid in the bosom of the wood, while the warriors skirmished at the edge to keep the trappers at bay.

The latter took their station in a ravine in front, from whence they kept up a scattering fire. As to Captain Wyeth, and his little band of "down-easters," they were perfectly astounded by this second specimen of life in the wilderness; the men being, especially, unused to bush-fighting and the use of the rifle, were at a loss how to proceed. Captain Wyeth, however, acted as a skillful commander. He got all his horses into camp and secured them; then, making a breastwork of his packs of goods, he charged his men to remain in garrison, and not to stir out of their fort. For himself, he mingled with the other leaders, determined to take his share in the conflict.

In the meantime, an express had been sent off to the rendezvous for reinforcements. Captain Sublette, and his associate, Campbell, were at their camp when the express came galloping across the plain, waving his cap, and giving the alarm; "Blackfeet! Blackfeet! a fight in the upper part of the valley!— to arms! to arms!"

The alarm was passed from camp to camp. It was a common cause. Every one turned out with horse and rifle. The Nez Perces and Flatheads joined. As fast as a horseman could arm and mount he galloped off; the valley was soon alive with white men and red men scouring at full speed.

Sublette ordered his men to keep to the camp, being recruits from St. Louis, unused to Indian warfare. He and his friend Campbell prepared for action. Throwing off their coats, rolling up their sleeves, and arming themselves with pistols and rifles, they mounted their horses and dashed forward among the first. As they rode along, they made their wills in soldierlike style; each stating how his effects should be disposed of in case of his death, and appointing the other his executor.

The Blackfeet warriors had supposed the brigade of Milton Sublette all the foe they had to deal with, and were astonished to behold the whole valley suddenly swarming with horsemen, galloping to the field of action. They withdrew into their fort, which was completely hid from sight in the dark and tangled wood. Most of their women and children had retreated to the mountains. The trappers now sallied forth and approached the swamp, firing into the thickets at random; the Blackfeet had a better sight at their adversaries, who were in the open field, and a half-breed was wounded in the shoulder.

When Captain Sublette arrived, he urged to penetrate the swamp and storm the fort, but all hung back in awe of the dismal horrors of the place, and the danger of attacking such desperadoes in their savage den. The very Indian allies, though accustomed to bush-fighting, regarded it as almost impenetrable, and full of frightful danger. Sublette was not to be turned from his purpose, but offered to lead the way into the swamp. Campbell stepped forward to accompany him.

Before entering the perilous wood, Sublette took his brothers aside, and told them that in case he fell, Campbell, who knew his will, was to be his executor. This done, he grasped his rifle and pushed into the thickets, followed by Campbell. Sinclair, the partisan from Arkansas, was at the edge of the wood with his brother and a few of his men. Excited by the gallant example of the two friends, he pressed forward to share their dangers.

The swamp was produced by the labours of the beaver, which, by damming up a stream, had inundated a portion of the valley. The place was all overgrown with woods and thickets, so closely matted and entangled, that it was impossible to see ten paces ahead, and the three associates in peril had to crawl along, one after another, making their way by putting the branches and vines aside; but doing it with caution, lest they should attract the eye of some lurking marksman. They took the lead by turns, each advancing about twenty yards at a time, and now and then hallooing to their men to follow. Some of the latter gradually entered the swamp, and followed a little distance in their rear.

They had now reached a more open part of the wood, and had glimpses of the rude fortress from between the trees. It was a mere breastwork, as we have said, of logs and branches, with blankets, buffalo robes, and the leathern covers of lodges, extended round the top as a screen. The movements of the leaders, as they groped their way, had been descried by the sharp-sighted enemy. As Sinclair, who was in the advance, was putting some branches aside, he was shot through the body. He fell on the spot. "Take me to my brother," said he to Campbell. The latter gave him in charge to some of the men, who conveyed him out of the swamp.

Sublette now took the advance. As he was reconnoitring the fort, he perceived an Indian peeping through an aperture. In an instant his rifle was levelled and discharged, and the ball struck the savage in the eye.

While he was reloading, he called to Campbell, and pointed out to him the hole; "Watch that place," said he, "and you will soon have a fair chance for a shot."

Scarce had he uttered the words, when a ball struck him in the shoulder, and almost wheeled him round. His first thought was to take hold of his arm with his other hand, and move it up and down. He ascertained to his satisfaction, that the bone was not broken. The next moment he was so faint that he could not stand. Campbell took him in his arms and carried him out of the thicket. The same shot that struck Sublette, wounded another man in the head.

A brisk fire was now opened by the mountaineers from the wood, answered occasionally from the fort. Unluckily, the trappers and their allies, in searching for the fort, had got scattered, so that Captain Wyeth, and a number of Nez Perces, approached the fort on the north-west side, while others did the same on the opposite quarter. A cross fire thus took place, which occasionally did mischief to friends as well as foes. An Indian was shot down, close to Captain Wyeth, by a ball which, he was convinced, had been sped from the rifle of a trapper on the other side of the fort.

The number of whites and their Indian allies, had by this time so much increased by arrivals from the rendezvous, that the Blackfeet were completely overmatched. They kept doggedly in their fort, however, making no offer of surrender.

An occasional firing into the breastwork was kept up during the day. Now and then, one of the Indian allies, in bravado, would rush up to the fort, fire over the ramparts, tear off a buffalo robe or a scarlet blanket, and return with it in triumph to his comrades. Most of the savage garrison that fell, however, were killed in the first part of the attack.

At one time it was resolved to set fire to the fort; and the squaws belonging to the allies, were employed to collect combustibles. This, however, was abandoned; the Nez Perces being unwilling to destroy the robes and blankets, and other spoils of the enemy, which they felt sure would fall into their hands.

58. The Rendezvous

General William H. Ashley, one of the principals of the Rocky Mountain Fur Company, was the organizer of the fur trading rendezvous that was held annually for six years in the region that is now southern Idaho and western Wyoming. These yearly assemblies were for the purpose of trading the year's catch for goods, buying supplies, debauching and frolicking. They were the trapper's holiday in which he broke the tedium of the long winter season, during much of which he had been holed up in a little cabin with no diversions whatever. For the trader they were a market for making a good profit—provided he got his goods to the rendezvous on time and was able to return safely to St. Louis with the packs of furs he purchased. Washington Irving accompanied Captain Bonneville to a rendezvous.

The Green river valley was at this time the scene of one of those general gatherings of traders, trappers, and Indians, that we have already mentioned. The three rival companies, which, for a year past had been endeavouring to out-trade, out-trap, and outwit each other, were here encamped in close proximity, awaiting their annual supplies. About four miles from the rendezvous of Captain Bonneville was that of the American Fur Company, hard by which, was that also of the Rocky Mountain Fur Company.

After the eager rivalry and almost hostility displayed by these companies in their late campaigns, it might be expected that, when thus brought in juxtaposition, they would hold themselves warily and sternly aloof from each other, and, should they happen to come in contact, brawl and bloodshed would ensue.

No such thing! Never did rival lawyers, after a wrangel at the bar, meet with more social goodhumour at a circuit dinner. The hunting season over, all past tricks and manoeuvres are forgotten, all feuds and bickerings buried in oblivion. From the middle of June to the middle of September, all trapping is suspended; for the beavers are then shedding their furs, and their skins are of little value. This, then, is the trapper's holiday, when he is all for fun and frolic, and ready for a saturnalia among the mountains.

At the present season, too, all parties were in good-humour. The year had been productive. Competition, by threatening to lessen their profits, had quickened their wits, roused their energies, and made them turn every favourable chance to the best advantage; so that, on assembling at their respective places of rendezvous, each company found itself in possession of a rich stock of peltries.

The leaders of the different companies, therefore, mingled on terms of perfect good fellowship; interchanging visits, and regaling each other in the best style their respective camps afforded. But the rich treat for the worthy captain was to see the "chivalry" of the various encampments, engaged in contests of skill at running, jumping, wrestling, shooting with the rifle, and running horses. And then their rough hunters' feastings and carousals. They drank together, they sang, they laughed, they whooped; they tried to outbrag and outlie each other in stories of their adventures and achievements. Here the free trappers were in all their glory; they considered themselves the "cocks of the walk," and always carried the highest crests. Now and then familiarity was pushed too far, and would effervesce into a brawl, and a "rough and tumble" fight; but it all ended in cordial reconciliation and maudlin endearment.

The presence of the Shoshonie tribe contributed occasionally to cause temporary jealousies and feuds. The Shoshonie beauties became objects of rivalry among some of the amorous mountaineers. Happy was the trapper who could muster up a red blanket, a string of gay beads, or a paper of precious vermilion, with which to win the smiles of a Shoshonie fair one.

The caravans of supplies arrived at the valley just at this period of gallantry and good fellowship. Now commenced a scene of eager competition and wild prodigality at the different encampments. Bales were hastily ripped open, and all their motley contents poured forth. A mania for purchasing spread itself throughout the several bands,—munitions for war, for hunting, for gallantry, were seized upon with equal avidity—rifles, hunting knives, traps, scarlet cloth, red blankets, garish beads, and glittering trinkets, were bought at any price, and scores run up without any thought how they were ever to be rubbed off. The free trappers, especially, were extravagant in their purchases. For a free mountaineer to pause at any paltry consideration of dollars and cents, in the attainment of any object that might strike his fancy, would stamp him with the mark of the beast in the estimation of his comrades. For a trader to refuse one of these free and flourishing blades a credit, whatever unpaid scores might stare him in the face, would be a flagrant affront scarcely to be forgiven.

Now succeeded another outbreak of revelry and extravagance. The trappers were newly fitted out and arrayed; and dashed about with their horses caparisoned in Indian style. The Shoshonie beauties also flaunted about in all the colours of the rainbow. A very freak of prodigality was indulged to its full extent, and in a little while most of the trappers having squandered away all their wages, and perhaps run knee deep in debt, were ready for another hard campaign in the wilderness.

During this season of folly and frolic, there was an alarm of mad wolves in the two lower camps. One or more of these animals entered the camps for three nights successively, and bit several of the people.

Captain Bonneville relates the case of an Indian, who was a universal favourite in the lower camp. He had been bitten by one of these animals. Being out with a party shortly afterwards, he grew silent and gloomy, and lagged behind the rest as if he wished to leave them. They halted and urged him to move faster, but he entreated them not to approach him, and, leaping from his horse, began to roll franticly on the earth, gnashing his teeth and foaming at the mouth. Still he retained his senses, and warned his companions not to come near him, as he should not be able to restrain himself from biting them. They hurried off to obtain relief; but on their return he was nowhere to be found. His horse and his accoutrements remained upon the spot. Three or four days afterwards, a solitary Indian, believed to be the same, was observed crossing a valley, and pursued; but he darted away into the fastnesses of the mountains, and was seen no more.

59. A Trip to the Prairies

An Italian nobleman Count Francesco Arese on a tour to the
United States penetrated deeply into the frontier. He saw the upper
Missouri country and traveled with the mountain men of John
Jacob Astor's American Fur Company. This urbane visitor to the
far western frontier was able to make penetrating observations on
life along the Missouri, and on the Indians. Traveling up the Missouri by steamboat in 1837 the Italian visitor was able to view the
widely opening gate of frontier transportation. Rapidly the steamboat was to replace the clumsy hand-propelled boats which had
been in use for almost a half century.

At last the boat was ready and I left. The deck gave an idea
of the sort of voyage the boat was setting out on: There were
anchors, chains, piles of rope, huge poles, planks, axes, and a
large beam to serve as a shore to hoist up the boat if it
grounded—a precaution which the sequel proved to be necessary. Except me, everybody aboard belonged to the American
Fur Company. Some of them were heads of factories and de-
pots, but the largest number was made up of hunters, trappers,
and voyageurs, mostly French, or to speak more precisely, of
French extraction, and well assorted for giving an idea of the
shades of human skin in Europeans—creoles, negroes, mulat-
tos of different degrees, half-breeds, and who knows what
not? A strict moralist or a Jesuit would term them lost souls;
but judging them less severely, one finds them good boys full
of life and activity, spry, in good trim, shrewd, and above all
preferring whisky to God, and not fearing the Devil so much
as the Indians' bullets and arrows. Certainly the life bristling
with danger, fatigue, and privation, which they lead for 11
months a year, gives them the right to make up to themselves

Conte Francesco Arese, *A Trip to the Prairies and in the Interior of
North America* (New York: The Harbor Press, 1934), 60–73.

for all that in the one month left them, during which they conscientiously follow the rule of spending everything they have earned the rest of the year. And why, after all, should they economize, not being very certain of coming back another time?

Despite distance, time, and the crossing of races, one recognizes in them the type of the Paris gamin: the same good humor under all circumstances, the same physical and moral elasticity: and I not only was pleased to see, but I enjoyed seeing that the *chahut* is not unknown in the New World.

Although their costumes are as bizarre as their behavior, they are not lacking in coquetry, especially in regard to their hair. Some like it very smooth and shiny like the Indians', others like to have long ringlets on their shoulders, for curling papers are not unknown among these men of the mountains and the forests. Their good-byes to their friends and acquaintances come to the levee to see them off on a journey they might well never return from, were much more comic than touching. It was like the conversations you hear in Carnival between the boxes and the gallery at the Franconi theatre.

The country from Saint Louis to where the Missouri enters the Mississippi is nothing startling; little towns and villages are scattered here and there on the river banks. I had supposed it impossible to find muddier, dirtier water than that of the Mississippi, but when I saw the Missouri, I was undeceived. I saw that it is the Missouri water that dirties the Mississippi, which is clean and clear above the junction. Our mountain streams after a Summer storm are as limpid as spring-water in comparison to the Missouri, which is almost chestnut in color: and the amount of earth and sand it carries is so great that a glass filled with its water at night is found in the morning to be one fourth sediment. And yet the water does not taste; it even is wholesome; it only requires a little courage to swallow it for a few days, and then one has the habit.

The currents of the two rivers run alongside each other

quite a distance before mingling. I have seen small rivers whose lovely clear water flowed in a solid stream through the Missouri, as if they avoided soiling their purity by touching the dark and muddy water of the big river.

The town of St. Charles makes a good appearance. After passing it you still for some while see villages. But farther up there are only log-houses, which is to say huts built of tree trunks. Soon after there are no dwellings, and will be no more to see before reaching Fort Leavenworth. The banks of the Missouri are flat and wooded. Only once in a while you see some limestone rocks which never are so much as a hundred feet high. One of these rocks, higher than the rest, which has a sort of cave in it, is known to the people thereabouts as *Tavern Rock,* and serves as a refuge for the crews of the flat-boats that go up and down the river.

Our trip as far as Fort Leavenworth went very well, although our keel frequently dragged along sand-bars, and now and then snags rubbed the sides of our boat. But we ran aground only one trifling time, and a very short while sufficed to set us afloat again. The next day a great roguish snag struck violently against the steamboat and water entered, and then the pump was working day and night, which is not particularly amusing, both because of the noise it makes, and because of the consequences that might ensue.

It would be perfectly impossible to have a captain better grounded, more active, more prudent, and at the same time more persistent than the one commanding the "St. Peter." He is a Mr. Pratte (son of the general of the same name), who is in charge of all the steamboats of the American Fur Company, of which he is one of the partners. It is purely to oblige his associates and to amuse himself that he is willing to take the job of commanding boats on the runs where a good captain is indispensable. He was one of the first to go in a steamboat as far up the Missouri as the Yellowstone. I will say nothing of his good nature, because having been overwhelmed by him with kindness and thoughtfulness, I should be too partial a judge; I will leave that to others who have

also had the good fortune of knowing him. Their judgment—
I have no doubt—will be the same as mine. But I really cannot refrain from speaking of the amazing cleverness of the
pilots, most of whom are half-breeds. In many places the river
was so clustered with snags that it really seemed as if it would
be absolutely impossible to find a way among them. The
difficulty was augmented by the strength of the current, which
made the effect of the tiller almost imperceptible. Despite all
of which our pilot has invariably steered his boat with the
same precision an able coachman would guide his vehicle
with. Sometimes the danger of collision was so great that
everybody was ready with axes and all other necessary implements in hand. But the only thing that was really alarming
for a moment was that 4 men on board were taken with terrible colic and vomiting. As there were in Saint Louis still
some few cases of cholera or cholerine, we thought that was
what ailed them.

What was very strange was that although everybody has
that idea, not a single mouth has pronounced the fatal word.
At the moment I write this, three of the men are nearly well
and the fourth is dying of an intestinal inflammation, according to what the captain tells me, and he is the ship's doctor.

Fort Leavenworth is the last American post. It has a regiment of dragoons and artillery to keep the savages respectful.
Some wretched barracks and a second-rate blockhouse is all
there is to what is called the military establishment. A long
time before we reached the fort, there were no more log-
houses of white men; and soon after the last one we began to
see Indians, who ran down to the shore to watch the steamboat go by. The evening of that day we called at a post of
the American Fur Company and landed the boss of the trading station, which is on the river bank. The boat was instantly flooded with savages, to whom tobacco and brandy
were given. They greeted the boss of the station affectionately,
wringing his hand and calling him "Papa, papa." They played
cards with great enthusiasm and even passion, and remained

on board very late that night; and three young Indian women
remained on board all night! . . . and with the consent of the
chief of the tribe. It was the tribe of Kickapoos.

The next day we saw a village of Sacs and Foxes, and that
night we stopped at Serpent Noir, a place inhabited by Iowas,
of whom we saw a few. At Fort Leavenworth there was a big
gathering of savages because it so happened that several chiefs
of different tribes were there then, who, on account of being
on their way to Washington to see the President, were all in
their finest costumes. But fine as they were, I much preferred
seeing them in lithographs. The first time I saw Indians and
was really, so to say, in contact with them, they caused me to
feel such disgust and fright (in Italian I would say *ribrezzo*,
but I do not know the equivalent word in French) as seemed
unconquerable; and I should never have suspected that within
three months I should be glad to sleep between two Indians
(males, of course), side by side so as to keep warm during a
night of North wind. Their heads are shaved except for one
little lock or a little queue, painted red and black, their faces
too painted in the same colors, and all shiny from the grease
that covered them. They are simply hideous. On their heads
they wear a lot of small feathers of various colors, and three
or four very long ones, standing up or hanging: to that they
add glass beads and pieces of deers' horn or bone; all of which
has some special meaning, and usually one referring to their
own exploits, that is, the number of men they have killed or
the number of horses they have stolen. In their ears, or around
them, they wear rings or strings of beads, under the weight
of which ornaments their ears bend down and sometimes are
completely closed, exactly like those of a hunting-dog.

These last few days we have seen several flocks of parakeets,
but of a small variety. They were entirely green except their
yellow heads. We have also seen a number of wild turkeys,
which are very much like our European turkeys, but larger
and of a very dark chestnut color and with a bunch of thick
hair, like horsehair, in the middle of the breast. At Black Snake

I saw some ducks much bigger than ours in Europe, with white, brown, and black plumage. In this part of the country they call them bustards, but they are totally different from the bustards I saw in Africa.

In conversations on board people told me two stories that show how insufficient the laws are in the United States, especially when public opinion is against them. A party of gamblers worked the Ohio and the Mississippi steamboats with great success. They reached Pittsburg (or Vicksburg, I don't remember which) and there the poor devils did very nicely—in fact too nicely, for the inhabitants massacred them in the most ruthless manner, and only two or three of the whole lot were able to run away. No legal attempt was made to punish a crime that cost the lives of a dozen people. The second story referred to Saint Louis. There somebody accused a negro of having tried to attack the constable, and another officer arrested him. As they were taking him to jail, the negro killed the two of them and got away. He was caught and put in jail. Before his trial friends and relatives of the constable went to the keeper and ordered him to turn the negro over to them. They got the poor chap and took him out of town to where they had a stake all ready. While they were lighting the fire, an elderly man remarked that the negro was going to be tried and would be found guilty and executed, and that consequently there was no need whatever for them to dirty their hands with blood, since the courts were there to see that he got the punishment his crime deserved. The answer he got to this was that if he didn't clear out right away, he would make a pair with the negro; and the honest man was obliged to pocket his philanthropy and trust to his legs, for otherwise he would certainly have shared the fate of the poor negro, who was cruelly burned slowly to death, without the public's trying to prevent it. Not the slightest attempt was made by the law to catch and punish the guilty. This took place in the Spring of 1836. I mention these two facts, because though I did not see them, they were related to me by persons seriously deserving to be believed. If one attempted to tell of all the outrages of that sort which have occurred, he would never finish.

To get back to my trip: when the boat stops at the trading posts, which are also called forts, it is very odd to see the hunters, trappers, and so on, who, before the boat is fast to the landing, jump over the railings and overrun the stockade, the field, and the house from cellar to garret. Maize, potatoes, everything, is looted, including dogs and cats; and all this is done in a flash, before the captain has time to call them back on board.

After 11 days on the Missouri we reached the Council Bluffs, which take their name from the fact that they used to be the place that served as a rendezvous for the Indians of the various tribes in the vicinity, who met there to hold war-councils. Today it is a trading post of the American Fur Company and consists of only three or four little houses and a few warehouses, the whole enclosed by a poorly built stockade. It is there that the Indians come to exchange furs and hides for cloth, beads, powder, lead, guns, and whisky, which they prefer to all the rest and which is given them in spite of a law forbidding it. It is furnished them not through cupidity, but for the sake of *morality* and in the *interests of the Indians*, or so one is told! (At Yellowstone the Company can buy a horse for two bottles of whisky, and it sells whisky to these men for 32 dollars a gallon). This is the explanation given: the Indians, they say, are mad for alcohol. If we do not furnish it to them, the ones in the North will go to get it from the Hudson Bay Company (an English company and therefore a rival of the American company's), and those in the South will go East to buy it at the first white settlement. To do either they must spend a long, long time, during which they abandon their families, do no hunting, and sell their goods to somebody else (and there you have the true explanation).

IX

Crossing the Continent

It would, of course, be unreasonable to pick out one aspect of the history of the westward movement and say this was the most exciting or significant. It is safe, however, to say that the era of long-range exploration and trailbreaking was one of immense excitement and meaning. The early trailbreakers served not only as the pathfinders across the continent, they were contemporary eyes through which the present day American gets a primary view of his continent. In the selections included in this segment nearly every journalist was within the context of his mission, a pioneer who was present at the opening of a new portion of the West.

Stephen Long and his party not only had the privilege of being scientific and official explorers and trailbreakers, they recorded in their famous reports some of the notions that Americans were to hold for almost a century about the physiographical nature of much of the continent. They as much as any other Americans created the myth of the "Great American Desert" which was to create a strange psychological barrier for Americans for at least two generations.

Once the domestic phase of the transcontinental folk movement got under way, an old dimension in a new and more expansive geographical setting was introduced to exploring and settling of the Trans-Mississippi West. In a sense the covered wagon became truly a vessel of exploration and travel for parties who moved families, meager property, and social mores across the land. Accompanying these early caravans were the makings for new cultural and domestic islands on the far-flung frontier beyond the Rockies. Edwin Bryant, a Louisville newspaper man, recorded eloquent descriptions of all the complexities of trying to transfer intact a semi-organized community over such vast distances, and with such severely limited knowledge of what the land and the elements offered in the way of divisive forces and hardships. No part of the westward movement touched the heartstrings of Americans so much as this domestic experience of people suspended between the two continental poles of settled society.

Before the wagon trains could fill the North and far West with population, the excitement of the Gold Rush not only added numbers to the movement, but likewise added speed, experience, and a dimension of geographical specificity. Certainly the Gold Rush with its myriad journals and personal accounts closed any information gap about the West which may have existed. Elisha Douglas Perkins was but one observer in this vast throng, but his journal hits close to the heart of this phase of western adventure with all of its intensive folk aspects.

Men like Samuel L. Clemens and A. D. Richardson saw the West through the discerning eyes of roving journalists. Clemens experienced the rawness of road travel on the way to an even rawer mining frontier, while Richardson viewed the land as the home of new settlers who came directly into both contact and conflict with the forces of nature. Both of these authors presented eloquent descriptions of life on a frontier that was evolving with all the strains and trauma of birth itself.

The far western trailbreakers and journalists were blood first-cousins to those who had come through Cumberland Gap less than a century before. They documented the fact that pioneer expansion across the vast North American Continent was part of a seamless web which duplicated, with but slight restringing of the loom of history, the designs that were set as far back on the trails as the valleys of Pennsylvania, New York, Virginia, and the Carolinas. Out of this basic experience came the roots at least of the heroics attached to pioneering of a people imbued with the hard challenge of a wilful land. This is the central theme of a large body of contemporary materials, written and published with a sense that they in fact documented the expansion of the Republic itself.

60. The Great Plains Above the Arkansas

The period 1815 to 1840 saw the emergence of a number of western military explorers. Chief among them was Major Stephen H. Long. In 1819 he commanded the most ambitious expedition to be sent to the far West since that of Lewis and Clark. And for the next several years he accumulated a body of data which finally became a major report on the West. With its publication, an American, for the first time, could get a dependable assessment of that part of his country which lay immediately east of the Rockies.

Aside from the vast herds of bisons which it contains, the country along the Platte is enlivened by great numbers of deer, badgers, hares, prairie wolves, eagles, buzzards, ravens, and owls: these, with its rare and interesting plants, in some measure relieved the uniformity of its cheerless scenery. We found a constant source of amusement in observing the unsightly figure, the cumbrous gait, the impolitic movements of the bison; we were often delighted by the beauty and fleetness of the antelope, and the social comfort and neatness of the prairie dog.

This barren and ungenial district appeared, at this time, to be filled with greater numbers of animals than its meagre productions are sufficient to support. It was, however, manifest that the bisons, then thronging in such numbers, were moving towards the south. Experience may have taught them to repair at certain seasons to the more luxuriant plains of Arkansa and Red river. What should ever prompt them to return to the inhospitable deserts of the Platte, it is not perhaps, easy to conjecture. In whatever direction they move, their parasites and dependants fail not to follow. Large herds are invariably attended by gangs of meagre, famine-pinched wolves, and flights of obscene and ravenous birds.

Stephen H. Long, "Account of an Expedition from Pittsburgh to the Rocky Mountains . . . ," Thwaites, ed., *Early Western Travels, 1748–1846,* vol. II, pp. 247–258.

We have frequently remarked broad shallow excavations in the soil, of the diameter of from five to eight feet, and greatest depth from six inches to eighteen. These are of rare occurrence near the Missouri, as far as Engineer cantonment, and in other districts where the bison is seldom seen at the present day; and when they do exist there, they are overgrown by grass and nearly obliterated. As you approach the country, still the constant residence of these animals, the excavations become more numerous, and are less productive of grass. They now are so numerous as to be of constant recurrence, offering a considerable impediment to the traveller, who winds his way amongst them, and are entirely destitute of grass, their surface being covered with a deep dust. Until recently, we had no opportunity to observe the cause which gives rise to these appearances; but we were now convinced that they were the result of the habit which the bulls have, in common with the domestic bull, of scraping up the earth with their fore feet, in the process of dusting themselves: they serve also as places for rolling and wallowing; a gratification which the bison bull indulges in as frequently, and in the same manner as the horse.

Some extensive tracts of land along the Platte, particularly those portions which are a little elevated, with an undulating or broken surface, are almost exclusively occupied by a scattered growth of several species of wormwood, (artemisia) some of which are common to this country, and that on the lower Missouri: we may enumerate the following—A. ludoviciana, A. longifolia, A. serrata, A. columbiensis, A. cernua, A. canadensis; most of these species have simple or finely divided compound leaves, which are long and slender, and canescent, like those of the A. absynthium, the common wormwood of the gardens. The peculiar aromatic scent, and the flavor of this well known plant, is recognized in all the species we have mentioned. Several of them are eaten by the bisons, and our horses were sometimes reduced to the necessity of feeding upon them.

The intense reflection of light and heat from the surface of many tracts of naked sand, which we crossed, added much to the fatigue and suffering of our journey. We often met with extensive districts covered entirely with loose and fine sand blown from the adjacent hills. In the low plains along the river, where the soil is permanent, it is highly impregnated with saline substances, and too sterile to produce any thing except a few stinted carices and rushes.

On the evening of the twenty-fourth, after we had en-camped, several bull bisons, being on the windward side, came so near us as to create a disturbance among our horses, who were not yet so familiarized to the formidable appearance of those animals, as to regard their near approach with indiffer-ence. The bulls at length became troublesome, approaching so near to smell at the horses, that some of the latter broke the cords by which they were fastened, and made their escape. A man was then sent to frighten away the bisons, who, in their turn, exhibited as much terror as they had occasioned to our horses.

. . . 26th. The weather had now been for some days fair. As we approached the mountains, we felt or fancied, a very mani-fest change in the character of the weather, and the tempera-ture of the air. Mornings and evenings were usually calm, and the heat more oppressive than in the middle of the day. Early in the forenoon, a light and refreshing breeze often sprung up, blowing from the west or south-west, which again subsided on the approach of night. This phenomenon was so often observed that we were induced to attribute it to the operation of the same local cause, which in the neighbourhood of the sea, pro-duces a diurnal change in the winds, which blow alternately to and from the shore. The Rocky Mountains may be con-sidered as forming the shore of that sea of sand, which is traversed by the Platte, and extends northward to the Missouri, above the great bend.

The rarefaction of the air over this great plain, by the rever-beration of the sun's rays during the day, causes an ascending current, which is supplied by the rushing down of the con-densed air from the mountains. Though the sun's rays in the middle of the day were scorching and extremely afflictive to

our eyes, the temperature of the air, as indicated by the ther-
mometer, had hitherto rarely exceeded 80° Fah.

In the forenoon we passed a range of hills more elevated
than any we had seen west of the Missouri. These hills cross
the Platte from north to south, and though inconsiderable in
magnitude, they can be distinguished extending several miles
on each side of the river. They consist principally of gravel,
intermixed with small waterworn fragments of granite and
other primitive rock, but are based on a stratum of coarse friable sand-stone, of a dark gray colour, which has been uncovered, and cut through by the bed of the Platte.

This range may perhaps be a continuation or spur from the
black hills mentioned by Lewis and Clarke, as containing the
sources of the Shienne, and other tributaries to the Missouri,
at no great distance to the north of the place where we now
were.

At evening we arrived at another scattering grove of cottonwood trees, among which we placed our camp, immediately
on the brink of the river. The trees of which these insulated
groves are usually composed, from their low and branching
figure, and their remoteness from each other, as they stand
scattered over the soil they occupy, revived strongly in our
minds the appearance and gratifications resulting from an
apple orchard; for which from a little distance they might
readily be mistaken, if seen in a cultivated region. At a few
rods distant on our right hand, was a fortified Indian camp,
which appeared to have been recently occupied. It was constructed of such broken half-decayed logs of wood as the place
afforded, intermixed with some skeletons of bisons recently
killed. It is of a circular form, enclosing space enough for
about thirty men to lie down upon. The wall is about five feet
high, with an opening towards the east, and the top uncovered.

At a little distance in front of the entrance of this breastwork, was a semicircular row of sixteen bisons skulls, with their
noses pointing down the river. Near the centre of the circle
which this row would describe, if continued, was another skull
marked with a number of red lines.

Our interpreter informed us that this arrangement of skulls and other marks here discovered, were designed to communicate the following information, namely, that the camp had been occupied by a war party of the Skeeree or Pawnee Loup Indians, who had lately come from an excursion against the Cumancias, Ietans, or some of the western tribes. The number of red lines traced on the painted skull indicated the number of the party to have been thirty-six; the position in which the skulls were placed, that they were on their return to their own country. Two small rods stuck in the ground, with a few hairs tied in two parcels to the end of each, signified that four scalps had been taken.

A record of facts, which may be important and interesting to others, is thus left for the benefit of all who may follow. For our part we were glad to be informed, that one lawless and predatory band of savages had lately left the country we were about to traverse. We were never without some anxiety on the subject of Indian war-parties; who are known frequently to remunerate themselves for any discomfiture or loss they may have sustained, by making free booty of the property and the scalps of the first weak or unguarded party they may meet.

At a late hour in the night, after our camp had become quiet, we were suddenly awakened by a loud rushing noise, which in a moment seemed to reach the centre of our encampment; immediately a piercing exclamation of terror was heard from one of our interpreters, which, from the peculiarity of its tone, seemed to have escaped from a throat under the grasp of death. It became immediately apparent that the cause of the alarm proceeded from our horses, all of whom had broken loose from their stakes, near the Indian fort, and had run in a state of fright through our camp, with the apparent desire to gain our protection against something in their rear. We proceeded in a cautious manner to reconnoitre the environs of the camp, stooping low, in order that the eye might be directed along the level of the top of the grass, which was here of a very luxuriant growth, in order to detect in the gloom, any inimical object that might rise above it; having thus convinced ourselves that nothing dangerous to our safety remained very near to us, the horses were again secured, and we betook ourselves to our beds, with the reflection, that they had probably been alarmed by the too near approach of bisons.

We had scarce fallen asleep, when we were aroused the second time, by the discharge of a gun close to our tent. This was the signal which we had all understood was to be given by the sentinel, in case of the hostile approach of Indians to the camp. We therefore bestirred ourselves, being well assured we had other business at hand, than the securing of horses. Several of the party went to reconnoitre the old fort above mentioned, but nothing was discovered and they returned.

After all were assembled at camp, Major Long informed us the alarm had been given by his order, and was intended to test the coolness and self-possession of the party, and to prepare us in some measure for an unpleasant occurrence, we all thought too likely to happen, which was no other than a serious attack from the Indians, to be made according to their custom at that highly unseasonable hour of the morning.

Since leaving the Missouri, we had never indulged a disposition to sluggishness, accustoming ourselves to rise every morning long before the sun; but we still found we left that small spot of earth, on which we had rested our limbs, and which had become warm and dry by the heat of our bodies, with as much reluctance as we have felt at quitting softer beds.

The mode of rallying now prescribed was the following; immediately after an alarm should be given, the party should seize their arms, and form in front of the tents, in the rear of the line of packs, and await any orders that might be given. The sentinel giving the alarm should proceed to the tent of the officers, in order to acquaint them with the cause. Major Long and Captain Bell should reconnoitre about the encampment, and if practicable ascertain the real occasion of the alarm. Farther movements to be regulated as the emergency might require.

This alarm was the occasion of our starting on the morning of the 26th at an earlier hour than usual. We rode on through the same uninteresting and dreary country as before, but were constantly amused at observing the motions of the countless thousands of bisons, by which we were all the time surrounded. The wind happening to blow fresh from the south, the scent of our party was borne directly across the Platte, and we could distinctly note every step of its progress through a distance of eight or ten miles, by the consternation and terror it excited among the buffaloes. The moment the tainted gale infected their atmosphere, they ran with as much violence as if pursued by a party of mounted hunters, and instead of running from the danger, turned their heads towards the wind; eager to escape from the terrifying scent, they pushed forward in an oblique direction towards our party, and plunging into the river they swam and waded, and ran with the utmost violence, in several instances breaking through our line of march, which was immediately along the left bank of the Platte.

It is remarked by hunters, and appears to be an established fact, that the odour of a white man is more terrifying to wild animals, particularly the bison, than that of an Indian. This animal, in the course of its periodic migrations, comes into the immediate neighbourhood of the permanent Indian villages, on the Missouri and the Platte. One was seen by our hunters within six miles of the Grand Pawnee village, and immediately about the towns we saw many heads and skeletons of such as had been killed there the preceding spring. They had come in while the Pawnees were absent on their winter's hunt, and at their return, we were informed, they found the bisons immediately about their villages. They disappeared invariably from the neighbourhood of the white settlements within a few years. We are aware that another cause may be found for this than the frightful scent of the white man, which is, the impolitic exterminating war which he wages against all unsubdued animals within his reach.

It would be highly desirable that some law for the preservation of game might be extended to, and rigidly enforced in the country where the bison is still met with; that the wanton destruction of these valuable animals, by the white hunters, might be checked or prevented. It is common for hunters to attack large herds of these animals, and having slaughtered as many as they are able, from mere wantonness and love of this barbarous sport, to leave the carcasses to be devoured by the wolves and birds of prey; thousands are slaughtered yearly, of which no part is saved except the tongues. This inconsiderate and cruel practice is undoubtedly the principal reason why the bison flies so far and so soon from the neighbourhood of our frontier settlements.

It is well known to those in the least degree conversant with the Indians, that the odour which their bodies exhale, though very strong and peculiar, is by no means unpleasant, at least to most persons. A negro in the employment of the Missouri Fur Company, and living at Fort Lisa, was often heard to complain of the intolerable scent of the squaws; in like manner, the Indians find the odour of a white man extremely offensive. In the language of the Peruvian Indians, are three words to express their idea of the smell of the European, the aboriginal American, and the negro. They call the first *Pezuna*, the second *Posco*, and the third *Grajo*.

After passing the range of hills above mentioned, the surface subsides nearly to a plain, having, however, manifestly a greater inclination than below. The velocity of the current of the river is much increased, the bed narrower, and the banks more precipitous. We passed several extensive tracts nearly destitute of vegetation. The surface of these consisted entirely of coarse sand and gravel, with here and there an insulated mass of clay, highly impregnated with salt, and gnawed and licked into various singular shapes, exhibiting the forms of massive insulated columns, huge buttresses, prominent angles, which are now gradually diminishing, under the action of the cause which produced them. The present surface upon which they repose, seems to be a stratum of a different earth, which does not afford the condiment so attractive to the animals; the consequence is, that the licking and chewing, principally, heretofore, affecting the surface on which the animal stood, is now directed against the upright portions of this singular grand excavation, and most remarkable of all known salt-licks.

Some extensive portions of the immediate bottom land, along the river, were white with an effloresced salt, but this being impure and but imperfectly soluble, did not appear to have been licked.

61. Salt Flats and Mirages

On August 3, 1846, Edwin Bryant's famous overland party reached the edge of the awesome Great Salt Desert and salt flats of Utah. They had made the journey up the Platte, across the Wyoming plains, over the Snowy Range, through the South Pass, and down Weber Canyon to the Great Salt Lake. Along most of the way, they had found both water and grass. Except for the great hardships of traveling down in the canyon, they had not known what it was like to endure the rugged environment of the western country to the crest of the western Sierras. Before them one morning lay some of the most treacherous country that any traveler had ever traversed on the North American Continent. They were to contend with salt flats, lack of water, grass, and food. Along the way they were to meet the miserable Digger Indians who introduced them to the lowest form of human subsistence on the continent. There are few more dramatic descriptions of the rigors of travel in the arid lands beyond the Salt Lake.

I rose from my bivouac this morning at half past one o'clock. The moon appearing like a ball of fire, and shining with a dim and baleful light, seemed struggling downwards through the thick bank of smoky vapor that overhung and curtained the high ridge of mountains west of us. The ridge, stretching far to the north and the south as the eye can reach, forms the western wall (if I may so call it) of the desert valley we had

Edwin Bryant, *What I Saw in California: Being the Journal of a Tour* (New York: D. Appleton and Company, 1848), 163–173.

crossed yesterday, and is composed of rugged, barren peaks
of dark basaltic rocks sometimes exhibiting mishapen outlines;
at others, towering upwards, and displaying a variety of archi-
tectural forms, representing domes, spires, and turreted fortifications.

Our encampment was on the slope of the mountain; and the
valley lay spread out at our feet, illuminated sufficiently by
the red glare of the moon, and the more pallid effulgence of
the stars, to display imperfectly its broken and frightful bar-
reness, and its solemn desolation. No life, except in the little
oasis occupied by our camp, and dampened by the sluggish
spring, by excavating which with our hands we had obtained
impure water sufficient to quench our own and our animal's
thirst, existed as far as the eye could penetrate over the mountain and plain. There was no voice of animal, no hum of insect,
disturbing the tomb-like solemnity. All was silence and death.
The atmosphere, chill and frosty, seemed to sympathise with
this sepulchral stillness. No wailing or whispering sounds sighed
through the chasms of the mountains, or over the gulf and
waterless ravines of the valley. No rustling zephyrs swept over
the scant dead grass, or disturbed the crumbling leaves of the
gnarled and stunted cedars, which seemed to draw a precarious
existence from the small patch of damp earth surrounding us.
Like the other elements sustaining animal and vegetable life,
the winds seemed stagnant and paralyzed by the universal
death around. I contemplated this scene of dismal and oppressive solitude until the moon sunk behind the mountain,
and object after object became shrouded in its shadow.

Rousing Mr. Jacob, who slept soundly, and after him the
other members of our party (nine in number), we commenced
our preparations for the long and much-dreaded march over
the great Salt Desert. Mr. Hudspeth, the gentleman who had
so kindly conducted us thus far from Fort Bridger as our pilot,
was to leave us at this point, for the purpose of exploring a
route for the emigrant wagons farther south. He was accompanied by three gentlemen, Messrs. Ferguson, Kirkwood, and
Minter. Consequently, from this time forward we are without

a guide, or any reliable index to our destination, except our course westward, until we strike Mary's river and the emigrant trail to California, which runs parallel with it, some two hundred miles distant. The march across the Salt Plain, without water or grass, was variously estimated by those with whom I conversed at Fort Bridger, at from sixty to eighty miles. Captain Walker, an old and experienced mountaineer, who had crossed it at this point as the guide of Captain Frémont and his party, estimated the distance at seventy-five miles, and we found the estimate to be nearly correct.

We gathered the dead limbs of the cedar which had been cut down by Captain Frémont's party when encamped here last autumn, and igniting them, they gave us a good light during the preparation and discussion of our frugal breakfast; which consisted today of bread and coffee, bacon being interdicted in consequence of its incitement to thirst– a sensation which at this time we desired to avoid, as we felt uncertain how long it might be before we should be able to gratify the unpleasant cravings it produces.

Each individual of the party busied himself around the blazing fires in making his various little but unimportant arrangements, until the first gray of the dawn manifested itself above the vapory bank overhanging the eastern ridge of mountains, when the word to saddle up being given, the mules were brought to the camp fires, and every arm and muscle of the party was actively employed in the business of saddling and packing "with care!"—with unusual care, as a short detention during the day's march to readjust the packs might result in an encampment upon the desert for the coming night, and all its consequent dangers, the death or loss by straying in search of water and grass of our mules, (next to death to us,) not taking into the account our own suffering from thirst, which for the next eighteen or twenty hours we had made up our minds to endure with philosophical fortitude and resignation. A small powder-keg, holding about three or four pints of coffee, which had been emptied of its original contents for the purpose, and filled with that beverage made from the brackish

spring near our camp, was the only vessel we possesed in which
we could transport water, and its contents composed our entire
liquid refreshment for the march. Instructions were given to
Miller, who had charge of this important and precious burden,
to husband it with miserly care, and to make an equitable
division whenever it should be called into use.

Everything being ready, Mr. Hudspeth, who accompanied
us to the summit of the mountain, led the way. We passed
upwards through the *Cañada* (pronounced Kanyeada) or
mountain gorge, at the mouth of which we had encamped, and
by a comparatively easy and smooth ascent reached the summit
of the mountain after traveling about six miles. Most of us were
shivering with cold, until the sun shone broadly upon us after
emerging, by a steep acclivity, from the gorge through which
we had passed to the top of the ridge. Here we should have
had a view of the mountain at the foot of which our day's
journey was to terminate, but for the dense smoke which hung
over and filled the plain, shutting from the vision all distant
objects.

Bidding farewell to Mr. Hudspeth and the gentleman with
him (Mr. Ferguson,) we commenced the descent of the mountain. We had scarcely parted from Mr. H. when, standing on
one of the peaks, he stretched out his long arms, and with a
voice and gesture as loud and impressive as he could make
them, called to us and exclaimed– "Now, boys, put spurs to
your mules and ride like hell!" The hint was timely given and
well meant, but scarcely necessary, as we all had a pretty just
appreciation of the trials and hardships before us.

The descent from the mountain on the western side was more
difficult than the ascent; but two or three miles, by a winding
and precipitous path through some straggling, stunted, and
tempest-bowed cedars, brought us to the foot and into the
valley where, after some search, we found a blind trail which
we supposed to be that of Captain Frémont, made last year.
Our course for the day was nearly due west; and following this
trail where it was visible, and did not deviate from our course,
and putting our mules into a brisk gait, we crossed a valley

some eight or ten miles in width, sparsely covered with wild sage (artemisia) and grease-wood. These shrubs display themselves and maintain a dying existence, a brownish verdure, on the most arid and sterile plains and mountains of the desert, where no other vegetation shows itself. After crossing the valley, we rose a ridge of low volcanic hills, thickly strewn with sharp fragments of basaltes and a vitreous gravel resembling junk-bottle glass. We passed over this ridge through a narrow gap, the walls of which are perpendicular, and composed of the same dark scorious materials as the debris strewn around. From the western terminus of this ominous-looking passage we had a view of the vast desert-plain before us, which, as far as the eye could penetrate, was a snowy whiteness, and resembled a scene of wintry frosts and icy desolation. Not a shrub or object of any kind rose above the surface for the eye to rest upon. The hiatus in the animal and vegetable kingdoms was perfect. It was a scene which excited mingled emotions of admiration and apprehension.

Passing a little further on, we stood on the brow of a steep precipice, the descent from the ridge of hills immediately below and beyond which a narrow valley or depression in the surface of the plain, about five miles in width, displayed so perfectly the wavy and frothy appearance of highly agitated water, the Colonel Russell and myself, who were riding together some distance in advance, both simultaneously exclaimed– "We must have taken a wrong course, and struck another arm or bay of the Great Salt Lake." With deep concern, we were looking around, surveying the face of the country to ascertain what remedy there might be for this formidable obstruction to our progress, when the remainder of our party came up. The difficulty was presented to them; but soon, upon a more calm and scrutinizing inspection, we discovered that what represented so perfectly the "rushing waters" was moveless, and made no sound! The illusion soon became manifest to all of us, and a hearty laugh at those who were the first to be deceived was the consequence; denying to them the merit of being good pilots or pioneers, etc.

62.   An Approach to the Southwest

By 1846 the road to Santa Fe was well known. Literally hundreds of travelers and traders had gone from Independence, Missouri to the Mexican city at the end of the sprawling southwestern trail. Many of them left accounts of their experiences on the way, and in the Mexican town assembled about its great cathedral. Buried in a drab governmental report is the graphic account of Lieutenant Colonel W. H. Emory's travels with the forces of Kearney and Doniphan in 1846. The colonel was more than a casual military traveler plugging along behind a dust laden army. He saw the countryside in vivid outline, and at the end of the trail was present at what amounted to the capitulation of Santa Fe.

August 2, 1846.– I looked in the direction of Bent's Fort, and saw a huge United States flag flowing to the breeze, and straining every fibre of an ash pole planted over the centre of a gate. The mystery was soon revealed by a column of dust to the east, advancing with the velocity of a fast walking horse– it was "the Army of the West." I ordered my horse to be hitched up, and, as the column passed, took my place with the staff.

A little below the fort, the river, where its bed slides over a black carbonaceous shale, which has been mistaken for coal, and induced some persons to dig for it.

Here we turned to the left, and pursued our course over an arid elevated plain for twenty miles without water. When we reached the Timpas, we found the water in puddles, and the grass bad.

Colonel Doniphan was ordered to pursue the Arkansas to near the mouth of the Timpas, and rejoin the army by following the bed of the stream.

W. H. Emory, *Notes of a Military Reconnoissance, from Fort Leavenworth in Missouri to San Diego in California* (Washington: Wendell and Van Bethuysen, 1848), 15–26.

Near where we left the Arkansas, we found on the other side of the slope several singular demi-spheroids, about the size of an umbrella, coated with carbonate of lime, in pyramids of crystals, which at a distance, resembled the bubbles of a huge boiling cauldron.

Along the Arkansas the principal growth consists of very coarse grass, and a few cotton woods, willows, and euphorbia marginata. The plains are covered with very short grass, sesleria dactyloides, now burnt to a cinder; artemisia, in abundance; Fremontia vermicularis; yucca augustifolia, palmillo, of the Spaniards; verbena; eurotia lanata, and a few menzelia nuda.

The only animals seen were one black-tailed rabbit and an antelope; both of which were killed.

Our march was 26 miles, that of the army 37; the last twenty miles without water.

The artillery arrived about 11 p.m.; both men and horses were parched with thirst. The teamsters, who had to encounter the dust, suffered very much. When water was near, they sprang from their seats and ran for it like mad men. Two sank under this day's march.

Our ascent was considerable today. The height, indicated by the barometer, being 4,523 feet above the level of the sea.

August 3.– We ascended the Timpas six and three quarter miles. Passing the rear wagons of the infantry, we found their horses almost worn out, and the teams followed by wolves.

Captain Cook of the 1st dragoons, was sent ahead the day before yesterday, to sound Armijo. Mr. Liffendorfer, a trader, married to a Santa Fé lady, was sent in the direction of Taos, with two Pueblo Indians, to feel the pulse of the Pueblos and the Mexican people, and, probably, to buy wheat if any could be purchased, and to distribute the proclamations of the colonel commanding.

Yesterday Wm. Bent, and six others, forming a spy-guard, were sent forward to reconnoitre the mountain passes. In this company was Mr. F. P. Blair, Jr., who had been in this country some months, for the benefit of his health. . . .

August 6.– Colonel Kearney left Colonel Doniphan's regiment and Major Clark's artillery at our old camp-ground of
last night, and scattered Sumner's dragoons three or four miles
up the creek, to pass the day in renovating the animals by nips
at the little bunches of grass spread at intervals in the valley,
with the Raton towering to the left. Pine trees (pinus rifida)
here obtain a respectable size, and lined the valley through
the whole day's march. A few oaks, (quercus olivaformis) big
enough for axles, were found near the halting place tonight.
When we left the camp this morning, we saw several clumps
of the piñon, (pinus monophyllus.) It bears a resinous nut,
eaten by Mexicans and Indians. We found also lamita in great
abundance. It resembles the wild currant, and is, probably,
one of its varieties; grows to the height of several feet, and
bears a red berry, which is gathered, dried, pounded, and then
mixed with sugar and water, making a very pleasant drink, resembling currant cordial. We were unfortunate in not being
able to get either the fruit or flower. Neither this plant, the
piñon, nor any of the plum trees, or grape vines, had any fruit
on them; which is attributable to the excessive drought. The
stream, which last year was a rushing torrent, is this year dry,
and in pools.

The view from our camp is unexpressibly beautiful, and reminds persons of the landscapes of Palestine. . . .

The rocks of the mountain were chiefly a light sandstone–
in strata not far from the horizontal; and the road covered with
many fragments of volcanic rocks, of purplish brown color,
porous, and melting over a slow fire.

The road is well located. The general appearance is something like the pass at the summit of the Boston and Albany
railroad, but the scenery bolder, and less adorned with vegetation.

An express returned from the spy-guard, which reported all
clear in front. Captain Cook and Mr. Liffendorfer have only
reached the Canadian river. It was reported to me that, at
Captain Sumner's camp, about 7 miles above where we encamped last night, and 12 miles from the summit, an intense

field of coal crops out; the seam being 30 feet deep. Tonight our animals were refreshed with good grass and water. . . .

August 7, camp 36.– We recommenced the ascent of the Raton which we reached with ease, with our wagons, in about two miles. The height of this point above the sea, as indicated by the barometer, is 7,500 feet. From the summit we had a beautiful view of Pike's Peak, the Whattahyah, and the chain of mountains running south from the Whattahyah. Several large white masses were discernible near the summits of the range, which we at first took for snow, but which, on examination with the telescope, were found to consist of white limestone, or granular quartz, of which we afterwards saw so much in this country. As we drew near, the view was no less imposing. To the east rose Raton, which appeared still as high as from the camp, 1,500 feet below. On the top of the Raton the geological formation is very singular, presenting the appearance of a succession of castles. As a day would be required to visit it, I was obliged to forego that pleasure, and examine it merely with the glass. The mountain appears to be formed chiefly of sandstone, disposed in strata of various shades of color, dipping gently to the east, until you reach near the summit, where the castellated appearance commences, the sides become perpendicular, and the seams vertical. The valley is strewed with pebbles and fragments of trap rock, and the fusible rock described yesterday, cellular lava, and some pumice.

For two days our way was strewn with flowers, exhilirated by the ascent, the green foliage of the trees in striking contrast with the deserts we had left behind, they were the most agreeable days of the journey. . . .

The descent is much more rapid than the ascent, and, for the first few miles, through a valley of good burned grass and stagnant water, containing many beautiful flowers. But frequently you come to a place where the stream (a branch of the Canadian) has worked itself through the mountains, and the road has to ascend and then descend in a sharp spur. Here the difficulties commence; and the road, for three or four miles, is just passable for a wagon; many of the trains were broken in the passage. A few thousand dollars judiciously expended here, would be an immense saving to the government if the Santa Fé country is to be permanently occupied, and Bent's Fort road adopted. A few miles from the summit we reached a wide valley where the mountains open out, and the inhospitable looking hills recede to a respectable distance to the left and right. Sixteen miles from camp 36 brought us to the main branch of the Canadian, a slow-running stream, discharging a volume of water the thickness of a man's waist. We found here Bent's camp. I dismounted under the shade of a cotton wood, near an ant hill, and saw something black which had been thrown out by the busy little insects; and, on examination, found it to be bituminous coal, lumps of which afterwards were found thickly scattered over the plain. After crossing the river, and proceeding about a mile and a quarter, I found the party from which I had become separated encamped on the river, with a plentiful supply of grass, wood, and water, and here we saw, for the first time, a few sprigs of the famous gama. . . .

The growth on today's march was piñon in small quantities, scrub oak, scrub pine, a few lamita bushes, and, on the Canadian, a few cottonwood trees; except at the camp, there was little or no grass. The evening threatened rain, but the clouds passed away, and we had a good night for observations. We have had no rain since we left cow creeks, thirty days ago.

We are now in what may be called the paradise of that part of the country between Bent's Fort and San Miguel; and yet he who leaves the edge of the Canadian or its tributaries must make a good day's march to find wood, water, or grass. . . .

Today commenced our half rations of bread; though not suffering for meat, we are anxious to seize on Santa Fé and its stock of provisions as soon as possible. . . .

August 9.– We broke up camp at 2½ o'clock, and marched with the colonel's staff and the first dragoons 10½ miles, and encamped under the mountains on the western side of the Canadian, on the banks of a small stream, a tributary of the Canadian. The grass was short, but good; the water in small quantities, and in puddles. Here we found a trap-dyke– course north 83 west– which shows itself on the Canadian, about four miles distant in the same course.

At the distance of six miles from last night's camp, the road forks– one fork running near the mountains to the west, but nearly parallel to the old road, and never distant more than four miles, and almost all the time in sight of it. The army was divided– the artillery, infantry, and wagon train ordered to take the lower, and the Missouri volunteers and the first dragoons the upper road. The valley here opens out into an extensive plain, slightly rolling, flanked on each side by ranges of perpendicular hills covered with stunted cedar and the piñon. In this extensive valley or plain may be traced by the eye, from any of the neighboring heights the valley of the Canadian and its tributaries, the Vermejo, the Poni, the Little Cimarron, the Rayada, and the Ocaté. We saw troops of antelopes, horses, deer &c.; also cacti in great abundance, and in every variety; also a plant which Dr. De Camp pointed out as being highly balsamic; and having collected quantities of it during his campaign to the Rocky Mountains, and tested its efficacy as a substitute for balsam crop.

Tonight we observed great numbers of insects, the first remarked since leaving the Arkansas. Birds were equally rare, with the exception of the cow bunting, which has been seen in great numbers on the whole route, and in a state so tame as to often alight on our horses. The horned frog (agama cornuta) also abounds here, as well as on the route westward from Choteau's Island. . . .

A halt was made at this point, and the colonel called up the lieutenant and lancers and said to them, "The road to Santa Fé is as now free to you as to myself. Say to General Armijo, I shall soon meet him, and I hope it will be as friends."

At parting the lieutenant embraced the colonel, Captain Turner and myself, who happened to be standing near.

The country today was rolling, almost mountainous, and covered in places with scoriae. Grass began to show itself. . . . As we emerged from the hills into the valley of the Vegas, our eyes were greeted for the first time with waving corn. The stream was flooded, and the little drains by which the fields were irrigated, full to the brim. The dry soil seemed to drink it in with the avidity of thirsty horses. The village, at a short distance, looked like an extensive brick kiln. On approaching, its outline presented a square with some arrangements for defence. Into this square the inhabitants are sometimes compelled to retreat, with all their stock, to avoid the attacks of the Eutaws and Navahoes, who pounce upon them and carry off their women, children, and cattle. Only a few days since, they made a descent on the town and carried off 120 sheep and other stock. As Captain Cook passed through the town ten days' since, a murder had just been committed on these helpless people. Our camp extended for a mile down the valley; on one side was the stream, and on the other the cornfields, with no fence or hedge interposing. What a tantalizing prospect for our hungry and jaded nags; the water was free, but a chain of sentinels was posted to protect the corn, and strict orders given that it should not be disturbed.

Captain Turner was sent to the village to inform the alcalde that the colonel wished to see him and the head men of the town. In a short time down came the alcalde and two captains of militia, with numerous servants, prancing and careering their little nags into camp.

63.   Through South Pass

In all its history the West found few better publicists than young John C. Frémont, who at twenty-nine led a War Department expedition into the Rocky Mountains. His report, published by the Congress, became a best-seller, as did his reports on two subsequent expeditions in 1843–1844 and 1845. Nothing escaped Frémont's

John C. Frémont, *Report of the Exploring Expedition to the Rocky Mountains in the Year, 1842, and to the Oregon and North California in Years 1843–'44* (Washington: Gales and Seaton, 1845), 106–110.

observation: Indians, plants, animals, topography. Fortunately Frémont had in his company men quite capable of making informed
and mature observations of terrain and fauna. In this particular
section the narrator gives a sense of the conditions that the emigrant
trains confronted on their way over the freshly opened trail to the
Pacific Northwest.

By making his deviation from the former route, the problem
of a new road to Oregon and California, in a climate more
genial, might be solved; and a better knowledge obtained of an
important river, and the country it drained, while the great
object of the expedition would find its point of commencement
at the termination of the former, which was at that great gate
in the ridge of the Rocky mountains called the South Pass, and
on the lofty peak of the mountain which overlooks it, deemed
the highest peak in the ridge, and from the opposite sides of
which four great rivers take their rise, and flow to the Pacific
or the Mississippi.

Various obstacles delayed our departure until the morning
of the 29th, when we commenced our long voyage; and at the
close of a day, rendered disagreeably cold by incessant rain,
encamped about four miles beyond the frontier, on the verge
of the great prairies.

Resuming our journey on the 31st, after the delay of a day
to complete our equipment and furnish ourselves with some of
the comforts of civilized life, we encamped in the evening
at Elm Grove, in company with several emigrant wagons, constituting a party which was proceeding to Upper California,
under the direction of Mr. J. B. Childs, of Missouri. The
wagons were variously freighted with goods, furniture, and
farming utensils, containing among other things an entire set
of machinery for a mill which Mr. Childs designed erecting
on the waters of the Sacramento river emptying into the bay
of San Francisco.

We were joined here by Mr. William Gilpin, of Missouri,
who, intending this year to visit the settlements in Oregon, had
been invited to accompany us, and proved a useful and agree-

able addition to the party. From this encampment, our route until the 3d of June was nearly the same as that described to you in 1842. Trains of wagons were almost constantly in sight; giving to the road a populous and animated appearance, although the greater portion of the emigrants were collected at the crossing, or already on their march beyond the Kansas river.

Leaving at the ford the usual emigrant road to the mountains, (which you will find delineated with considerable detail on one of the accompanying maps,) we continued our route along the southern side of the Kansas, where we found the country much more broken than on the northern side of the river, and where our progress was much delayed by the numerous small streams, which obliged us to make frequent bridges. On the morning of the 4th, we crossed a handsome stream, called by the Indians Otter creek, about 130 feet wide, where a flat stratum of limestone, which forms the bed, made an excellent ford. We met here a small party of Kansas and Delaware Indians, the latter returning from a hunting and trapping expedition on the upper waters of the river; and on the heights above were five or six Kansas women, engaged in digging prairie potatoes, (psoralea esculenta.) On the afternoon of the 6th, while busily engaged in crossing a wooded stream, we were thrown into a little confusion by the sudden arrival of Maxwell, who entered the camp at full speed at the head of a war party of Osage Indians, with gay red blankets, and heads shaved to the scalp lock. They had run him a distance of about nine miles, from a creek on which we had encamped the day previous, and to which he had returned in search of a runaway horse belonging to Mr. Dwight, which had taken the homeward road, carrying with him saddle, bridle and holster pistols. The Osages were probably ignorant of our strength, and, when they charged into the camp, drove off a number of our best horses; but we were fortunately well mounted, and, after a hard chase of seven or eight miles, succeeded in recovering them all. This accident, which occasioned delay and trouble, and threatened danger and loss, and broke down some good horses at the start, and actually endangered the expedition was a first fruit of having gentlemen in company —very estimable, to be sure, but who are not trained to the care and vigilance and self-dependence which such an expedition required, and who are not subject to the orders which enforce attention and exertion. We arrived on the 8th at the mouth of the Smokyhill fork, which is the principal southern branch of the Kansas; forming here, by its junction with the Republican, or northern branch, the main Kansas river. Neither stream was fordable, and the necessity of making a raft, together with bad weather, detained us here until the morning of the 11th; when we resumed our journey along the Republican fork. By our observations, the junction of the streams is in latitude 39°03′38″, longitude 96°24′56″, and at an elevation of 926 feet above the gulf of Mexico. For several days we continued to travel along the Republican, through a country beautifully watered with numerous streams, handsomely timbered; and rarely an incident occurred to vary the monotonous resemblance which one day on the prairies here bears to another, and which scarcely require a particular description. Now and then, we caught a glimpse of a small herd of elk; and occasionally a band of antelopes, whose curiosity sometimes brought them within rifle range, would circle round us, and then scour off into the prairies. As we advanced on our road, these became more frequent; but as we journeyed on the line usually followed by the trapping and hunting parties of the Kansas and Delaware Indians, game of every kind continued very shy and wild. The bottoms which form the immediate valley of the main river were generally about three miles wide; having a rich soil of black vegetable mould, and, for a prairie country, well interspersed with wood. The country was everywhere covered with a considerable variety of grasses—occasionally poor and thin, but far more frequently luxurious and rich. We had been gradually and regularly ascending in our progress westward, and on the evening of the 14th, when we encamped on a little creek in the valley of the Republican, 265 miles by our travelling road from the mouth of the Kansas, we were at an elevation of 1,520 feet. That part of the river where we were now encamped is called by the Indians the *Big Timber.* Hitherto our route had been laborious and extremely slow, the unusually wet spring and constant rain having so saturated the whole country that it was necessary to bridge every watercourse, and, for days together, our usual march averaged only five or six miles. Finding that at such a rate of travel it would be impossible to comply with your instructions, I determined at this place to divide the party, and, leaving Mr. Fitzpatrick with 25 men in charge of the provisions and heavier baggage of the camp, to proceed myself in advance, with a light party of 15 men, taking with me the howitzer and the light wagon which carried the instruments.

Accordingly, on the morning of the 16th, the parties separated; and, bearing a little out from the river, with a view of heading some of the numerous affluents, after a few hours' travel over somewhat broken ground, we entered upon an extensive and high level prairie, on which we encamped towards evening at a little stream, where a single dry cottonwood afforded the necessary fuel for preparing supper. Among a variety of grasses which today made their first appearance, I noticed bunch grass, (*festuca,*) and buffalo grass, (*sesleria dactyloides.*) Amorpha canescens (*lead plant*) continued the characteristic plant of the country, and a narrow-leaved *lathyrus* occurred during the morning in beautiful patches. *Sida coccinea* occurred frequently, with a *psoralia* near *psoralia floribunda,* and a number of plants not hitherto met, just verging into bloom. The water on which we had encamped belonged to Solomon's fork of the Smoky-hill river, along whose tributaries we continued to travel for several days.

The country afforded us an excellent road, the route being generally over high and very level prairies; and we met with no other delay than being frequently obliged to bridge one of the numerous streams, which were well timbered with ash, elm, cottonwood, and a very large oak—the latter being, occasionally five and six feet in diameter, with a spreading summit. *Sida coccinea* is very frequent in vermillion-colored patches on the high and low prairie; and I remarked that it has a very pleasant perfume.

The wild sensitive plant (*schrankia angustata*) occurs frequently, generally on the dry prairies, in valleys of streams, and frequently on the broken prairie bank. I remark that the leaflets close instantly to a very light touch. *Amorpha,* with the same *psoralea,* and a dwarf species of *lupinus,* are the characteristic plants.

On the 19th, in the afternoon, we crossed the Pawnee road to the Arkansas, and, travelling a few miles onward, the monotony of the prairies was suddenly dispelled by the appearance of five or six buffalo bulls, forming a vanguard of immense herds, among which we were travelling a few days afterwards. Prairie dogs were seen for the first time during the day; and we had the good fortune to obtain an antelope for supper. Our elevation had now increased to 1,900 feet. *Sida coccinea* was a characteristic on the creek bottoms, and buffalo grass is becoming abundant on the higher parts of the ridges.

June 21.– During the forenoon we travelled up a branch of the creek on which we had encamped, in a broken country, where, however, the dividing ridges always afforded a good road. Plants were few; and with the short sward of the buffalo grass, which now prevailed every where, giving to the prairies a smooth and mossy appearance, were mingled frequent patches of a beautiful red grass, (*aristida pallens,*) which had made its appearance only within the last few days.

We halted at noon at a solitary cottonwood in a hollow, near which was killed the first buffalo, a large old bull.

Antelope appeared in bands during the day. Crossing here to the affluents of the Republican, we encamped on a fork, about forty feet wide and one foot deep, flowing with a swift current over a sandy bed, and well wooded with ash-leaved maple, (*negunda fraxinifolium,*) elm, cottonwood, and a few white oaks. We were visited in the evening by a very violent storm, accompanied by wind, lightning, and a thundershower; a cold rain falling in torrents. According to the barometer, our elevation was 2,130 feet above the gulf.

At noon, on the 23d, we descended into the valley of a principal fork of the Republican, a beautiful stream with a dense
border of wood, consisting principally of varieties of ash, forty
feet wide and four feet deep. It was musical with the notes of
many birds, which, from the vast expanse of silent prairie
around, seemed all to have collected here. We continued during the afternoon our route along the river, which was populous with prairie dogs, (the bottoms being entirely occupied
with their villages,) and late in the evening encamped on its
banks. The prevailing timber is a blue-foliaged ash, (*fraxinus,*
near *F. Americana,*) and ash-leaved maple. With these were
fraxinus Americana, cottonwood, and long-leaved willow. We
gave to this stream the name of Prairie Dog river. Elevation
2,350 feet. Our road on the 25th lay over high smooth ridges,
3,100 feet above the sea; buffalo in great numbers, absolutely
covering the face of the country. At evening we encamped
within a few miles of the main Republican, on a little creek,
where the air was fragrant with the perfume of *artemisia fili-
folia,* which we here saw for the first time, and which was now
in bloom. Shortly after leaving our encampment on the 26th,
we found suddenly that the nature of the country had entirely
changed. Bare sand hills every where surrounded us in the
undulating ground along which we were moving; and the
plants peculiar to a sandy soil made their appearance in abundance. A few miles further we entered the valley of a large
stream, afterwards known to be the Republican fork of the
Kansas, whose shallow waters, with a depth of only a few
inches, were spread out over a bed of yellowish white sand
600 yards wide. With the exception of one or two distant and
detached groves, no timber of any kind was to be seen; and the
features of the country assumed a desert character, with which
the broad river, struggling for existence among quicksands
along the treeless banks, was strikingly in keeping. On the
opposite side, the broken ridges assumed almost a mountainous
appearance; and, fording the stream, we continued on our
course among these ridges, and encamped late in the evening
at a little pond of very bad water, from which we drove away

a herd of buffalo that were standing in and about it. Our encampment this evening was 3,500 feet above the sea. We travelled now for several days through a broken and dry sandy region, about 4,000 feet above the sea, where there were no running streams; and some anxiety was constantly felt on account of the uncertainty of water, which was only to be found in small lakes that occurred occasionally among the hills. The discovery of these always brought pleasure to the camp, as around them were generally green flats, which afforded abundant pasturage for our animals; and here were usually collected herds of the buffalo, which now were scattered over all the country in countless numbers.

64.   Roughing It

In 1864, Samuel L. Clemens and his brother Orion set out across the plains to reach Nevada. Orion had been appointed territorial secretary and Sam was going along as his assistant. In *Roughing It,* Clemens described his experiences. The trails had already been established. Already multitudes had gone overland to the far West, and the road down the Humboldt was worn by the grindings of hundreds of wheels. Many an anxious traveler before Samuel Clemens had made notes on overland travels, but none viewed the scenes with quite the same sense of grim reality on the one hand and humor on the other. Already the image of the West was forming, and Clemens added another cubic to its measure.

On the seventeenth day we passed the highest mountain peaks we had yet seen, and although the day was very warm the night that followed upon its heels was wintry cold and blankets were next to useless.

On the eighteenth day we encountered the eastward-bound telegraph-constructors at Reese River station and sent a mes-

Samuel L. Clemens, (Mark Twain), *Roughing It.* (Hartford: F. G. Gilman, 1886), 150–156.

sage to his Excellency Gov. Nye at Carson City (distant one hundred and fifty-six miles).

On the nineteenth day we crossed the Great American Desert—forty memorable miles of bottomless sand, into which the coach wheels sunk from six inches to a foot. We worked our passage most of the way across. That is to say, we got out and walked. It was a dreary pull and a long and thirsty one, for we had no water. From one extremity of this desert to the other, the road was white with the bones of oxen and horses. It would hardly be an exaggeration to say that we could have walked the forty miles and set our feet on a bone every step! The desert was one prodigious graveyard. And the log-chains, wagon tyres, and rotting wrecks of vehicles were almost as thick as the bones. I think we saw logchains enough rusting there in the desert, to reach across any State in the Union. Do not these relics suggest something of an idea of the fearful suffering and privation the early emigrants to California endured?

At the border of the Desert lies Carson Lake, or The "Sink" of the Carson, a shallow, melancholy sheet of water some eighty or a hundred miles in circumference. Carson River empties into it and is lost—sinks mysteriously into the earth and never appears in the light of the sun again—for the lake has no outlet whatever.

There are several rivers in Nevada, and they all have this mysterious fate. They end in various lakes or "sinks," and that is the last of them. Carson Lake, Humboldt Lake, Walker Lake, Mono Lake, are all great sheets of water without any visible outlet. Water is always flowing into them; none is ever seen to flow out of them, and yet they remain always level full, neither receding nor overflowing. What they do with their surplus is only known to the Creator.

On the western verge of the Desert we halted a moment at Ragtown. It consisted of one loghouse and is not set down on the map.

This reminds me of a circumstance. Just after we left Julesburg, on the Platte, I was sitting with the driver, and he said:

"I can tell you a most laughable thing indeed, if you would like to listen to it. Horace Greeley went over this road once. When he was leaving Carson City he told the driver, Hank Monk, that he had an engagement to lecture at Placerville and was very anxious to go through quick. Hank Monk cracked his whip and started off at an awful pace. The coach bounced up and down in such a terrific way that it jolted the buttons all off of Horace's coat, and finally shot his head clean through the roof of the stage, and then he yelled at Hank Monk and begged him to go easier—said he warn't in as much of a hurry as he was awhile ago. But Hank Monk said, 'Keep your seat, Horace, and I'll get you there on time!'—and you bet you he did, too, what was left of him!"

A day or two after that we picked up a Denver man at the cross roads, and he told us a good deal about the country and the Gregory Diggings. He seemed a very entertaining person and a man well posted in the affairs of Colorado. By and by he remarked:

"I can tell you a most laughable thing indeed, if you would like to listen to it. Horace Greeley went over this road once. When he was leaving Carson City he told the driver, Hank Monk, that he had an engagement to lecture at Placerville and was very anxious to go through quick. Hank Monk cracked his whip and started off at an awful pace. The coach bounced up and down in such a terrific way that it jolted the buttons all off of Horace's coat, and finally shot his head clean through the roof of the stage, and then he yelled at Hank Monk and begged him to go easier—said he warn't in as much of a hurry as he was awhile ago. But Hank Monk said, 'Keep your seat, Horace, and I'll get you there on time!'—and you bet you he did, too, what was left of him!"

At Fort Bridger, some days after this, we took on board a cavalry sergeant, a very proper and soldierly person indeed. From no other man during the whole journey, did we gather such a store of concise and well-arranged military information. It was surprising to find in the desolate wilds of our country a man so thoroughly acquainted with everything useful to

know of his line of life, and yet of such inferior rank and un-
pretentious bearing. For as much as three hours we listened
to him with unabated interest. Finally he got upon the subject of trans-continental travel, and presently said:

"I can tell you a very laughable thing indeed, if you would
like to listen to it. Horace Greeley went over this road once.
When he was leaving Carson City he told the driver, Hank
Monk, that he had an engagement to lecture at Placerville
and was very anxious to go through quick. Hank Monk cracked
his whip and started off at an awful pace. The coach bounced
up and down in such a terrific way that it jolted the buttons
all off of Horace's coat, and finally shot his head clean through
the roof of the stage, and then he yelled at Hank Monk and
begged him to go easier—said he warn't in as much of a
hurry as he was awhile ago. But Hank Monk said, 'Keep
your seat, Horace, and I'll get you there on time!'—and you
bet you he did, too, what was left of him!"

When we were eight hours out from Salt Lake City a Mormon preacher got in with us at a way station—a gentle, soft-
spoken, kindly man, and one whom any stranger would warm
to at first sight. I can never forget the pathos that was in his
voice as he told, in simple language, the story of his people's
wanderings and unpitied sufferings. No pulpit eloquence was
ever so moving and so beautiful as this outcast's picture of
the first Mormon pilgrimage across the plains, struggling sor-
rowfully onward to the land of its banishment and marking
its desolate way with graves and watering it with tears. His
words so wrought upon us that it was a relief to us all when
the conversation drifted into a more cheerful channel and the
natural features of the curious country we were in came under
treatment. One matter after another was pleasantly discussed,
and at length the stranger said:

"I can tell you a most laughable thing indeed, if you would
like to listen to it. Horace Greeley went over this road once.
When he was leaving Carson City he told the driver, Hank
Monk, that he had an engagement to lecture in Placerville,

and was very anxious to go through quick. Hank Monk cracked his whip and started off at an awful pace. The coach bounced up and down in such a terrific way that it jolted the buttons all off of Horace's coat, and finally shot his head clean through the roof of the stage, and then he yelled at Hank Monk and begged him to go easier—said he warn't in as much of a hurry as he was awhile ago. But Hank Monk said, 'Keep your seat, Horace, and I'll get you there on time!'—and you bet you he did, too, what was left of him!"

Ten miles out of Ragtown we found a poor wanderer who had lain down to die. He had walked as long as he could, but his limbs had failed him at last. Hunger and fatigue had conquered him. It would have been inhuman to leave him there. We paid his fare to Carson and lifted him into the coach. It was some little time before he showed any very decided signs of life; but by dint of chafing him and pouring brandy between his lips we finally brought him to a languid consciousness. Then we fed him a little, and by and by he seemed to comprehend the situation and a grateful light softened his eye. We made his mail-sack bed as comfortable as possible, and constructed a pillow for him with our coats. He seemed very thankful. Then he looked up in our faces, and said in a feeble voice that had a tremble of honest emotion in it:

"Gentlemen, I know not who you are, but you have saved my life; and although I can never be able to repay you for it, I feel that I can at least make one hour of your long journey lighter. I take it you are strangers to this great thoroughfare, but I am entirely familiar with it. In this connection I can tell you a most laughable thing indeed, if you would like to listen to it. Horace Greeley—"

I said, impressively:

"Suffering stranger, proceed at your peril. You see in me the melancholy wreck of a once stalwart and magnificent manhood. What has brought me to this? That thing which you are about to tell. Gradually but surely, that tiresome old anecdote has sapped my strength, undermined my constitution,

withered my life. Pity my helplessness. Spare me only just this
once, and tell me about young George Washington and his
little hatchet for a change."

We were saved. But not so the invalid. In trying to retain
the anecdote in his system he strained himself and died in
our arms.

I am aware, now, that I ought not to have asked of the
sturdiest citizen of all that region, what I asked of that mere
shadow of a man; for, after seven years' residence on the
Pacific coast, I know that no passenger or driver on the Overland ever corked that anecdote in, when a stranger was by,
and survived. Within a period of six years I crossed and re-
crossed the Sierras between Nevada and California thirteen
times by stage and listened to that deathless incident four
hundred and eighty-one or eight-two times. I have the list
somewhere. Drivers always told it, conductors told it, land-
lords told it, chance passengers told it, the very Chinamen
and vagrant Indians recounted it. I have had the same driver
tell it to me two or three times in the same afternoon. It has
come to me in all the multitude of tongues that Babel bequeathed to earth, and flavored with whiskey, brandy, beer,
cologne, sozodont, tobacco, garlic, onions, grasshoppers—
everything that has a fragrance to it through all the long
list of things that are gorged or guzzled by the sons of men.
I never have smelt any anecdote as often as I have smelt that
one. And you never could learn to know it by its smell, because every time you thought you had learned the smell of it,
it would turn up with a different smell. Bayard Taylor has
written about this hoary anecdote, Richardson has published
it; so have Jones, Smith, Johnson, Ross Browne, and every
other correspondence-inditing being that ever set his foot
upon the great overland road anywhere between Julesburg
and San Francisco; and I have heard that it is in the Talmud.
I have seen it in print in nine different foreign languages; I
have been told that it is employed in the inquisition in Rome;
and I now learn with regret that it is going to be set to music.
I do not think that such things are right.

Stage-coaching on the Overland is no more, and stage drivers are a race defunct. I wonder if they bequeathed that bald-headed anecdote to their successors, the railroad brakemen and conductors, and if these latter still persecute the helpless passenger with it until he concludes, as did many a tourist of other days, that the real grandeurs of the Pacific coast are not Yo Semite and the Big Trees, but Hank Monk and his adventure with Horace Greeley.°

65. Spanning the Continent by Rail

By 1850 so many sectional rivalries had developed over the location of railroads that this became an active political issue in Congress. The South wished to locate the eastern terminus of a transcontinental railroad within its boundaries. Promoters about Lake Michigan sought the same advantage, as did those all along the Mississippi. An effort was made at objectively determining the best routes for railroads across the continent. One party, led by Howard Stansbury, made the survey across the Salt Lake Flat of Utah. This party was by no means the first either to cross or to describe this tremendously rugged territory, but Stansbury's description is a precise account of the courage demonstrated to bring it under economic conquest. Also, it did as much to bring long stretches of the Great Basin West under intelligent observation as did the Frémont explorations. Crossing the continent with a railroad required something more than materials, capital, and the location of a suitable route.

° And what makes that worn anecdote the more aggravating, is, that the adventure it celebrates *never occurred.* If it were a good anecdote, that seeming demerit would be its chiefest virtue, for creative power belongs to greatness; but what ought to be done to a man who would wantonly contrive so flat a one as this? If I were to suggest what ought to be done to him, I should be called extravagant—but what does the thirteenth chapter of Daniel say? Aha!

Howard Stansbury, *Exploration and Survey of the Valley of the Great Salt Lake of Utah* (Philadelphia: Government Printing Office, 1852), 55, 56, 70, 71, 74.

Thursday, July 19.—Bar. 25.68; Ther. 80°. Leaving the valley of the Warm Spring Branch, the road crosses over to a branch of Bitter Creek, an affluent of the Platte, down the valley of which it winds until it reaches the main stream. We followed this valley the whole day, crossing the stream several times, and encamped on its left bank after a short march of ten and a-half miles. We were detained here the following day by the extreme illness of Auguste, who was unable to be removed. We passed to-day the nearly consumed fragments of about a dozen wagons that had been broken up and burned by their owners; and near them was piled up, in one heap, from six to eight hundred weight of bacon, thrown away for want of means to transport it farther. Boxes, bonnets, trunks, wagon-wheels, whole wagon-bodies, cooking utensils, and, in fact, almost every article of household furniture, were found from place to place along the prairie, abandoned for the same reason. In the evening, Captain Duncan, of the Rifles, with a small escort, rode into camp. He had left Fort Laramie in the morning, and was in hot pursuit of four deserters, who had decamped with an equal number of the best horses belonging to the command.

Bitter Creek is a fine clear stream, about fifty feet wide, with a swift current, and seems, from the great heaps of drift-wood piles upon its banks, to discharge a large quantity of water in the spring.

Upon examining the bluff on the opposite side of the stream, the strata were found to be composed of sandstone and clay with sand. There was also a layer of sulphate of lime about four inches thick and crystalline. In some of the layers of sandstone there were ripple-marks of water; others were thickly studded with oval bodies about the size of pigeons' eggs. Other strata were formed of more compact sandstone, not in layers but in irregular shaped masses, as if composed of bones, much resembling what we had remarked near Chimney Rock. Some fossils were collected, but in not a very perfect state. In some of the sandstones there were evidently a great many, but in the more friable they were rotten; and in others the stone, in the endeavour to get them out, split in every direction. A crystalline mass of what was thought to be sulphate of lime was also found, with dark crystals interspersed. The top of the hill was covered with masses of primitive rock, probably from the decomposition of conglomerate. The hunters brought in the choice parts of three fat buffalo-cows today, which fairly loaded down their pack-mules. The meat was estimated to weigh upward of one thousand pounds. . . .

Monday, August 6.– Leaving the valley of the Sweetwater, we crossed this morning through the South Pass over to the head branches of Sandy Creek, an affluent of the Colorado, or Green River of the West, and nooned at the "Pacific Springs," at the foot of the pass, on the western side. This celebrated depression through the Rocky Mountains is now so well known that any further description of it would be superfluous. That of Frémont conveys a very accurate idea of the locality, which has nothing remarkable in its features. The water at the Pacific Springs is not very good, but is quite cold. It is a favourite camping ground of the emigrants on account of the grass. Encamped for the night on the banks of Dry Sandy, where we had to dig in the bed of the stream for water; but a very scanty supply was obtained; and the grass moreover was so scarce that our animals were allowed to run loose all night under the protection of the guard, instead of being picketed as usual. In the afternoon, one of our best mules died from the bite of a snake. In the morning her jaws and fauces had been observed to be very much swollen, and before sundown she became so weak that we were obliged to release her from the wagon, when she lay down by the side of the road and in a short time expired.

Between the Sweetwater and the South Pass, the soil for some four or five miles presented the same disintegrated dark shales as had been observed on the other side of the river. It then became more sandy, and portions of weathered marble were found on the surface. On ascending some low hills on the left of the road, and within about a mile of the Pass, marble was found in place, containing a considerable incrustation of silex. It evidently cropped out on the south side of these hills, on the top of one of which was found a stratum of gray sandstone, in which the remains of encrinites were observed. It was quite horizontal, not conformable with the marble under it, and was undoubtedly a continuation of the secondary formation which had been observed up the whole valley of the Sweetwater. On the left of the road, and a few miles distant, were some high hills, which, from their appearance, seemed to be capped by the reddish clay which forms the isolated masses in the valley of the Platte. Shortly after passing the summit we found a stratum of apparently metamorphic clay, horizontal, with an east and west direction. Over this were strata of gray sandstone, horizontal, or with a slight dip to the east. Descending the western side of the Pass, the soil was composed principally of red sand. No rocks were visible. About a mile from Dry Sandy, some masses of rock were observed on the right of the road, standing up like pillars; they were found to be composed of a coarse sandstone, of an ochrey colour. Under them were white and red shales, apparently horizontal. The surface of the ground appeared to be the result of the decomposition of this ochrey rock.

I witnessed, at the Pacific Springs, an instance of no little ingenuity on the part of some emigrant. Immediately alongside of the road was what purported to be a grave, prepared with more than usual care, having a headboard on which was painted the name and age of the deceased, the time of his death, and the part of the country from which he came. I afterward ascertained that this was only a ruse to conceal the fact that the grave, instead of containing the mortal remains of a human being, had been made a safe receptacle for divers casks of brandy, which the owner could carry no farther. He afterward sold his liquor to some traders farther on, who, by his description of its locality, found it without difficulty. . . .

Saturday, August 11.– Ther. at 6 o'clock, 40°. A drive of thirty-two miles, during which we crossed Ham's Fork and Black's Fork three times, brought us to Fort Bridger—an Indian tradingpost, situated on the latter stream, which here

branches into three principal channels, forming several extensive islands, upon one of which the fort is placed. It is
built in the usual form of pickets, with the lodging apartments
and offices opening into a hollow square, protected from attack
from without by a strong gate of timber. On the north, and
continuous with the walls, is a strong high picket-fence, enclosing a large yard, into which the animals belonging to
the establishment are driven for protection from both wild
beasts and Indians. We were received with great kindness and
lavish hospitality by the proprietor, Major James Bridger,
one of the oldest mountain-men in this entire region, who
has been engaged in the Indian trade, here, and upon the
heads of the Missouri and Columbia, for the last thirty years.
Several of my wagons needing repair, the train was detained
five days for the purpose, Major Bridger courteously placing
his blacksmith-shop at my service.

X

Age of the Argonauts

No part of the frontier saga was more dramatic than the great Gold Rush of 1849 by way of the overland and isthmus pass routes to California. Not only did the discovery of gold on the American River at Sutter's Mill late in 1848 and the spread of its news excite the entire populace and hasten thousands of gold seekers across the continent to seek personal fortunes, it unleashed on the frontier a veritable army of journalists, humble and able, who were determined the saga would be recorded in detail if not always with eloquence. No part of the westward movement was so completely described by contemporaries as the California gold rushers.

These journalists came from everywhere and experienced about as many hardships and frustrations as there were gold-seekers. Basically, three experiences were common to all of them: they had a hard time getting to California, they found little gold, and most of them hastened home, even though they were embarrassed to admit failure.

The mineral rushes colored the history of the frontier in many ways. There was neighborliness as tender as any newly settled community ever experienced, and there was violence which knew no bounds. Out beyond the arm of law enforcement, men threw off all civilized restraints and misbehaved in animalistic fashion. Others took the law into their hands and meted "justice" with a speed and definity that defied human belief. This was "justice" beyond appeal to any court, even to that of humanity itself. This was all a part of the rapidity with which American civilization found itself hurtled across space to settle the Pacific Coast and to create a new state.

66.   The Great Trail, Independence to San Francisco

Edwin Bryant, a Kentucky journalist with wanderlust, undertook to lead a party of emigrants from Missouri to California in the summer of 1846. The conquest of California passed through its early stages while Bryant's party was enroute; it arrived to find the supposed Mexican territory already a province of the United States. The emigrants took part in bringing order to the new territory, and Bryant became an alcalde in San Francisco. But he had the privilege of seeing California before it was heavily under American influence, and he wrote an engaging account of life there at the moment Spanish customs began to surrender to American customs.

We left Los Angeles late in the afternoon of the 29th of January, with two Indian vaqueros, on miserable, broken-down horses, (the best we could obtain,) and encamped at the deserted rancho at the foot of Couenga plain, where the treaty of peace had been concluded. After we had been here some time, two Indians came to the house, who had been sent by the proprietor of the rancho to herd cattle. Having nothing to eat with us, a tempting offer prevailed upon the Indians to milk one of the cows; and we made our supper and breakfast next morning on milk. Both of our Indian vaqueros departed in the night, carrying with them sundry articles of clothing placed in their charge. A few days have made a great change in the appearance of the country. The fresh grass is now several inches in height, and many flowers are in bloom. The sky is bright, and the temperature delightful.

On the 30th of January, leaving the mission of San Fernando on our right, at a distance of eight or ten miles, we followed

Edwin Bryant, *What I Saw in California: Being the Journal of a Tour, by the Emigrant Route and South Pass of the Rocky Mountains, Across the Continent of North America, the Great Desert Basin, and Through California, in the Years 1846, 1847* (New York: A. Appleton, 1848), 417–422.

the usually traveled trail next to the hills, on the western side of the plain. As we were passing near a rancho, a well-dressed Californian rode out to us; and after examining the horses of our miserable *caballada*, politely claimed one of them as his property. He was told that the horse was drawn from the public *caballada*, at Los Angeles, and could not be given up. This seemed to satisfy him. After some further conversation, he informed us that he was Don Andres Pico, the late leader and general of the Californians. The expression of his countenance is intelligent and prepossessing; and his address and manners courteous and pleasing. Shaking hands and bidding us a very earnest *adios*, he put spurs to his horse and galloped away.

We were soon after overtaken by a young Californian, who appeared at first rather doubtful whether or not he should make our acquaintance. The ice being broken, however, he became very locquaxcious and communicative. He stated that he was returning home, near Santa Barbara, from the wars, in which he had been engaged against his will. The language that he used was, that he with many others of his acquaintances, were forced to take up arms by the leading men of the country. He was in the two battles of the 8th and 9th of January, below Los Angeles; and he desired never to be in any more battles. He was heartily rejoiced that there was peace, and hoped that there would never be any more wars. He traveled along with us until afternoon, when he fell behind, and we did not see him again until the next day.

After passing two or three deserted houses, we reached an inhabited rancho, situated at the extremity of a valley, and near a narrow gorge in the hills, about four o'clock, and our jaded animals performing duty with reluctance, we determined to halt for the night, if the prospect of obtaining anything to eat (of which we stood in much need) was flattering. Riding up to the house, a small adobe, with one room, and a shed for a kitchen, the *ranchero* and the *ranchera* came out and greeted us with a hearty "*Buenas tardes Señores, paisanos, amigos*", shaking hands and inviting us at the same time to alight and remain for the night, which invitation we accepted. The kind-hearted *ranchera* immediately set about preparing supper for us. An Indian *muchacha* was seated at the *metáte*, (hand mill,) which is one of the most important articles of the California culinary apparatus. While the *muchacha* ground, or rather crushed the wheat between the stones, the *ranchera*, with a platter-shaped basket, cleansed it of dust, chaff, and all impure particles, by tossing the grain in the basket. The flour being manufactured and sifted through a *cedazo*, or coarse sieve, the labor of kneeding the dough was performed by the *muchacha*. An iron plate was then placed over a rudely constructed furnace, and the dough being beaten by hand into *tortillas*, (thin cakes,) was baked upon this. What would American housewives say to such a system as this? The viands being prepared, they were set out upon a small table, at which we were invited to seat ourselves. The meal consisted of *tortillas*, stewed jerked-beef, with *chile* seasoning, milk, and *quesadillas*, or cheesecakes, green and tough as leather. However, our appetites were excellent, and we enjoyed the repast with a high relish.

Our host and hostess were very inquisitive in regard to the news from below, and as to what would be the effects of the conquest of the country by the Americans. The man stated that he and all his family had refused to join the late insurrection. We told them that all was peaceable now; that there would be no more wars in California; that we were all Americans, all Californians– *hermanos, hermanas, amigos.* They expressed delight at this information by numerous exclamations.

We asked the woman how much the dress which she wore, a miserable calico, cost her? She answered, *"seis pesos,"* (six dollars.) When we told her that in a short time, under the American government, she could purchase as good a one *"por un pesos,"* she threw up her hands in astonishment, expressing by her features at the same time the most unbounded delight. Her entire wardrobe was soon brought forth, and the price paid for every article named. She then enquired what would be the cost of similar clothing under the American government, which we told her. As we replied, exclamation followed upon exclamation, expressive of her surprise and pleasure, and the whole was concluded with "*Viva los Americanos-viva los Americanos!*" I wore a large coarse woollen peajacket, which the man was very desirous to obtain, offering for it a fine horse. I declined the trade.

In the evening several of the brothers, sisters, and brothers and sisters-in-law of the family collected, and the guitar and violin, which were suspended from a beam in the house, were taken down, and we were entertained by a concert of instrumental and vocal music. Most of the tunes were such as are performed at fandangos. Some plaintive airs were played and sung with such pathos and expression, the whole party joining in the choruses. Although invited to occupy the only room in the house, we declined it, and spread our blankets on the outside.

The next morning (January 31) when we woke the sun was shining bright and warm, and the birds were singing gaily in the grove of evergreen oaks near the house. Having made ready to resume our journey, as delicately as possible we offered our kind hostess compensation for the trouble we had given her, which she declined, saying, that although they were not rich, they nevertheless had enough and to spare. We however insisted, and she finally accepted, with the condition that we would also accept of some of her *quesadillas* and *tortillas* to carry along with us. The *ranchero* mounted his horse and rode with us three or four miles, to place us on the right trail, when, after inviting us earnestly to call and see him again, and bidding us an affectionate *adios*, he galloped away.

Traveling over a hilly country and passing the ruins of several deserted ranchos, the grounds surrounding which were strewn with the bones of slaughtered cattle, we reached, about five o'clock, p. m., a cluster of houses in the valley of Santa Clara river, ten miles east of mission San Buenaventura. Here we stopped at the house of a man named Sanchez. Our arrival was thought to be worthy of notice, and it was accordingly celebrated in the evening by a fandango given at one of the houses, to which we were invited. The company, to the number of some thirty or forty persons, young and old, were assembled in the largest room of the house, the floor being a hard clay. The only furniture contained in the room was a bed and some benches, upon which the company seated themselves when not engaged in dancing.

Among the *señoritas* assembled, were two daughters of an American named Chapman, who has been a resident of the country for many years. They were fair-skinned, and might be called handsome. An elder and married sister was also present. They called themselves Americans, although they did not speak our language, and seemed to be more proud of their American than their Spanish blood.

A singular custom prevails at these fandangos. It is this: during the intervals between waltzes, quadrilles, and other dances, when the company is seated, a young lady takes the floor *solus*, and after showing off her graces for general observation a few minutes, she approaches any gentleman she may select and performs a variety of pirouettes and other Terpischorean movements before him for his special amusement and admiration, until he places on her head his hat or cap, as the case may be, when she dances away with it. The hat or cap has afterwards to be redeemed by some present, and this is usually in money. Not dancing ourselves, we were favored with numerous special exhibitions of this kind, the cost of each which was *un peso*. With a long journey before us, and with purses in a nearly collapsed condition, the drafts upon us became so frequent, that at an early hour, under the plea of fatigue and want of rest, we thought it prudent to beat a retreat, leaving our fair and partial *fandangueras* to bestow their favors upon others better able to bear them. The motions of the California females of all classes in the dance are highly graceful. The waltz is their favorite measure, and in this they appear to excel as the men do in horsemanship. During the progress of the dance, the males and females improvise doggerel rhymes complimentary of the personal beauties and graces of those whom they admire, or expressive of their love and devotion, which are chanted with the music of the instruments, and the whole company join in the general chorus at the end of each verse. The din of voices is sometimes almost deafening.

Our host accompanied us to our lodgings on the opposite side of the way. Beds were spread down under the small porch outside, and we laid our bodies upon them, but not to sleep, for the noise of the fandango dancers kept us awake until broad daylight, at which time it broke up.

Hiring fresh horses here, and a vaquero to drive our tired animals after us, we started about nine o'clock in the morning, and passing through San Buenaventura, reached Santa Barbara, 45 miles, a little after two in the afternoon. We stopped at the house of Mr. Sparks, who received us with genuine hospitality. Santa Barbara presented a more lively appearance than when we passed here on our way down, most of its population having returned to their homes. Procuring fresh but miserably poor horses, we resumed our journey on the afternoon of the 2nd of February, and encamped at the rancho of Dr. Den, situated on the Plain of Santa Barbara, near the seashore. The soil of this plain is of the most fertile composition. The fresh grass is now six or eight inches high, and the varieties numerous. Many of these early flowers are in bloom. I noticed a large wheat field near the house, and its appearance was such as to promise a rich harvest.

67. The Road to California

In 1849 one of North America's most exciting dramas was enacted on that vast stage between the eastern states and California. The great mass of the actors was strung out along the trail from Independence, Missouri to Sacramento, California. This great road led up

From Joseph L. Stephens to Beman Gates, *Marietta* [Ohio] *Intelligencer*, September 6, 1849.

the Platte by way of old Fort Laramie, up the northern Platte to the headwaters of the Sweetwater, across South Pass, around the Great Basin rim, and up the Humboldt, and across the Sierras into the Sacramento Valley. Hundreds of people making this arduous passage wondered why they left home in the first place, and in California they failed to find gold. Prices of commodities were exorbitant, living conditions all but intolerable, competition intense.

In the following section Joseph L. Stephens described for Beman Gates, editor of the Marietta (Ohio) *Intelligencer,* the travails of the Elisha Douglas Perkins's party of inexperienced travelers in making the overland crossing. Young Stephens wrote with the intimate feelings of a callow youth who found himself thrust into the clutches of a wicked environment from which he could escape only by serving out the time required by the heartless trail (and then facing failure in the gold fields), but with thankfulness in his heart he had not dragged a family westward with him.

This morning I have unexpectedly found time to write. I have been too busy in preparing for the mines to write by the last steamer, which left here on the first of the month. Chesbro and myself have been here two weeks, but have not yet heard a word from the other boys, and, as I wrote you from Fort Laramie fear they will see the *Elephant* before they reach the mines, though they may be here in a few days. The Harmar Company have not yet arrived, and I think it will be some time before they do: but in this I only judge from what I have seen myself. I had made arrangements to start to the mines (125 miles from this place) this morning, but owing to a subsequent arrangement I am to start in a wagon this evening. Chesbro is not going to the mines with me, but will be on in a day or two. . . .

The trip over the plains and mountains is of such magnitude that it would take quires instead of this sheet, to give you an *idea* of it; so I will give little on that head. We started from St. Josephs behind *seven thousand wagons*– some had left two months before, and some only two days before– but to say that only 500 of them reached this city before us looks unreasonable; but such is a fact. We made the trip in

85 days, which is nearly the shortest time on the route. Our reason for such a rush was, that to be at the end of 7000 teams we thought we should never get through; for there is not grass enough for more than half the stock so we thought it better to get through alive, with dead mules, than to perish on the road. Unless something be done to relieve the families which are back on the road there will be intense suffering this winter. Emigrants here who have friends on the road, are sending word, and are going back themselves, to turn the teams to Oregon, or the Salt Lake (Mormon City) or to have them stop in the valleys where there is sufficient grass to winter. If an early winter sets in they would undoubtedly perish in the mountains; for it snowed on the 15th of August where we were, and it was not a sprinkle only, for it laid in the hot sun a long time. The sun was oppressively hot in the mountains, but as soon as hidden by a cloud, or below the horizon, it became chilly and begins to freeze. But enough of this– and now something of California.

This "beautiful and fertile valley of the Sacramento," of which Col. Frémont speaks, is an outrageously hot country, and has to be watered to raise anything whatever. Those who have the inclination to cultivate the land in this way may do so– but I shall not. The greater part that you read in relation to this country is *false*; and this everyone who knows will testify. The gold is here, but no man ever *dug* a dollar who did not earn it– The gold digging is a lottery sure enough– Some men make a fortune in a short time, but others in ten years would not make a cent. Of those who will leave here, the proportion will scarcely be one in five will leave with any money; though it is within the power of every man in California to make a small fortune. Any man who has the health and energy can make ten dollars per day at almost anything he chooses to do– Our clothing costs us but little. We wear nothing that costs more than two dollars– Vegetables are *tolerably* well up– for instance; melons from two to six dollars each, onions, one dollar each– potatoes one dollar per pound– squashes, one dollar each– everything else in proportion.

substantials are as follows: flour, nine dollars per hundred–
sugar, 18 cents per pound– coffee, 12½– tea, one dollar–
beef, 25 cents– hams, 60. Mules and horses are worth from
fifty to three hundred dollars each, and hay ten cents a pound.
Money is nothing here. One hundred dollars is not worth
more than ten cents in Marietta. Some persons in this city
are making money as fast as they can count it.– but they
are those who had a start at the beginning. . . .

The hardships of the overland route to California are beyond conception. Care and suspense, pained anxiety, fear of
losing animals and leaving one to foot it and pack his "duds"
on his back, begging provisions, fear of being left in the
mountains to starve and freeze to death, and a thousand other
things which no one thinks of until on the way, or things
which I may write and you may read, but they are nothing
to the *reality*. Still I am in as good health as I ever was, and
weigh more by four pounds than I ever did before. I have
come to the conclusion that it would be child's play to do
as some are doing– to turn around a few times and then go
home because they cannot pick up gold under their feet as
they walk along. This will not be my course. I have spent
four hundred dollars, but I am going to have it back again
with *big interest* before I quit the country. Some of my
Kentucky friends are at the mines making from $100 to $200
per week. But to stick to business is the only way to make it
pay– at least this is what the old miners tell me. If I hit a
rich spot, a fortune can be made in a day, as many have done;
but if I do not, it will count up in a year or two. If I am any
thing like lucky I will leave this country so as to cross the
Isthmus after the sickly season of 1850– if not I may stay
another year. . . .

You will almost doubt what I am going to say– but nevertheless it is true. When we packed from Fort Laramie, we
started with but little provisions, as we wished to get along as
fast as possible, thinking we could buy of the teams on the
road. Our provisions lasted us but 1500 miles, and we had to
go hunting. A great many had thrown away their bacon and

bread, and had only enough to last them through, and others had to buy as we did. For a hundred miles in places men would not answer us when we asked for anything– many would not give us a decent answer at other times. And some again would not sell to a *packer,* because as they said, packers could travel faster than they could. Many times I have sat down and eaten dry crackers, in a powdered state, without even water; and often ate raw bacon sides, powdered crackers, and water, for days together. We have been refused a cup of coffee repeatedly– and have often begged men to sell us a pound of bread and could not get it.

But now to give the devil his due. I have seen some Kentuckians that were gentlemen– and others not. From Ohio the same– and the same from Missouri. And indeed the same from almost every state in the Union save Yankeedom. Never have we met the first soul of these that were not as brothers to us– they would not always divide with us to the last morsel. The Irish were on a par with the Yankees– and the Germans came next to them. At one time we got out of chocolate and tried to buy from every wagon– but no one would sell us an ounce. At last we came to an Irish train. I told Chesbro I thought we could get something there. At the first wagon we reached we asked to buy some chocolate. A *lady* said she could let us have some; and the wagon we stopped until she could get at it. She got two pounds and gave it to us refusing to take any pay. Another wagon in the same train gave a tea pot. So much upon this head– but you cannot imagine the reality.– When you are suffering from starvation and ask a man, a brute in the shape of a man, to sell you a meal of victuals, or even a cup of coffee, and he coldly refuses, if the tears would not come then I am mistaken.

We have been on the Humboldt River where the Indians were scattered through the bushes shooting their poisoned arrows at man and cattle. We camped alone several nights where we dare not build a fire lest we should be discovered; and we had to do so because we had traveled as far as our mules could take us, without coming up with any wagons.

In such cases we stopped as if it was in a bear's den. To lose our mules by travel was almost certain death to us, and we tried always to be on the safe side. But writing about these things is nothing, when one has had them to *feel*. In consequence, however, of these trials, we have had fine times since we reached this place, where everything to eat is plenty. I do not of course say that all have had as hard time as we met with.

For my part I would not have the feelings of the people we passed on the road, many of whom had their families with them, and who are now 400 or 500 miles behind (with not a spear of grass in their way) for all the gold in this country. Though all of them get through alive. It is with these persons that we have had comparatively "fine times."

68.   Gold in the Rockies

On May 6, 1859, John H. Gregory, a Georgia gold miner, made a rich gold strike on the headwaters of Clear Creek in present Colorado. This was an exciting event in this newest gold producing area, and it touched off the great Pike's Peak gold rush which tempted so many goldseekers to this part of the West. Among the band of rushing miners and prospectors were three newspaper men: Horace Greeley of the New York *Tribune,* Henry Villard of the Cincinnati *Commercial,* and Albert D. Richardson, a New York freelance writer. These observers contributed heavily to the excitement generated by the Gregory strike. Some of Greeley's stories verified in the minds of the gold seekers the fact that they would find riches at the foot of Pike's Peak. In June 1859, Richardson visited the new town of Golden which was springing up under the shadow of Table Mountain. There he was to experience all the excitement that accompanied the building of a western mineral Babylon. He produced a vivid description of his visit to this exciting new gold scene.

Albert D. Richardson, *Beyond the Mississippi, from the Great Ocean* (Hartford: Webster, 1867), 197–201.

In the evening I reached the diggings. A single month had changed them greatly. An incredible amount of work had been expended in seeking for gold. The same labor would have converted hundreds of miles of Kansas or Minnesota prairies into one continuous garden. Gregory Gulch now rejoiced in the hum and bustle of a city. Ravines were vocal with the crash of falling pine and hemlock, and the ring of hammer ax pick and spade. The women had increased to more than a hundred. Every mechanical trade and every traffic was pursued. A single 'town' lot had sold for five hundred dollars. When I asked a miner if there was any church, he replied:

'No; but we are going to build one before next Sunday.'

Erecting a temple of worship in a week was in thorough accordance with the prevailing spirit.

Thousands of miners were busy at the sluices, which now numbered several hundred. All reported gold-bearing rock abundant; but as yet there were no mills for crushing the quartz within a thousand miles. The 'pay dirt' was brought from the hillsides to the sluices in coffee sacks, borne upon the shoulders or drawn on rough sleds along smooth freshly-peeled pine trunks– a rudimentary inclined-plane railway.

Several miners were each taking out two hundred dollars per day; but not more than one in four was obtaining five dollars. By the established regulations the size of a claim was fifty feet by one hundred; and some were selling at from ten to forty thousand dollars. Generally only a few hundred dollars of the purchase money was paid down; if the claim did not yield the balance it was never liquidated.

Climbing a hill side, I obtained a vivid evening view of the Alpine city. Beyond it a fire was raging upon an isolated peak. The flame swept even higher and higher, till at the summit, striking a single dead tree, it ran fiercely up the trunk into a perfect cone of fire, against a background of mountain and cloud.

At my feet the valley was lighted with scores of camp fires, casting the shadows of tall pines and firs in every direction, and throwing a lurid glare upon the swarthy faces of the miners. Some were cooking in the open air, some taking their evening meal upon tables of pine bark, and others sitting upon logs or reclining upon the ground smoking and talking.

From one camp issued the lively notes of a violin; and from another, 'Home, sweet home' floating upon the evening air in a low, plaintive voice, told that the heart of the singer was with dear ones far away.

On Sunday morning, a walk through the diggings revealed nearly all the miners disguised in clean clothing. Some were reading and writing letters, some ministering to the sick, and some enacting the part of Every-man-his-own-washer-woman– rubbing valiantly away at the tub. Several hundred men, in the open air, were attending public religious worship– perhaps the first ever held in the Rocky Mountains. They were roughly clad, displaying weapons at their belts; and represented every section of the Union and almost every nation of the earth. They sat upon logs and stumps, a most attentive congregation, while the clergyman upon a rude log platform, preached from the text: 'Behold, I bring you good tidings of great joy.' It was an impressive spectacle– that motley gathering of gold-seekers among the mountains, a thousand miles from home and civilization, to hear the 'good tidings' forever old and yet forever new.

During the two weeks I spent in the mines the unhealthy diet and miasma arising from the freshly-broken earth, produced much fever. Many a poor fellow weak and listless, on straw bunk in squalid cabin, waited the approach of that grim specter with whom ancients found prayers and sacrifices alike unavailing. Many with folded arms and rigid faces were consigned by strangers to hill-side graves, with no child's voice to prattle its simple sorrow, no woman's tear to bedew their memory.

We slept upon the ground under fir boughs. The sweetest of all the rest is on the bosom of mother earth, watched by sentinel stars, lulled by the sad-hearted pine and falling water.

I found in one camp a party of Kansas acquaintances living upon ham and eggs. The latter were a rare luxury, costing two dollars and fifty cents per dozen. My friends had packed several barrels in Leavenworth, pouring liquid lard around the eggs, which forming a mold enabled them to sustain with admirable composure their wagon-journey of seven hundred miles.

Flour sold at twenty dollars per hundred, and milk at fifty cents a quart. Flapjacks were the substitute for bread. I think enough were made during the season to pave the road from Leavenworth to the mines. At every camp one saw perspiring men bending anxiously over the griddle, or turning the cake by tossing it skillfully in the air. To a looker-on, such masculine feats were decidedly amusing. Four years later, in rebel prisons, I found practical cookery far less entertaining.

Many professional men were hard at work in the diggings. One often heard sunburnt miners while resting upon their spades, discussing Shakespeare, the classics, religion, and political economy.

The stream beds abounded in mica, which old miners called 'fools' gold. A shrewd German washed out and secreted an immense quantity, supposing he had discovered a new Golconda. Upon learning that it was not the precious metal he started back in disgust to the Pennsylvania coal mines.

When the melancholy John Phenix occupied the tripod of the San Diego *Herald,* he advertised for a lad to bring water, black his boots and keep the sanctum in order– one by whom obtaining a knowledge of the business would be deemed a sufficient compensation. The caution which he added– 'No young woman in disguise need apply'– was needful in a mining country. I encountered in the diggings several women dressed in masculine apparel, and each telling some romantic story of her past life. One averred that she had twice crossed the plains to California with droves of cattle. Some were adventurers; all were of the wretched class against which Society shuts its iron doors, bidding them to hasten un-cared-for to destruction.

The Utes killed a number of the miners. William M. Slaughter a Denver pioneer, was out prospecting with two friends, when these savages, after dining with them in apparent friendliness, attacked the party, killing and scalping two. Slaughter though repeatedly shot at, sprang into the bushes, concealed himself two days, and finally escaped.

After spending six weeks in the new gold region, my published impression of the mines was thus summed up:

> I have absolute confidence in the permanency extent and richness of these diggings. I believe that the mountain ranges, *from Salt Lake to Mexico,* abound in gold and the secondary metals, and that their yield will be the richest ever known in the world. Yet those who are doing moderately well at home should remember that not more than one man in ten meets with success in any mining country, and that the prairies of Kansas, Nebraska, and Missouri offer much stronger inducements to settlers than the gold regions.

I also hazarded the prediction that with proper cultivation the valleys of the Platte and its tributaries within fifty miles of Denver, would produce enough small grains and vegetables to support a population of two hundred thousand. This was scoffed at; and the arid sands did look unpromising. But now the settlers of Colorado have tested the agriculture of their new state, and yearly they raise enough farm produce for their own consumption.

Returning down the mountains I found opportunity to contrast the two classes common to all gold regions. The newcomers going into the mines were sanguine and cheery, climbing with elastic step, and beguiling the way with song and laughter. But the stampeders turning homeward, convinced that gold digging was hard and unremunerative, left their packs and shovels behind, and trudged mechanically with downcast woebegone faces.

69. Vigilantism

Gold rush communities of western Montana, during the Civil War years, were infested with cutthroats and highwaymen. Most famous were members of Plummer's Gang. As gold was shipped out of the region by stage coach and freight wagons, travel became dangerous. Numerous stories of murders and robberies drifted into the camps. By 1864, crime had reached such a peak that either the highwaymen would have to be destroyed or the mining camps would be forced to close. Virginia City, Bannack, Last Chance Gulch, Blackfoot, and other places were threatened. The list of highwaymen included such worthies as George Ives, Henry Plummer, Ned Ray, Boone Helm, Jack Gallagher, Cyrus Skinner, Dutch John Waggoner, Joe Pizanthia, and Buck Stinson. Thomas J. Dimsdale described the fate dealt three of them by the vigilantes on January 10, 1864, in Bannack City.

At dusk, three horses were brought into town, belonging severally and respectively to the three marauders so often mentioned, Plummer, Stinson, and Ray. It was truly conjectured that they had determined to leave the country, and it was at once settled that they should be arrested that night. Parties were detailed for the work. Those entrusted with the duty performed admirably. Plummer was undressing when taken at his house. His pistol (a self-cocking weapon) was broken and useless. Had he been armed, resistance would have been futile; for he was seized the moment the door was opened in answer to the knocking without. Stinson was arrested at Toland's, where he was spending the evening. He would willingly have done a little firing, but his captors were too quick for him.

Thomas Josiah Dimsdale, *The Vigilantes of Montana: Trial, Capture and Execution of Henry Plummer's Notorious Road Agent Band; Forming the only Reliable Work ever offered to the Public by Prof. Thos. J. Dimsdale* (Virginia City, Montana Territory: D. W. Hilton & Co., Book and Job Printers, 1866).

Ray was lying on a gambling table when seized. The three details marched their men to a given point, en route to the gallows. Here a halt was made. The leader of the Vigilantes and some others, who wished to save all unnecessary hard feeling, were sitting in a cabin, deigning not to speak to Plummer, with whom they were so well acquainted. A halt was made, however, and at the door appeared Plummer. The light was extinguished; when the party moved on, but soon halted. The crisis had come. Seeing that the circumstances were such as admitted of neither vacillation nor delay, the citizen leader, summoning his friends, went up to the party and gave the military command, "Company! forward– march!" This was at once obeyed. A rope taken from a noted functionary's bed had been mislaid and could not be found. A nigger boy was sent off for some of that highly necessary but unpleasant remedy for crime, and the bearer made such good time that some hundreds of feet of hempen necktie were on the ground before the arrival of the party at the gallows. On the road Plummer heard the voice and recognized the person of the leader. He came to him and begged for his life, but was told, "It is useless for you to beg for your life; that affair is settled and cannot be altered. You are to be hanged. You cannot feel harder about it than I do; but I cannot help it if I would." Ned Ray, clothed with curses as with a garment, actually tried fighting, but found that he was in the wrong company for such demonstrations; and Buck Stinson made the air ring with the blasphemous and filthy expletives which he used in addressing his captors to spare his life. He begged to be chained down in the meanest cabin; offered to leave the country forever; wanted a jury trial; implored time to settle his affairs; asked to see his sister-in-law, and, falling on his knees, with tears and sighs declared to God that he was too wicked to die. He confessed his numerous murders and crimes, and seemed almost frantic at the prospect of death.

The first rope being thrown over the cross-beam and the noose being rove, the order was given to "Bring up Ned Ray."

This desperado was run up with curses on his lips. Being loosly pinioned, he got his fingers between the rope and his neck, and thus prolonged his misery.

Buck Stinson saw his comrade robber swinging in the death agony, and blubbered, "There goes poor Ed Ray." Scant mercy had he shown to his numerous victims. By a sudden twist of his head at the moment of his elevation, the knot slipped under his chin, and he was some minutes dying.

The order to "Bring up Plummer" was then passed and repeated; but no one stirred. The leader went over to this "perfect gentleman," as his friends called him, and was met by a request to "Give a man time to pray." Well knowing that Plummer relied for a rescue upon other than Divine aid, he said briefly and decidedly, "Certainly; but let him say his prayers up here." Finding all efforts to avoid death were useless, Plummer rose and said no more prayers. Standing under the gallows which he had erected for the execution of Horan, this second Haman slipped off his necktie and threw it over his shoulder to a young friend who had boarded at his house, and who believed him innocent of crime, saying as he tossed it to him, "Here is something to remember me by." In the extremity of his grief, the young man threw himself weeping and wailing upon the ground. Plummer requested that the men would give him a good drop, which was done, as far as circumstances permitted, by hoisting him up as far as possible in their arms, and letting him fall suddenly. He died quickly and without much struggle.

It was necessary to seize Ned Ray's hand, and by a violent effort to draw his fingers from between the noose and his neck before he died. Probably he was the last to expire of the guilty trio.

The news of a man's being hanged flies faster than any other intelligence in a Western country, and several had gathered around the gallows on that fatal Sabbath evening– many of them friends of the road agents. The spectators were allowed to come up to a certain point, and were halted by the guard, who refused permission either to depart or to approach nearer than the "dead line," on pain of their being instantly shot.

The weather was intensely cold, but the party stood for a long time round the bodies of the suspended malefactors, determined that rescue should be impossible.

Loud groans and cries uttered in the vicinity attracted their attention, and a small squad started in the direction from which the sound proceeded. The detachment soon met Madam Hall, a noted courtesan– the mistress of Ned Ray– who was "making the night hideous" with her doleful wailings. Being at once stopped, she began inquiring for her paramour, and was thus informed of his fate, "Well, if you must know, he is hung." A volcanic eruption of oaths and abuse was her reply to this information; but the men were on "short time," and escorted her towards her dwelling without superfluous display of courtesy. Having arrived at the brow of a short descent, at the foot of which stood her cabin, stern necessity compelled a rapid and final progress in that direction.

Soon after, the party formed and returned to town, leaving the corpses stiffening in the icy blast. The bodies were eventually cut down by the friends of the road agents and buried. The "Reign of terror" in Bannack was over.

70. Law and Order in Virginia City

There is some truth in the contention of historians that frontiersmen often regressed in their social relationships as they moved out to the raw edge of the spreading boundaries of civilization. They no doubt lost their perspectives, allowed rougher elements to grab freer hands in setting the tone of newly formed communities, and created false standards of values. Samuel L. Clemens saw life at its rawest in Virginia City, Nevada. Murder was commonplace, and the local leaders were men, who under other conditions of society,

Samuel L. Clemens (Mark Twain), *Roughing It* (Hartford: Webster, 1872), 339–343.

would have been consigned low social positions. Clemens also saw the American system of law and order being subverted by a literal interpretation of qualifications for jury duty.

The first twenty-six graves in the Virginia [City] cemetery were occupied by murdered men. So everybody said, so everybody believed, and so they will always say and believe. The reason why there was so much slaughtering done, was, that in a new mining district the rough element predominates, and a person is not respected until he has "killed his man." That was the very expression used.

If an unknown individual arrived, they did not inquire if he was capable, honest, industrious, but—had he killed his man? If he had not, he gravitated to his natural and proper position, that of a man of small consequence; if he had, the cordiality of his reception was graduated according to the number of his dead. It was tedious work struggling up to a position of influence with bloodless hands; but when a man came with the blood of half a dozen men on his soul, his worth was recognized at once and his acquaintance sought.

In Nevada, for a time, the lawyer, the editor, the banker, the chief desperado, the chief gambler, and the saloon keeper, occupied the same level in society, and it was the highest. The cheapest and easiest way to become an influential man and be looked up to by the community at large, was to stand behind a bar, wear a cluster-diamond pin, and sell whisky. I am not sure but that the saloon-keeper held a shade higher rank than any other member of society. His opinion had weight. It was his privilege to say how the elections should go. No great movement could succeed without the countenance and direction of the saloon-keepers. It was a high favor when the chief saloon-keeper consented to serve in the legislature or the board of aldermen. Youthful ambition hardly aspired so much to the honors of the law, or the army and navy as to the dignity of proprietorship in a saloon.

To be a saloon-keeper and kill a man was to be illustrious. Hence the reader will not be surprised to learn that more than one man was killed in Nevada under hardly the pretext of provocation, so impatient was the slayer to achieve reputation and throw off the galling sense of being held in indifferent repute by his associates. I knew two youths who tried to "kill their men" for no other reason—and got killed themselves for their pains.

"There goes the man that killed Adams" was higher praise and a sweeter sound in the ears of this sort of people than any other speech that admiring lips could utter.

The men who murdered Virginia [City's] original twenty-six cemetery-occupants were never punished. Why? Because Alfred the Great, when he invented trial by jury, and knew that he had admirably framed it to secure justice in his age of the world, was not aware that in the nineteenth century the condition of things would be so entirely changed that unless he rose from the grave and altered the jury plan to meet the emergency, it would prove the most ingenious and infallible agency for defeating justice that human wisdom could contrive. For how could he imagine that we simpletons would go on using his jury plan after circumstances had stripped it of its usefulness, any more than he could imagine that we would go on using his candle-clock after we had invented chronometers? In his day news could not travel fast, and hence he could easily find a jury of honest, intelligent men who had not heard of the case they were called to try—but in our day of telegraphs and newspapers his plan compels us to swear in juries composed of fools and rascals, because the system rigidly excludes honest men and men of brains.

I remember one of those sorrowful farces, in Virginia [City], which we call a jury trial. A noted desperado killed Mr. B., a good citizen, in the most wanton and cold-blooded way. Of course the papers were full of it, and all men capable of reading, read about it. And of course all men not deaf and dumb and idiotic, talked about it. A jury-list was made out, and Mr. B. L., a prominent banker and a valued citizen, was questioned precisely as he would have been questioned in any court in America:

"Have you heard of this homicide?"

"Yes."

"Have you held conversations upon the subject?"

"Yes."

"Have you formed or expressed opinions about it?"

"Yes."

"Have you read the newspaper accounts of it?"

"Yes."

"We do not want you."

A minister, intelligent, esteemed, and greatly respected; a merchant of high character and known probity; a mining superintendent of intelligence and unblemished reputation; a quartz mill owner of excellent standing, were all questioned in the same way, and all set aside. Each said the public talk and newspaper reports had not so biased his mind but that sworn testimony would overthrow his previously formed opinions and enable him to render a verdict without prejudice and in accordance with the facts. But of course such men could not be trusted with the case. Ignoramuses alone could mete out unsullied justice.

When the peremptory challenges were all exhausted, a jury of twelve men was impaneled—a jury who swore they had neither heard, read, talked about nor expressed an opinion concerning a murder which the very cattle in the corrals, the Indians in the sage-brush and the stones in the streets were cognizant of! It was a jury composed of two desperadoes, two low beer-house politicians, three bar-keepers, two ranchmen who could not read, and three dull, stupid, human donkeys! It actually came out afterward, that one of these latter thought that incest and arson were the same thing.

The verdict rendered by this jury was, Not Guilty. What else could one expect?

XI

Impact of the Frontier

In analyzing the contents of the United States Census for the end of the decade 1890, the editorial staff undertook to sound out the changes that had occurred in the rapidly expanding republic. This new census count had come on the heels of one of the great land rushes, a period of intensive internal population movement of railroad expansion, and of some national concern about the land resource. For the first time, perhaps, the nation could begin to make some accurate predictions about the relationships of land and human history. Looking backward in 1890 it seemed a remarkably short time since backwoodsmen first penetrated the great wooded shoulders of the frontier east of the Appalachian ranges. Now the great bulk of the land had been claimed, the roster of states was almost completed, and the question had arisen about future impacts of men upon the land. The returns of the 1890 census supplied the raw statistical data from which all sorts of interested specialists, including historians, could draw significant inferences.

Mere statistical tables hardly tell the story of a frontier or of human pioneering conditions. What was revealing, however, was how fast Americans had exploited many of the natural resources of the continent. Great areas of virgin forest lands already lay in waste, and frankly no one knew with any certainty when they would be restored, or if, in fact, they could be restored. New lines of settlement still were reaching out from older areas, and population density was growing with the passing decades. By 1890 the superintendent of the census could read clearly on positional maps the fact that in the future the advance of population would be more in the form of working out from settled bases rather than from long straggling lines of wagon trains and settler groups. The frontier, of course, was not closed by a mere positioning of persons in tables and on maps, but rather by the changes in approaches to the future. Already Americans were beginning to learn about and to apply the new scientific knowledge of farming, stock breeding, marketing, and forestry. It was a combination of many forces and human facts which brought about the closing of the frontier. One of these was the subtlety which occurred in the folk nature of social organization, and this subtlety, in the case of the closing frontier, was indeed significant.

71. Western America

Two foreigners, Alexis de Tocqueville and Lord James Bryce, made sound observations on the fundamental meanings of life and democracy in America. Tocqueville saw the country in the 1830s and Lord Bryce in the 1860s and 1880s. Lord Bryce viewed western America as a land of change and promise. Its great land and mineral resources, its vast space, and the inflow of individuals from all over the nation would shape a society with its own peculiar flavor and personality. The Westerner appeared to him to have great confidence, and therein lay the success of the region. Like the superintendent of the census in 1890, Lord Bryce looked upon settlement of the Northwest as somewhat the closing of the frontier gate. When the last of this region was exploited, then the American would have to turn inward to find a new frontier. That inward frontier was to a large extent the adaptations of the forms of a democratic government to the virgin lands of the West.

Western America is one of the most interesting subjects of study the modern world has seen. There has been nothing in the past resembling its growth, and probably there will be nothing in the future. A vast territory, wonderfully rich in natural resources of many kinds; a temperate and healthy climate fit for European labor; a soil generally, and in many places marvellously, fertile; in some regions mountains full of

James Bryce, *The American Commonwealth,* 2 vols. (New York: MacMillan, 1910), vol. I, pp. 891–896.

minerals, in others trackless forests where every tree is over two hundred feet high; and the whole of this virtually unoccupied territory thrown open to a vigorous race, with all the appliances and contrivances of modern science at its command,—these are phenomena absolutely without precedent in history, and which cannot recur elsewhere, because our planet contains no such other favoured tract of country.

The Spaniards and Portuguese settled in tropical countries, which soon enervated them. They carried with them the poison of slavery; their colonists were separated, some by long land journeys, and all by still longer voyages, from the centres of civilization. But the railway and the telegraph follow the Western American. The Greeks of the sixth and seventh centuries before Christ, who planted themselves all round the coasts of the Mediterranean, had always enemies, and often powerful enemies, to overcome before they could found even their trading-stations on the coast, much less occupy the lands of the interior. In Western America the presence of the Indians has done no more than give a touch of romance or a spice of danger to the exploration of some regions, such as Western Dakota and Arizona, while over the rest of the country the unhappy aborigines have slunk silently away, scarcely even complaining of the robbery of lands and the violation of plighted faith. Nature and time seem to have conspired to make the development of the Mississippi basin and the Pacific slope the swiftest, easiest, completest achievement in the whole record of the civilizing progress of mankind since the founder of the Egyptian monarchy gathered the tribes of the Nile under one government.

The details of this development and the statistics that illustrate it have been too often set forth to need re-statement here. It is of the character and temper of the men who have conducted it that I wish to speak, a matter which has received less attention, but is essential to a just conception of the Americans of to-day. For the West is the most American part of America; that is to say, the part where those features which distinguish America from Europe come out in the strongest relief. What

Europe is to Asia, what England is to the rest of Europe, what America is to England, that the Western States are to the Atlantic States, the heat and pressure and hurry of life always growing as we follow the path of the sun. In Eastern America there are still quiet spots, in the valleys of the Alleghanies, for instance, in nooks of old New England, in university towns like Princeton or Amherst, Ithaca or Ann Arbor. In the West there are none. All is bustle, motion, and struggle, most so of course among the native Americans, yet even the immigrant from the secluded valleys of Thuringia, or the shores of some Norwegian fjord, learns the ways almost as readily as the tongue of the country, and is soon swept into the whirlpool.

It is the most enterprising and unsettled Americans that come West! and when they have left their old haunts, broken their old ties, resigned the comforts and pleasures of their former homes, they are resolved to obtain the wealth and success for which they have come. They throw themselves into work with a feverish yet sustained intensity. They rise early, they work all day, they have few pleasures, few opportunities for relaxation. I remember in the young city of Seattle on Puget Sound to have found business in full swing at seven o'clock A.M.: the shops open, the streets full of people. Everything is speculative, land (or, as it is usually called, "real estate") most so, the value of lots of ground rising or falling perhaps two or three hundred per cent in the year. No one has any fixed occupation; he is a storekeeper to-day, a ranchman to-morrow, a miner next week. I once found the waiters in the chief hotel at Denver, in Colorado, saving their autumn and winter wages to start off in the spring "prospecting" for silver "claims" in the mountains. Few men stay in one of the newer cities more than a few weeks or months; to have been there a whole year is to be an old inhabitant, an oracle if you have succeeded, a by-word if you have not, for to prosper in the West you must be able to turn your hand to anything, and seize the chance to-day which every one else will have seen to-morrow. This venturesome and shifting life strengthens the reckless and heedless habits of the people. Every one thinks so much of gaining that he thinks little of spending, and in the general dearness of commodities, food (in the agricultural districts) excepted, it seems not worth while to care about small sums. In California for many years no coin lower than a ten-cent piece (5d.) was in circulation; and even in 1881, though most articles of food were abundant, nothing was sold at a lower price than five cents. The most striking alternations of fortune, the great *coups* which fascinate men and make them play for all or nothing, are of course commoner in mining regions than elsewhere. But money is everywhere so valuable for the purposes of speculative investment, whether in land, live stock, or trade, as to fetch very high interest. At Walla Walla (in what was then the Territory of Washington) I found in 1881 that the interest on debts secured on good safe mortgages was at the rate of fourteen per cent per annum, of course payable monthly.

The carelessness is public as well as private. Tree stumps were left standing in the streets of a large and flourishing town like Leadville, because the municipal authorities cannot be at the trouble of cutting or burning them. Swamps were left un-drained in the suburbs of a populous city like Portland, which every autumn were breeding malarial fevers; and the risk of accidents to be followed by actions does not prevent the rail-ways from pushing on their lines along loosely heaped embank-ments, and over curved trestle bridges which seem as if they could not stand a high wind or the passage of a heavy train.

This mixture of science and rudeness is one of a series of singular contrasts which runs through the West, not less con-spicuous in the minds of the people than in their surroundings. They value strong government, and have a remarkable faculty for organizing some kind of government, but they are tolerant of lawlessness which does not directly attack their own interest. Horse-stealing and insults to women are the two unpardonable offences; all others are often suffered to go unpunished. I was in a considerable Western city, with a population of 70,000 people, some years ago, when the leading newspaper of the place, commenting on one of the train robberies that had been frequent in the State, observed that so long as the brigands had confined themselves to robbing the railway companies and the express companies of property for whose loss the companies must answer, no one had greatly cared, seeing that these companies themselves robbed the public; but now that private citizens seemed in danger of losing their personal baggage and money, the prosperity of the city might be compromised, and something ought to be done—a sentiment delivered with all gravity, as the rest of the article showed. Brigandage tends to disappear when the country becomes populous, though there are places in comparatively old States like Illinois and Missouri where the railways are still unsafe. But the same heedlessness suffers other evils to take root, evils likely to prove permanent, including some refinements of political roguery which it is strange to find amid the simple life of forests and prairies.

Another such contrast is presented by the tendency of this shrewd and educated people to relapse into the oldest and most childish forms of superstition. Fortune-telling, clairvoyance, attempts to pry by the help of "mediums" into the book of fate, are so common in parts of the West that the newspapers devote a special column, headed "astrologers," to the advertisements of these wizards and pythonesses. I have counted in one issue of a San Francisco newspaper as many as eighteen such advertisements, six of which were of simple fortune-tellers, like those who used to beguile the peasant girls of Devonshire. In fact, the profession of a soothsayer or astrologer is a recognized one in California now, as it was in the Greece of Homer. Possibly the prevalence of mining speculation, possibly the existence of a large mass of ignorant immigrants from Europe, may help to account for the phenomenon, which as California is deemed an exceptionally unreligious State, illustrates the famous saying that the less faith the more superstition.

All the passionate eagerness, all the strenuous effort of the Westerners is directed towards the material development of the country. To open the greatest number of mines and extract the greatest quantity of ore, to scatter cattle over a thousand hills, to turn the flower-spangled prairies of the North-west into wheat-fields, to cover the sunny slopes of the South-west with

vines and olives: this is the end and aim of their lives, this is
their daily and nightly thought—

> juvat Ismara Baccho
> Conserere atque olea magnum vestire Taburnum

The passion is so absorbing, and so covers the horizon of public
as well as private life that it almost ceases to be selfish—it takes
from its very vastness a tinge of ideality. To have an immense
production of exchangeable commodities, to force from nature
the most she can be made to yield, and send it east and west by
the cheapest routes to the dearest markets, making one's city a
centre of trade, and raising the price of its real estate—this,
which might not have seemed a glorious consummation to
Isaiah or Plato, is preached by Western newspapers as a kind
of religion. It is not really, or at least it is not wholly, sordid.
These people are intoxicated by the majestic scale of the nature
in which their lot is cast, enormous mineral deposits, boundless
prairies, forests which, even squandered—wickedly squandered
—as they now are, will supply timber to the United States for
centuries; a soil which, with the rudest cultivation, yields the
most abundant crops, a populous continent for their market.
They see all round them railways being built, telegraph wires
laid, steamboat lines across the Pacific projected, cities springing up in the solitudes, and settlers making the wilderness to
blossom like the rose. Their imagination revels in these sights
and signs of progress, and they gild their own struggles for
fortune with the belief that they are the missionaries of civilization and the instruments of Providence in the greatest work the
world has seen.

72. End of the Statistical Frontier

In 1890 the superintendent of the United States Bureau of the
Census presented an extensive summary of population movement
by each decade since 1790. This changing spread and density of
settlement of the national population as it advanced westward was
charted on a series of density maps. Not only was the population
located but likewise the islands where the settled density fell below
two persons per square mile. The total national population was
62,622,250, and the average density had risen to 32.16 per square
mile. To all intents and purposes the frontier was closed as a practical statistical consideration, even though vacant lands remained.
These were either in rugged mountainous areas, in deserts, or, as
in the case of the Florida frontier, in uninhabitable swamps. In a
century the great westward movement had seen settlers bring under exploitation almost two million square miles of land, and, as
the superintendent of the Census Bureau said, "into the service
of man."

This census completes the history of a century; a century
of progress and achievement unequaled in the world's history.
A hundred years ago there were groups of feeble settlements
sparsely covering an area of 239,935 square miles, and num-
bering less than 4,000,000. The century has witnessed our
development into a great and powerful nation; it has witnessed the spread of settlement across the continent until not
less than 1,947,280 square miles have been redeemed from the
wilderness and brought into the service of man, while the
population has increased and multiplied by its own increase
and by additions from abroad until it numbers 62,622,250.

   During the decade just past a trifling change has been made
in the boundary between Nebraska and Dakota by which the
area of Nebraska has been slightly increased. Dakota terri-

Eleventh Census of the United States, Population (Washington: The
Government Printing Office, 1891), Part I, pp. XXVII, XXVIII.

tory has been cut in two and the states of North Dakota and South Dakota admitted. Montana, Wyoming, Idaho, and Washington have also been added to the sisterhood of states. The territory of Oklahoma has been created out of the western half of the Indian territory, and to it has been added the strip of public land lying north of the panhandle of Texas.

The most striking fact connected with the extension of settlement during the past decade is the numerous additions which have been made to the settled area within the Cordilleran region. Settlements have spread westward up the slope of the plains until they have joined the bodies formerly isolated in Colorado, forming a continuous body of settlement from the east to the Rocky mountains. Practically the whole of Kansas has become a settled region, and the unsettled area of Nebraska has been reduced in dimensions to a third of what it was ten years ago. What was a sparsely settled region in Texas in 1880 is now the most populous part of the state, while settlements have spread westward to the escarpment of the Staked Plains. The unsettled regions of North Dakota and South Dakota have been reduced to half their former dimensions. Settlements in Montana have spread until they now occupy one-third of the state. In New Mexico, Idaho, and Wyoming considerable extensions of area are to be noted. In Colorado, in spite of the decline of the mining industry and the depopulation of its mining regions, settlement has spread, and two-thirds of the state are now under the dominion of man. Oregon and Washington show equally rapid progress, and California, although its mining regions have suffered, has made great inroads upon its unsettled regions, especially in the south. Of all the western states and territories Nevada alone is at a standstill in this respect, its settled area remaining practically the same as in 1880. When it is remembered that the state has lost one-third of its population during the past ten years, the fact that it has held its own in settled area is surprising until it is understood that the state has undergone a material change in occupations during the decade, and that the inhabitants, instead of being closely grouped and engaged in mining pursuits, have become scattered along its streams and have engaged in agriculture.

Settlement is spreading with some rapidity in Maine, its unsettled area having dwindled from 12,000 to about 4,000 square miles. The unsettled portion of the Adirondack region in New York has also diminished, there being now but 1,000 square miles remaining. The frontier has been pushed still farther southward in Florida, and the unsettled area has been reduced from 20,800 to 13,000 square miles.

Lumbering and mining interests have practically obliterated the wilderness of Michigan and have reduced that of Wisconsin to less than one-half of its former area. In Minnesota the area of the wild northern forests has been reduced from 34,000 to 23,000 square miles. The population is 62,622,250, and the average density of settlement 32.16 to the square mile.

Index